Modernism, Fashion and Interwar Women Writers

Modernism, Fashion and Interwar Women Writers

Vike Martina Plock

EDINBURGH
University Press

Edinburgh University Press is one of the leading university presses in the UK. We publish academic books and journals in our selected subject areas across the humanities and social sciences, combining cutting-edge scholarship with high editorial and production values to produce academic works of lasting importance. For more information visit our website: edinburghuniversitypress.com

© Vike Martina Plock, 2017

Edinburgh University Press Ltd
The Tun – Holyrood Road,
12(2f) Jackson's Entry,
Edinburgh EH8 8PJ

Typeset in 11/14 Adobe Sabon by
IDSUK (DataConnection) Ltd

A CIP record for this book is available from the British Library

ISBN 978 1 4744 2741 8 (hardback)
ISBN 978 1 4744 2743 2 (webready PDF)
ISBN 978 1 4744 2744 9 (epub)

The right of Vike Martina Plock to be identified as the author of this work has been asserted in accordance with the Copyright, Designs and Patents Act 1988, and the Copyright and Related Rights Regulations 2003 (SI No. 2498).

Contents

List of Figures	vi
Acknowledgements	vii
List of Abbreviations	x
Introduction	1
1 Novelty and the Market: Edith Wharton	37
2 Conformity and Idiosyncrasy: Jean Rhys	73
3 Patterns: Rosamond Lehmann	110
4 Ties: Elizabeth Bowen	145
5 Uniforms and Uniformity: Virginia Woolf	181
Envoi	217
Bibliography	223
Index	239

List of Figures

Figure 1	*Century Advertisements: Laddie: A True Blue Story*, 1913, Edith Wharton Collection, 1862–1937, Beinecke Rare Book and Manuscript Library, YCAL MSS 42 1/10/268	38
Figure 2	*Vogue* Pattern Service, *Vogue*, 55:4 (1920): 79, Vogue © The Condé Nast Publications Ltd	118
Figure 3	Cover of Uniform Edition of Virginia Woolf's *To the Lighthouse*, 1930. Mortimer Rare Book Room, Smith College	203
Figure 4	Advert for the Hogarth Press's Virginia Woolf: New Uniform Edition, 1929. Mortimer Rare Book Room, Smith College	204

Acknowledgements

This is a book about fashion. But it is also a book about the professional and personal affiliations that fashion brings into play, and this is the place where its author wishes to acknowledge the people whose friendship, support or knowledge has contributed in one way or another to its composition. First, I want to thank colleagues at the University of Exeter, who read or provided feedback on work in progress. It is due to the input provided by Siân Harris, Kirsty Martin and Peter Riley that this project was able to take its final shape. Jana Funke, Gabriella Giannachi, Jo Gill, Helen Hanson, Daisy Hay, Felicity Henderson, Kate Hext, Elliot Kendall, James Lyons, Sinéad Moynihan, Alex Murray, Henry Power, Laura Salisbury, Florian Stadtler, Adam Watt, Phil Wickham and Patricia Zakreski were around at different stages of the writing process, and it is their company and intellectual curiosity that continue to make everyday working life much more enjoyable.

Arguments relating to this project were first presented at conferences and symposia, and I have been fortunate to meet other scholars who share my interests in fashion, modernism or related areas of research. At Modernist Studies Association Conferences in Montréal, Brighton, Pittsburgh and Boston, Jane Garrity, Celia Marshik, Sophie Oliver, Ilya Parkins, Elizabeth Sheehan, Emma West and Alice Wood were enthusiastic fellow panellists and discussion partners. Equally important for directing the course of my work were activities related to the AHRC-funded research network, *Tailored Trades: Clothes, Labour and Professional Communities, 1880–1939*, which I co-directed with Nicole Robertson from 2012 to 2014 and which offered opportunities to engage in specialist conversations with scholars from different disciplinary backgrounds. Editorial work for *Literature & History* provided an equally important context for thinking about and producing interdisciplinary research, and many thanks are due to the other members of the editorial team, especially Andrew Thacker and Ryan Sweet, for years of congenial collaborative work on the journal.

At Edinburgh University Press, Jackie Jones expressed an early interest in this project and saw it to completion with patience and enthusiasm. I thank her for her professionalism and her kindness. Two anonymous readers gave thoughtful and meticulous feedback on the manuscript and helped to make it a much better book, while Adela Rauchova and Rebecca Mackenzie helped with queries during the production process. Before this monograph could go to press, however, considerable archival work had to be undertaken and some of it was facilitated by research fellowships from the Harry Ransom Center at the University of Texas at Austin (2010; 2014) and the Beinecke Rare Book and Manuscript Library at Yale University (2011). Staff in these research centres provided assistance as did archivists and librarians in the following institutions: Library & Archive, Girton College, Cambridge; Modern Archives Centre, King's College, Cambridge; McFarlin Library, University of Tulsa; University of Reading, Special Collections; University of Sussex, Special Collections at the Keep. While pursuing archival work, I was also fortunate to meet a number of researchers with whom I was able to discuss my ideas for this book. Lise Jaillant offered advice on uniform editions and patiently answered questions about book history and interwar print culture, conversations with Ariela Freedman at conferences in different parts of the world continue to inspire and Lara Feigel's optimistic outlook on life can only impress. Closer to home, Rowena Kennedy-Epstein is an important collaborator who has become a good friend, someone who knows how to mix professional commitments with a good amount of common sense and humour.

Outside of these academic circles, a number of individuals provided essential distraction. My mother Gabriele Plock and my sister Nele Müller-Plock have done little to influence the research for this project, but I do not think it could have been written without them. Nobody, however, has contributed as much to my happiness over the last few years as my husband Jason David Hall and my son Jeremy Maarten Hall. Neither of them shares my interests in modernism or fashion but their loud voices and resounding laughter are welcome reminders that life takes place in the present.

Extracts from Edith Wharton's unpublished correspondence and manuscripts have been published by permission of The Edith Wharton Estate and the Watkins/Loomis Agency. The Society of Authors as the Literary Representative of the Estate of Rosamond Lehmann has kindly granted permission to use unpublished material from her correspondence, while the Estate of Wogan Philipps also allowed me to quote from his unpublished letters. Passages from Elizabeth Bowen's letters and unpublished typescripts have been reproduced with permission of Curtis Brown Group Ltd, London on behalf of The Estate of Elizabeth Bowen, Copyright © The Estate of Elizabeth Bowen 2016. I would also like to thank the University of Sussex and the Society of Authors as the Literary Representative of the Estate of Leonard and Virginia Woolf for letting me publish extracts from the Monks House Papers and from their letters. Aspects of Chapters 3 and 4 have previously been published in academic journals, and I thank the relevant editors and publishers for permission to publish new versions: material from the Rosamond Lehmann chapter was originally published as '"I Just Took It Straight from *Vogue*": Fashion, Femininity, and Literary Modernity in Rosamond Lehmann's *Invitation to the Waltz*', *Modern Fiction Studies*, 59:1 (2013): 83–106 but the argument has been considerably expanded by more research on Lehmann's early critical reception and her relationship with the interwar publishing industry. Material from the Elizabeth Bowen chapter was originally published as 'Sartorial Connections: Fashion, Clothes, and Character in Elizabeth Bowen's *To the North*', *Modernism/Modernity*, 19:2 (2012): 287–302. Like the Lehmann material, it has been substantially developed by pursuing further archival research on Bowen's professional correspondence with editors and publishers and by analysing her views of the twentieth-century literary marketplace.

List of Abbreviations

AK	Alfred A. Knopf Inc. Records, Harry Ransom Center, The University of Texas at Austin
EB	Elizabeth Bowen Collection, 1923–1975, Harry Ransom Center, The University of Texas at Austin
HPA	The Hogarth Press Business Archive, University of Reading, Special Collections
JC	Records of Jonathan Cape Ltd, University of Reading, Special Collections
JRA	Jean Rhys Archive, McFarlin Library, The University of Tulsa
KV2	British Online Archives, Right-Wing Extremists: Sir Oswald Mosley/Lady Mosley, Security Service: Personal Files (accessed 17 April 2014)
MHP	Monk's House Papers, University of Sussex, Special Collections at the Keep
RNL	Rosamond Nina Lehmann Papers, Archives Centre, King's College, Cambridge
YCAL MSS 42	Edith Wharton Collection, Beinecke Rare Book and Manuscript Library, Yale University Library
YCAL MSS 361	Anna Catherine Bahlmann Collection, Beinecke Rare Book and Manuscript Library, Yale University Library

Introduction

This book argues that fashion mattered to anglophone women novelists of the interwar period for two distinct yet interrelated reasons. First, it suggests that fashion provided them with a rich conceptual framework for analysing the complex processes of identity formation in a time of significant social and cultural change. Unlike any other social practice, fashion structures the relationship between individuals and between an individual and adjacent collectives. For this reason, it facilitates the analysis of modern subject identity as a psychological composite at once receptive and defensive towards external influences and pressures. Originality in dress can generate admiration in everyday encounters. But as Mabel Waring, the protagonist of Virginia Woolf's short story 'The New Dress' (1924), has to learn the hard way,[1] too much extravagance in clothing ostracises. Because group identity is often maintained by a certain degree of uniformity in dress, sartorial conspicuousness can lead to isolation from communities with which the individual seeks affiliation.

This apparent contradiction between individual expression and community building through the use of clothes is a topic to which my chosen novelists consistently return, and it is the first aim of this book to analyse what aspects of fashion's conceptual apparatus they employ to discuss the ways in which their characters position themselves in relation to new and established gender dynamics that were propagated or challenged in the early decades of the twentieth century. During a time when women's clothing underwent radical changes, the rhetoric provided by the fashion discourse offered these writers a particularly relevant set of thematic clusters to analyse the construction of female subjectivity in a world in which people were relentlessly held up for comparison with others but in which individuals also worried about being swallowed up by the crowds populating the vast metropolitan centres that were the setting of so much of modern fiction.[2] In the work of the included women writers, the analysis of this dialectic between assimilation and differentiation, between conformity and rebellion, facilitates discussions about identity politics. Fashion, as these authors noted, was a social practice that could be easily seized for political ends. And it is these politically motivated appropriations of fashion that are comprehensively discussed and often critiqued in their writing.

But there is another reason why fashion mattered to these women novelists. Fashion, as I explained above, decisively organises the individual's position in social configurations through the processes of assimilation and differentiation. And this idea about the relationship between the part and the whole manifesting itself through visual signifiers obviously exceeds the conceptual terrain of clothes and sartorial markers. It is equally applicable to broader questions of style, taste and appearance and it affects, as such, the production, dissemination and reception of other cultural goods – books or novels, for instance. Pierre Bourdieu has therefore proposed to look for structural similarities between '*haute couture*' and '*haute culture*', and this project attends to his suggestion that there is an obvious 'homology between the field of production of one particular category of luxury goods, namely fashion garments and the field of production of that other category of luxury goods, the goods of legitimate culture such as music, poetry, philosophy and so on' (Bourdieu 1995: 132). Only if the resemblances in the promotional logic dealing with such presumably distinct cultural productions as garments and books are acknowledged as factual reality, in other words, can we subject the 'legitimate' art forms (music, painting, literature, philosophy) that are 'protected by their legitimacy' to a critical analysis that investigates not only the intellectual but also the professional and economic motivations of their producers (1995: 132). Following Bourdieu, my second aim in *Modernism, Fashion and Interwar Women Writers* will therefore be to investigate how the included novelists – Edith Wharton, Jean Rhys, Rosamond Lehmann, Elizabeth Bowen and Virginia Woolf – who were very clearly interested in sartorial fashions, developed their novels and authorial personas in response to contemporary market demands. If fashion brings into productive play the antagonistic relationship between assimilation and differentiation, an obvious question to ask would be how these women novelists affiliated themselves (or not) with the literary collectives of their time. How, in other words, did decisions about forming intellectual and professional affiliations inform the development of their self-images, their social performances and their modes of writing? Fashion, I maintain throughout, helpfully focuses these, often dissimilar, stories about a woman novelist's writing practices and her authorial self-formation – her position, that is, in the 'network of objective relations (of domination or subordination, of complementarity or antagonism' that Bourdieu has identified as constitutive in the formation of a 'field of cultural production' (1996: 231). Because I am particularly interested in examining the place of these authors in the literary field of the interwar period, significant parts of the following chapters will therefore be dedicated to the question of how these writers created their novelistic scripts and authorial personas in response to contemporary expectations about artistic standards. If fashion regulated contemporary clothes styles in no subtle manner, *Modernism, Fashion and Interwar Women Writers* shows that it was also becoming an unassailable force in the interwar period, organising an embattled field of cultural production and with it the working practices of the included women writers.

Both of these intersecting critical narratives take as their point of departure the premise that fashion was relevant for authors of the interwar period because this was a time when the marketing of books became increasingly tied to the cultivation of a celebrity culture that developed exorbitantly at the beginning of the twentieth century. New publishing ventures fundamentally changed the ways in which books were produced and marketed, and it suffices to say here that the author's image became increasingly visible in publishers' publicity campaigns. Women writers, especially when they were good-looking, were particularly targeted in these campaigns – an obvious reason why successful image cultivation was of such significance to a female author who hoped to sell her books. When Anita Loos rose to meteoric fame after the publication of *Gentlemen Prefer Blondes* (1925), her status as bestselling author was further confirmed by articles and features in Britain's periodical press (Anon. 1926a: 170–1) that used her biography as a Hollywood screenwriter of humble origins as an effective means of promotion. What helped to sell a book was its author's image and reputation – an issue that certainly worried Wharton, who would reject the possibility of Woolf's writerly talents simply because she objected to the publicity campaign that followed in the wake of *Orlando*'s publication in 1928 (R. W. B. Lewis 1975: 483). In this cultural climate, celebrity authorship was carefully manufactured, and it was managed by negotiating exactly the kind of tensions that fashion brings into play: the relationship between individual and collective identity and between originality and social approval. A book or its author had to be seen to differ significantly from competing products to be sought after and marketable, but too much extravagance in writing or authorial posturing could easily lead to the same results as extravagance in dress: incomprehension and possible rejection by an intended target audience. It is hardly surprising that women authors of the period, whose images and biographies were used strategically for marketing purposes, were aware that fashion determined more than the choice of one's clothes. None of the ones in *Modernism, Fashion and Interwar Women Writers* failed to see how much it determined her working life as a writer.

The responses of a number of interwar women novelists to contemporary fashion are the focus of the analysis. In view of that – because I propose to investigate these writers' attitudes towards the ways in which fashion structured their historical moment – I am less interested in applying recent fashion theory to their writing. Although there can be no doubt that this particular body of scholarship has very productively underlined the relationship between fashion studies and feminist politics, queer studies or eco-criticism,[3] this monograph deliberately prioritises discussing the conceptions of fashion that were or could have been available to the women writers whose work is analysed this study. What interests me, above all, is what aspects of a contemporary fashion discourse these women writers incorporated into their fiction. The question of how they experienced sartorial and literary fashions will determine the construction of the arguments in subsequent chapters, and more than once fashion is brought into dialogue with the rhetoric of reactionary gender politics (Rhys, Lehmann) that might sound outdated by now but that was of immense relevance at the time when these authors were writing their novels. But it is precisely these narratives about the various entanglements that existed between the chosen women writers and the fashion discourse of their time that I hope to recuperate, and the historical focus, which I maintain throughout, is the reason why more recent writing on fashion is less applicable to the arguments in *Modernism, Fashion and Interwar Women Writers* than the work of some nineteenth- and early twentieth-century cultural theorists that will be referenced throughout in debates about these writers' artistic and professional affiliations.

Commercially successful writing is thereby identified as one of the two significant literary formations affecting the ways in which the selected novelists considered their own position in the literary field of the interwar period. The other, equally significant one for my purpose is literary modernism because it presented itself, ostensibly at least, as commercial literature's determined adversary. Obviously, the critical narrative about modernism's rejection of commodity culture has often been told, and it continues to be the subject of discussions that hope to problematise the notion of a polarised literary culture establishing itself in the interwar years (Rainey 1998; Cooper 2004; Goldman 2011). In much of its original conception, however, modernist writing showed little, if any, determination to cater to the public taste, and it is for this particular reason that I use it as commercial literature's conceptual obverse in the discussions of interwar women's writing that follow. In these, I am less concerned with determining if and why a particular novelist qualifies for inclusion in the modernist canon. Instead, *Modernism, Fashion and Interwar Women Writers* proposes to use modernism as a critical shorthand for writing produced by the period's avant-garde to show how the attempts made by these artists to deliberately and self-consciously set themselves apart from marketable crowd-pleasers affected the way in which other authors negotiated their working relationships with the contemporary cultural economy.

In both cases, I am aware that these terms – modernism and commercially successful writing – are reductive and potentially problematic abstractions. But as we shall see, these concepts are still immensely helpful when analysing the work of the selected novelists because these women often adhered to this kind of dialectic reading of interwar literary culture when they called attention to the concealed connections between the two literary formations (Wharton) or when they helped to promote the narrative of high culture and exclusivity that was to become so central to modernism's self-promotion (Lehmann, Bowen). In fact, Aaron Jaffe has recently shown the effectiveness of this specific promotional narrative disseminated by the high modernists. Following Fredric Jameson, he has suggested that the (male) modernists of the 1920s used the concept of an inimitable 'textual signature' as a 'means of promotion', to 'create and expand a market for [their] elite literary works' in campaigns that seemingly circumvented 'celebrity and its fetish of biography' in the very process of creating them (Jaffe 2005: 2–3). *Modernism, Fashion and Interwar Women Writers* builds on Jaffe's critical suggestions by investigating how the creation of the modernist 'imprimatur', as he has called it (20), influenced the self-conception and the public profiles of the selected women writers working alongside or in the immediate vicinity of the (male) modernists. Not many at the time would have been as aware as Wharton that fashion moulded the production of both, mainstream literature and modernism. Rather, they would have thought of these two literary configurations as the opposing ends of a spectrum on which work as different as that produced by Woolf or the Golden Age crime writer Agatha Christie was placed in marketing campaigns.

This, then, is the two-pronged argument developed in *Modernism, Fashion and Interwar Women Writers*. The selected novelists investigated how fashion determined the existence and the experiences of their female characters, and they criticised it as an often problematic but inescapable force in women's lives that undermined attempts at individual self-styling by the irreconcilable intention to standardise appearance and behaviour. Commenting on fashion, in other words, was one way in which they could intervene in contemporary debates about identity politics. But as the critical explorations that follow will show, the included writers also feared that their professional lives as authors were increasingly subjected to fashion's forceful interventions. They knew that their work would be measured by publishers and by their readers according to opinions about what was deemed sufficiently new but, at the same time, reassuringly familiar in the same manner in which a sartorial composition could decide about an individual's well-being and social success. No wonder, then, that they used their assessments of contemporary sartorial protocols as the starting point to think self-reflexively about their positions in the literary field of the interwar period. Wharton was, as we shall see, by no means the only one who found the thought unbearable that an author's creative impulses could be appropriated by marketing campaigns that insisted on discovering new talent every year. For her, as for many of her contemporaries with similarly romantic notions about authorship, writing remained synonymous with an urgent need for self-expression. This book will discuss how such different novelists as Wharton, Rhys, Lehmann, Bowen and Woolf thought about, defended or redefined creative individualism at a time when a capitalist imperative for uniformity in products and features was very effectively managed, if not concealed, by fashion's crusade for novelty, originality and individual difference.

Fashioning authorial identities: interwar celebrity culture

It is well known that the manufacturing of celebrity authorship was by no means a new phenomenon at the turn of the twentieth century. One only needs to think of the extensive publicity campaigns catapulting to fame Lord Byron or Charles Dickens to find examples of nineteenth-century authors whose celebrity status was successfully manufactured.[4] Conventionally, however, critical examinations of celebrity culture argue that this phenomenon significantly accelerated at the turn of the twentieth century when the emergence of mass media technologies and the establishment of an all-encompassing commodity culture in Western countries facilitated the strategic dissemination of easily recognisable images of people of public renown.[5] 'Conspicuous consumption', the phenomenon identified by Thorstein Veblen as the compulsion to publicly display one's wealth and social status with the help of consumer articles (86–7), is certainly the offspring of this modern fascination with celebrities that motivates consumers to aspire to the images of famous people mass-circulated in turn-of-the-century magazines and, increasingly, in Hollywood's cinematic productions – an industry that would soon become the most influential producer and manipulator of this new obsession with stars.[6] When Virginia Woolf suggested in the early 1940s that the 'extraordinary display' of 'slashed cloaks', 'stiff ruffs', 'wrought chains' and 'loops of pearls', which characterised Elizabethan garments was meant to 'enforce the individual' and 'concentrated in the body' the 'fame' of the Renaissance subject, she explicitly acknowledged that contemporary celebrity culture relying on 'the publicity of the paper, of the photograph' differently managed the production of cultural icons (2011: 588).

To these technological and socio-cultural developments, fashion with its insistence on perpetual change should be added as another important influence on this early twentieth-century fascination with stars. As the fashion historian Elizabeth Wilson argues, 'fashion is dress in which the key feature is rapid and continuous changing of styles. Fashion', she continues, 'in a sense *is* change' (3). If modern celebrity culture created the conditions for the meteoric rise of (literary) artists and performers, fashion seems to add an insistence on novelty to the story about the fabrication of celebrities. Indeed, since Charles Baudelaire had identified the 'the transient, the fleeting, the contingent' in 1863 as the modern painter's remit (403), cultural modernity has been repeatedly aligned with an emerging interest in immediacy and with explorations of that which is new. And fashion, as it is registered by the artist's absorbing consciousness, was seen by Baudelaire as the visible manifestation of change.[7] The fleeting nature of the present moment can be located in those subtle variations that determine new elements in the sartorial grammar of each year.[8] In theory, at least, fashion as an industry can only sustain itself by proclaiming the divorce of the present from the past. Seasonal renewal is its quintessential imperative.[9] Unsurprisingly, therefore, a number of early twentieth-century sociologists and cultural critics consistently returned to the suggestion that novelty, obsolescence and change were modern fashion's constitutive features. It was felt by many at this point that tastes and trends were changing more rapidly and randomly than ever before, and Walter Benjamin clearly identified himself as one of them when he declared that 'the ephemerality of fashions has increased in our days as the means for their diffusion have expanded via our perfect communication techniques'. When he suggested that the 'duration of a fashion is inversely proportional to the swiftness of its diffusion' (75), Benjamin further related the speed with which fashion abandons earlier styles and forms to the rise of modern media technologies. In his view, the onset of industrial modernity was responsible for a perpetually quicker turnover of fashions with increasingly briefer durability.

It is this insistence on novelty – fashion's most discernible, programmatic feature – that had significant consequences for the construction of celebrities in the twentieth century. As the critic Pamela Church Gibson suggests, in its dependence 'upon built-in obsolescence taken to the point of "instant throwaway"', modern, 'fashion-centred consumption' requests a completely different construction of fame (3), one that makes rapid change of content and a continuous search for something new and different its most significant incentives. Taken to its logical conclusion, this suggestion implies that a celebrated author, actor or performer can not hope to hold the public's attention for more than a few years unless he or she is exceptionally resourceful in the constant re-invention of his or her public persona.[10] Countless contemporary examples, some of which are perceptively analysed by Church Gibson, support this view that the rise of fashion forever altered the make-up of a modern celebrity culture that is democratic but capricious. Anyone – independent of class, race or social status – might become the temporary focus of the media's attention. But the rules of a fashion-centred market, which demands a new face, story or headline with increasing frequency, will make the upkeep of (global) fame an equally if not more impressive achievement.

The above remarks make it sound as if the rise of modern celebrity culture in some ways preceded that of fashion. This is, of course, by no means the case. Both phenomena are mutually constitutive.[11] They have shared historical origins in the long eighteenth century when theatrical institutions began to manufacture such celebrity actresses and actor-managers as Sarah Siddons or David Garrick, and when the onset of the Industrial Revolution significantly updated the conception of fashion.[12] Accelerated modes of production lowered the price of fabrics and clothes, which in turn facilitated that rapid turnover of sartorial codes that we associate with fashion today.[13] However, I want to suggest that the intersection between the two, fashion and celebrity culture, and the former's influence on the latter, only became apparent at a time when fashion was given more focused attention. As its ascendancy was observed with progressive interest during the long nineteenth and early twentieth centuries, its social and cultural resonances could be more extensively discussed. Only when fashion itself became a discourse to be scrutinised, in other words, could its effect on related cultural phenomena be detected and analysed. The flourishing of an impulsive celebrity culture that offered its sponsorship seemingly at random was one, very obvious, example of fashion's impact on related cultural fields that could be considered by contemporary theorists and critics.

In many early twentieth-century explorations that established fashion as a subject for critical inquiry, the Benjaminian insistence on exponential change was thereby an often-used refrain (Sombart 1902: 8; Kracauer 1995: 67). But as the work of the German socio-economist Werner Sombart very clearly shows, some theorists also believed that fashion's determined emphasis on novelty was meant to conceal those standardised appearances that had become ubiquitous with the rise of modern capitalism – a suggestion with significant consequences for literary texts produced under the patronage of an expanding interwar entertainment industry that manufactured celebrities with distinct personas precisely because its products were beginning to look increasingly alike. '[F]ashion is capitalism's favorite offspring' (23), Sombart accordingly argued in 1902 when he proposed that a causal relationship between change and standardisation determined the quick turnover with which product designs are first invented but then abandoned. What is available on the market looks exceedingly alike. But the consumer's need for variation and diversion – a psychological condition diagnosed by Sombart as epidemic in capitalist modernity – will soon call for alternatives. The demand is met but only if sufficient trade can be guaranteed through the sale of more mass-produced goods. Novelty is therefore quickly checked by standardisation, a competing traction but one that will inevitably bring about renewed demands for new styles. In this manner, new forms have to be created with the same promptness with which others are adopted, leading to a complex interplay of change and assimilation that, for Sombart, explains the organisation of a consumer culture effectively organised by modern fashion's accelerated temporality.

Sombart's economically motivated examination of modern fashion is conceptually extended by Siegfried Kracauer's work on interwar mass culture and its standardised productions. Fashion, Kracauer accordingly argued in 1925 'effaces the intrinsic value of the things that come under its dominion by subjecting the appearance of these phenomena to periodic changes that are not based on any relation to the things themselves' (1995: 67). The modern entertainment industry demands regular alteration of content in all of its productions and thereby discounts the same individuality it seems to venerate. Precisely because novelty and difference have become the motivating principles for cultural productivity in capitalist market societies, creative outputs are in danger of losing their particularity and with it any kind of significance that exceeds the present moment. Literature, produced under these particular market conditions, is, to borrow Kracauer's words, reduced to an endless series of 'literary hits whose relevance is limited to their topicality' (1995: 90). It is also increasingly considered, for marketing purposes, in relation to trends that can be analysed, discussed and predicted. As Rosamond Lehmann acerbically wrote in 1946, it seemed to her 'that trend-hunting has become a profession in itself', 'smacking of pseudo-scholarship and short cuts to culture and all the modern paraphernalia of reading about books instead of reading books' (6). It is little surprising that an almost forty-year-old Woolf would worry in 1921 that she was 'out of fashion; old' (1980a: 106). If Kracauer and Lehmann are correct, writers' textual productions were subjected to exactly the same kind of scrutiny that was applied to all other cultural forms that flooded the interwar marketplace, their value tested by an ability to carefully conceal the promise of mass appeal behind the attractively packaged suggestion of novelty and difference.[14]

No doubt, readers can already foresee why literary modernism is an essential reference point for this study. Its insistence on novelty and individual difference, captured most succinctly in Ezra Pound's famous mantra 'make it new', obviously requires revisiting in light of Kracauer's observations about interwar literature's subjection to the laws of modern fashion. As Fredric Jameson has argued, modernism was 'predicated on the invention of a personal, private style, as unmistakable as your fingerprint' (5–6), and this modernist belief in a unique self, in individuality, has become as much of a critical given as modernism's equally well-known insistence on breaking with artistic traditions. In many recent critical reconstructions of interwar literary culture, modernism's lack of alignment with the market has, of course, been challenged, and I have already alluded to Aaron Jaffe's suggestion that the modernist insistence on textual idiosyncrasy assisted in turning the work of its producers into prestige commodities. Jonathan Goldman has recently extended this argument by suggesting that the personality rather than the work of the modernist author became an effective tool in publicity campaigns. Anglo-American modernism was 'situated in the newly mechanised society saturated with reproducible images' and participated, he proposes, 'in the phenomenon of celebrity' by making the 'ideal of the exceptional personality available to popular culture' (Goldman 2011: 2). Reading modernism through the critical lens provided by early twentieth-century theories of fashion advances these revisionist attempts by scholars to unearth modernism's affiliations with the interwar culture industry. As Sombart's thoughts on fashion have shown, a deep-seated suspicion of uniformity, which was the ghostly by-product of democracy, propelled demands for novelty, change and, above all, new styles that were meant to index individuality through the singularity of the subject's particular, at times even peculiar, tastes. But this suggestion that artistic independence was designable through a radical break with accepted cultural forms and productions was fraught and riddled with complexities – above all because the insistence on individuality and difference was itself a carefully controlled dynamic by which the operations of the capitalist market, the producer of standardised forms and tastes, could be maintained. Viewed in this light, Pound's demand for novelty and change can hardly be read as oppositional. Instead, it evidences, as Wharton saw with such clarity, an obvious compliance or rather a shrewd manipulation of a market that would eventually absorb and promote modernism's countercultural creations as attractive new products available for profitable dissemination.[15]

Modernism, Fashion and Interwar Women Writers is influenced by this body of scholarship on modernism and celebrity culture but extends existing debates in two ways. In the first place, it analyses how a number of women novelists writing in the shadow of modernism's effective marketing campaigns fashioned their literary works and authorial personas in response to modernist and mainstream literature. In this manner, it deliberately looks beyond the group of high (male) modernist writers who have been the subject of much current scholarship on the topic. This is important because such an analysis of authors adjacent to the modernists can help to examine the mechanisms by which the story about modernist exclusivity and stylistic idiosyncrasy was disseminated in the interwar period. In refracting it, writers such as Lehmann and Bowen promoted modernism's insistence on exclusive difference and actively assisted in turning its countercultural impetus into an aspect of mainstream culture. Not only the self-styling of individual women novelists is at stake in what follows, therefore, but some of my chapters also demonstrate how a number of interwar women writers helped the high modernists in shaping their critical afterlives through their own intellectual engagements with some of modernism's programmatic concerns.

In the second place, I propose that the critical focus on fashion can significantly advance debates about the creation of interwar (celebrity) authorship. Not only is this particular discourse extremely relevant for female writers of the time – I have more to say about this issue in the paragraphs that follow – but fashion's obvious association with assimilation and differentiation as relational but mutually exclusive concepts for identity formation productively underlines the demands made on aspiring writers who worked in a literary economy that pitted the presumed individuality of the celebrity author and his or her work against the drabness of other, uniform-looking cultural products. Fashion's conceptual vocabulary, that is, provides a new and extremely expedient set of critical tools for analysing the professional choices of interwar women writers working within a literary field that was shaped by the celebrity discourse as a particularly dominant expression of modern capitalism – women writers who were aware that their critical and commercial success hinged on correctly negotiating the relationship between idiosyncrasy and conformity, between attacking and confirming expectations about literary standards. It will be the task of subsequent chapters to determine how the assembled writers engaged with the demands of the contemporary market. They will also examine if these authors were influenced or even persuaded by the suggestion that modernism's carefully crafted narrative about idiosyncratic otherness could offer them an effective model for authorial and textual self-styling that defied mainstream culture's reliance on standardised products and forms.[16]

'Speaking crudely, football and sport are "important"; the worship of fashion, the buying of clothes "trivial"': male and female writers and the discourse of fashion

But why focus exclusively on women writers? Clearly, the cultural and commercial conditions outlined above would have advocated an energetic 'production of exceptional author figures' that made no difference between male and female writers (Rosenquist 2013: 438). At first glance, this might appear to be the case. But the long-standing association of women with mass and consumer culture, which has already been the focus of significant critical attention (Huyssen 1986: 62; Felski 1995: 29), was responsible for gendering the celebrity discourse, differently affecting the ways in which women and men were constructing their images as successful yet serious writers in the interwar period. When Woolf insisted in 1931 that modern women writers needed to kill the 'Angel in the House' (2011: 481), she graphically illustrated that the Victorian ideology of the separate spheres continued to make its influence felt: women, if they wanted to be published writers, were even now expected to conform to accepted cultural standards, producing books for other women that followed the literary formulas commonly found in such popular genres as the romance or the domestic novel. Women writers' professional authority was often premised, that is, on conditions that many of them wanted to supersede: an association with popular literary traditions that seemingly circumnavigated the public sphere entirely because they had both their origin and intended endpoint in the lady's drawing room. As the example of Woolf's 'Angel in the House' critique demonstrates, for female authors with intellectual ambitions, the process that allowed them access to the domain of professional authorship was therefore complex. Although it could liberate them from the stifling domestic realm by allowing access, as Amy Kaplan put it in her work on Wharton, to 'a specialized province of experts' (72), cultural expectations similarly tied them to the very same domestic realm by making popular appeal among female readers a required building block of their professional success. Often, trivialisation was the inevitable outcome of a woman writer's achievements, and it is no wonder that such authors as Woolf or Bowen, who wanted to be recognised as serious artists, could find commercial success similarly empowering and disabling.[17] Seen as perishable and intellectually vacuous, their work, if associated too firmly with mainstream or female literary culture, could be easily dismissed as inconsequential.[18]

However, if this problematic association with popular culture proved a difficult position to transcend for female authors with intellectual ambitions, fashion, aligned very firmly in the popular imagination of the early twentieth century with women on the one hand and with superficiality and capriciousness on the other, further enforced this narrative about the alleged inferiority of women's cultural interests and achievements. It should not surprise, therefore, that Virginia Woolf noted in 1929 that 'football and sport are "important"; the worship of fashion, the buying of clothes "trivial"', because in life and in fiction 'it is the masculine values that prevail' (Woolf 1992b: 96). A year later, J. C. Flügel's psychoanalytical study, *The Psychology of Clothes*, which was published by the Hogarth Press, could therefore incontrovertibly offer the concept of the 'great masculine renunciation' as its authoritative interpretation of recent fashion history (111), a theory of clothing that explicitly proposed that men's professionalism and seriousness were indexed by their austere and increasingly uniform clothing: the formal, standardised business suit that had started to dominate men's sartorial appearances in the nineteenth century (Shannon 2006: 53). It can easily be inferred to what kind of conclusions readers of Flügel's gendered taxonomy of clothes styles would have been steered. By associating women's garments of the same period with ornateness, changefulness but also with an exhibitionism that invites 'the charge of immodesty' (Flügel 1966: 108), this fashion theorist proposed, in no uncertain terms, a particular type of public visibility for women – one that emphasised superficial sexual attractiveness rather than professional or intellectual competence.[19]

Needless to say, this gendered narrative about clothes styles and leisure activities that insisted on indirectly linking masculinity with prowess and femininity with frivolity, immensely complicated the process of image marketing for interwar women novelists with highbrow ambitions. For them, it would have been extremely difficult to make clothes and fashion a signature of subversive intellectualism in the same manner in which such male contemporaries as James Joyce, Wyndham Lewis or F. T. Marinetti could make the focus on sartorial matters an index of the countercultural currents pervading their work and thinking.[20] If an excessive interest in fashion had little to do with men's conventional remits, it could, of course, be employed to great effect in their writing to signal disagreement with accepted conventions and further emphasise the gulf between their work and popular literary productions.[21] In the hands of male writers, fashion could be deployed, therefore, to work against cultural hegemonies and assumptions – a process that was much harder to emulate by anglophone women writers of the same period. There are notable exceptions, of course, and Edith Sitwell springs to mind as the obvious example of a woman author who used the newly established fascination with celebrities and fashionable notoriety to great effect to advance her career as female intellectual.[22] In general, however, women's long-standing, negative association with commodity culture made it much harder for female writers to employ fashion as a means to signal non-conformity, originality and difference as the trademarks of a mode of writing that hoped to challenge rather than confirm existing views about gender hierarchies.

Modernism, Fashion and Interwar Women Writers privileges a gendered approach to investigate, in a series of detailed case studies, how a select group of interwar women novelists rose to the challenge of making the thematic focus on such an allegedly feminine pursuit as fashion an important aspect of their reputation building as serious writers. Each section of this book can thus be read independently as one writer's particular tussle with an interwar culture industry that tended to downgrade the cultural work of women. Collectively, however, the following chapters perform an even more important critical task. By introducing the chosen novelists as fashion critics they hope to address an imbalance in those conceptualisations of fashion that were available at the time when these women were writing. As this introduction's discussion of such fashion theories as Flügel's has already revealed, women were generally marginalised in debates that identified them as the receivers rather than the analysts of fashion's cultural imperatives.[23] As implicated subjects, the authors I have selected for study were therefore confronting an authoritative, androcentric narrative that all but insisted on excluding women from its discursive spaces. It is for this particular reason that a critical engagement with fashion could become a politically significant gesture for female writers with intellectual ambitions – even if they did not resemble Rhys and Lehmann in explicitly associating it with the preservation of patriarchal values. By producing diagnostic evaluations about a discourse that assisted in confining women to the position of inferior cultural workers, female writers could inspect and also call into question the very same discursive practices that deemed them incapable of producing the analytical work associated with men's superior intelligence. In making fashion an important reference point for their work, in other words, these women writers were drawing attention to the gendered logic that continued to affect the professional lives and creative pursuits of those women who had chosen careers in the arts in the years between the wars.

Modernism, middlebrow literature and the interwar literary market

If the previous passages have explained why *Modernism, Fashion and Interwar Women Writers* privileges a gendered approach to the study of interwar literature and fashion, the purpose of the following paragraphs is to show how this study understands the relationships among commercial literature, literary modernism – initially associated by critics with a predominantly male tradition of experimental writing – and the work of the female novelists included. Throughout this introduction, I have proposed that Wharton, Rhys, Lehmann, Bowen and to a certain extent even Woolf, had to negotiate the tensions between two main literary collectives: commercially successful prose and literary modernism as its conceptual antithesis – literary formations identified respectively by Bourdieu as 'the *field of large-scale cultural production*, specifically organised with a view to the production of cultural goods destined for non-producers of cultural goods, "the public at large"' and 'the *field of restricted production* as a system producing cultural goods (and instruments for appropriating these goods) objectively destined for a public of producers of cultural goods' (1993: 127).[24] Given recent attempts made by critics to diversify our notions of the modernist canon, this idea to propose modernism as a discrete critical category might, of course, appear counterproductive. What scholarship on the relationship between modernism and middlebrow literary culture has demonstrated is that the boundaries between these ostensibly opposing categories were permeable and easily negotiable.[25] Even more recently, Kristin Bluemel's term 'intermodernism' has offered useful nomenclature for further expanding our critical vocabulary for studying twentieth-century literature (2009: 5).[26] But I maintain that modernism is a necessary term in the chapters to come – less so because it should be used as a critical paradigm today but because it was seen as a separate literary tradition that was promoted as such in the interwar period as a counterpoint to the work produced by writers who were little concerned about their commercial entanglements with the market. One only needs to look at critical explorations dealing with late modernism to see how much the towering reputation of writers such as Pound, Eliot or Joyce influenced authors writing alongside or in the wake of the high modernists. Rod Rosenquist, for instance, uses the term 'ascendant' or 'hegemonic modernism' for referencing exactly the kind of 'dominant mode of critical values led by the cultural and institutional power of, most obviously, Eliot and, to varying extents, Pound, Joyce and others' (2009: 4). Although I do not adopt Rosenquist's proposed terms, I am indebted to his proposition that 'the contemporaries of the high modernists viewed them as forming a coherent and dominant group of writers' (2009: 17).[27] Naturally, modernism's insistence on intellectual exclusivity would thereby have been the most forceful strategy of demarcating the movement's intellectual contours, confirming it as a literary tradition in its own right. As Rosenquist argues, those 'who found themselves marginalized by the establishment of high modernism' would also be the ones to 'speak most clearly of the nature of the literary field in the modernist period' (2009: 18).

In what follows, I certainly do not propose that we should revert to the kind of monolithic version of literary modernism that has been rejected in the wake of recent interest in middlebrow or intermodernist literature. Even if these all-inclusive designations are sometimes in danger of submerging into critical collectives too many different voices that defy – each in their own way – the development of conceptual universals, these scholarly attempts to redraw the interwar literary field have been immensely helpful because they have brought back into view the work of many all-but-forgotten (female) writers who deserve our attention. But I do suggest that the understanding of an exclusive modernism was one that was available to the writers examined in *Modernism, Fashion and Interwar Women Writers* – some of whom actively defined its critical afterlife and helped to transform it from avant-garde movement into prestige commodity. When Bowen published her study *English Novelists* in 1946, for instance, she suggested that E. M. Forster and Woolf 'epitomize English tradition', moving 'forward along lines of their own' (47). Years later, in a preface for a 1960 edition of *Orlando*, she would make this point even more emphatically, suggesting that a younger generation of writers 'were not only the author's most zealous readers, but, in the matter of reputation, most jealous guardians. Her aesthetic became a faith; we were believers' (1952b: 40). Although she does not apply the term 'modernist' to their work, Bowen nonetheless presents, in comments such as the ones cited above, the work of these writers as a literary tradition in its own right.[28] Lehmann, in her obituary notice for Woolf, which will be discussed in more detail in Chapter 3, similarly cemented the reputation of the older writer as a paragon of the modernist literary tradition. These examples, taken from the work of two of the novelists included, demonstrate the extent to which these authors were involved in defining modernism as an aesthetic category determining the literary field of their time. The myth of an exclusive modernism that based its right of existence on formal difficulty, novelty and the cult of the individual was explicitly cultivated in the interwar period, and it was a myth further propagated, as we shall see, by some of the writers included in this study. As such, modernism can best be seen as one of Bourdieu's 'pseudo-concepts' or '*practical* classifying tools' that created 'resemblances and differences' 'in the *struggle for recognition* by the artists themselves or their accredited critics' (1993: 106). Like mainstream or commercially successful writing, modernism was created as an effective marker of distinction that organised into relational categories literary activity in the interwar period. It is in this manner that both terms are understood and used in *Modernism, Fashion and Interwar Women Writers*.

Indeed, accepting that this particular logic of distinction between modernism and mainstream culture informed contemporary writers' conception of literature is particularly important, I suggest, for studies that are, like the current one, interested in historicising the mechanisms by which opinions about literary tastes and aesthetic values were created, articulated and challenged in the interwar period. And the fact that my own study does not endorse or reiterate but rather aims to historicise the cultural associations attached to these artistic formations has hopefully become apparent by my choice of authors. Purposely, I have selected a range of different female authors for analysis – ranging from Wharton, the bestselling writer of novels of manners, to Woolf, the most canonised female modernist of the interwar period – to show that the diversity inherent in these interwar literary productions actually contradicted the reality of such literary binaries as modernism and popular prose writing. Although these conceptual absolutes were certainly endorsed by some of the writers I study in *Modernism, Fashion and Interwar Women Writers*, the appearance of many of their texts very clearly problematises the logic of such classificatory systems. To what extent is Lehmann's comfortable association with commercially successful literary traditions unsettled by her use of themes borrowed from a high modernist precursor? And how does Bowen's focus on exteriors and surfaces challenge the preoccupation with interiority that supposedly characterised modernist literary aesthetics? To address questions such as these, modernism as a terminological construct will be used in the chapters to come because it helps to demarcate those conceptual boundaries that the chosen women authors endorsed or transgressed in their writing.

Affiliations

This study obviously establishes a dialogue with but also departs significantly from existing work on modernist literature and fashion, and before concluding these introductory passages, I want to clarify how my project differs from these other critical explorations. Doing so will provide an opportunity to explain the logic that has motivated the choice of authors included, and it will also allow me to reference the work of another fashion theorist that will be of immense importance in subsequent chapters. Fashion, it is worth re-emphasising at this point, is understood in this study as a discourse about affiliations. And at the beginning of the twentieth century, Georg Simmel was the sociologist who most succinctly described fashion's social hermeneutics, arguing in 1904 that 'adaptation' and 'differentiation' were its 'two antagonistic principles' (1971: 295–6).[29] In the case studies that follow, I will repeatedly return to these propositions made by Simmel when I suggest that fashion is identified by the included writers as a cultural force that brings individuals into associative connections. Bowen, in fact, goes as far as visualising fashion's ability to encourage connective sociability in her use of the sartorial image of the tie. Reading fashion imagery in the work of Wharton, Rhys, Lehmann, Bowen or Woolf, that is, is to realise that these novelists were exceptionally committed to exploring how different, at times contending, social forces determined and transformed subjective experiences. For these writers, I shall argue, identity formation and community building were complex processes thoroughly tied up with sartorial practices.

Because it sets out to investigate how the chosen novelists described and at times criticised social protocols determined by fashion, *Modernism, Fashion and Interwar Women Writers* parts ways with an existing strand of scholarship that derives its critical purchase from identifying reductionist aesthetics as the common motif of modernist literature and women's early twentieth-century dress designs. The simple, economic Flapper dress, Judith Brown accordingly proposes, 'finds its ideal condition in the clean (synthetic, cold, abstract) lines of high modernism' (2009: 1). As Brown argues, modernist aesthetics shares with glamour a reliance on abstraction and a fascination with surface impressions. Modernist style, in this particular critical construction, is associated with detachment rendered visible in the clarity and simplicity of its form, in the 'cool precision' of Wallace

Stevens's poetic language, for instance (Brown 2009: 16). Related to Brown's argument is Jessica Burstein's reading of 'cold modernism' as a variety of different art forms – among which she also lists fashion – that prioritise surfaces, the mechanical and the inhuman as thematic accents. Individuality, the self and subjectivity are dismissed in what Burstein calls modernism's 'vocabulary of the clinical'. 'Eliot's endorsement of a depersonalized art' and Pound's 'aesthetic of properly modernist language, with his emphasis on the clean phrase' are cited by Burstein as particular pertinent examples (2002: 230). Compatible with the language of the scientist, *Imagisme*'s verbal economy and directness recall the minimalism and the clear geometrical lines of the new couture of the early twentieth century. Pound's recommendation to '[u]se either no ornament or good ornament' would find many visual parallels in contemporary fashion plates (Rainey 2005: 96).

There is no doubt that modernist work can be organised according to Burstein's distinction between 'hot' and 'cold' modernism,[30] but this critical mandate would probably lead to some problematic (albeit intriguing) contradictions if followed too rigorously. It would be fascinating to see, for instance, where individual episodes of Joyce's *Ulysses* (1922) end up in this relational reading of modernist forms. However, it is not my intention to question Burstein's attempt to create new critical subdivisions in modernist studies. What interests me is that the bulk of existing criticism seems to use fashion (and conceptually related fields) to propose a particular version of modernism, one that emphasises impersonality, detachment and emotional austerity as its programmatic concerns.[31] No doubt, this conjoined reading of modernism and fashion owes a lot to the deathly glamour we associate with displays on catwalks in contemporary fashion shows. The androgyny of fashion models and the inexpressiveness of their faces create the impression of mute impersonality. Individual bodies disappear to become surfaces for the display of sartorial creations. It is understandable, therefore, that a particularly evocative image of modern fashion is that of translucent deathliness that discounts individuality to display scenes of stylish detachment. In what follows, however, I offer an alternative account of modernist literature and fashion, one that comprehends fashion first and foremost as a set of sartorial practices that brings into view an individual's social affiliations. Thus far, emotive and stylistic penury has been considered the common purview of modernist literature and fashion. *Modernism, Fashion and Interwar Women Writers*, I want to stress at this juncture, conversely registers an interest in fashion's social causalities in the work of the included writers.[32] By examining how they used fashion to think about identity formation and community building in the interwar period, this monograph purposefully presents their works as socially embedded literary texts interested in exploring the place of the individual in a complexly structured modern world.[33]

To date, the only critic who has addressed the issue of modernism's investments in the social dynamics produced by contemporary garment culture is Celia Marshik, who states that British literature of the interwar period uses a particular set of garments (the evening gown, the mackintosh, fancy dress and second-hand clothing) to unsettle anthropocentric notions about subject-object relations. '[W]riters of the period', she states, 'employ clothing to challenge the fantasy that the human subject is in control of or privileged in the material world. Authors repeatedly stage conflicts', she concludes, 'between subjects and garments to suggest that clothing *damages*, *reduces*, and even *erases* subjects' (2017: 8). My work is in sympathy with her suggestion that clothing has agency and can occasionally resist 'the desires of the human subject who wears it' (2017: 13). But as my chapter on Bowen illustrates particularly well, this study also suggests that women writers of the interwar period were not always fearful about clothes' tendency to destabilise the place of the human subject in the world of material objects. At times, they optimistically registered clothing's ability to bring individuals into contact in diverse, unexpected and often meaningful ways. By noting that sartorial objects can have conjunctive functions, the writers studied here therefore offer a different and, at times, less pessimistic view on contemporary garment culture. It is true, the results of the social interactions produced by fashion are not always desirable, and these are the moments when my selected authors astutely criticise fashion's interventions in contemporary gender politics. Overall, however, their engagement with fashion shows that we do not have to read everyday garments exclusively as sites for making manifest early twentieth-century anxieties about subject-object relationships. Rather, I suggest, women writers of the period saw fashion first and foremost as an important agent in producing intersubjective relations – dynamic social processes that were rife with both perils and pleasures.[34]

How individual authors responded to the suggestion that fashion organised the modern subject's social relations is detailed below. Before this introduction can be concluded by offering a chapter-by-chapter synopsis, however, a word needs to be said about the affiliations among the writers that this study proposes to establish by reading their work side by side. Evidently, not all of them can or would have wanted to be associated with the modernist movement. Wharton is the most obvious case in point but even Bowen or Lehmann's place in the modernist canon has yet to be confirmed. In fact, one problem for scholars interested in establishing new critical paradigms for the study of anglophone women writers of the interwar period seems to be that there existed, as Jane Garrity explains, 'no organized group of women literary practitioners in Britain during the period of high-modernist activity comparable with the female expatriate communities in Paris' or one that resembled 'the system of patronage that was foundational to the institutional structure of male modernism' (2003: 19). As the owner of the Hogarth Press, Woolf had the ability and the institutional position but not the inclination to establish a canon of female writing in Britain.[35] Noteworthy connections, both personal and professional, were established among some of the novelists included in this study and some of these are discussed in my chapter on Lehmann. But it is certainly correct that no distinct movement of interwar female writers existed in Britain that could have been used to determine this project's selection of authors.

As a result, the main organising principle for *Modernism, Fashion and Interwar Women Writers*'s choice of authors was – apart from their apparent interest in fashion and their historical or in some cases also their geographical co-existence – these women's professional decision to self-identify as novelists who *engaged*, in one way or another, with modernist experimentation: Rhys, Lehmann and Bowen wrote in the wake of the high modernists; Wharton was, as we shall see below, an astute critic of modernism; and Woolf's position as the principal female writer of the 1920s literary avant-garde in Britain was one, I show in Chapter 5, that she carefully guarded but also reconsidered in the political climate of the 1930s. And the focus on novelistic prose writing easily proposed itself because of an obvious etymological connection between the two expressions 'novel' and 'novelty', the latter being fashion's essential, albeit complexly composed, refrain.[36] Moreover, both fashion and the novel are cultural productions whose histories share many common threads: democratisation, secularisation, technological innovations and middle-class aspirations that were reflected in increased literacy rates are among the cultural tractions responsible, from the eighteenth century onwards, for the mass production of affordable consumer articles. Books and clothes were equally popular commodities that started to be manufactured and sold in increasing quantities – one reason why the novel was subsequently denigrated as light-hearted entertainment that lacked the intellectual clout of poetry and other established prose forms. Its emphasis on the quotidian, the everyday world of the reader, additionally associates the novel, throughout English literary history, with ephemerality and obsolescence. Its subject material, it was often suggested, is of short-lived interest as much as its moral substance is irrelevant or questionable.[37] Like fashion, its conceptually related double, the novel was seen as the flimsy by-product of commodity culture developing in the aftermath of the Industrial Revolution.[38]

For all its complex origins as an eighteenth-century commodity, the novel was nonetheless valued by some interwar writers as a textual site that could render visible – in a manner that poetry simply could not – social synergies and emotional connections among individuals. Bowen, in fact, was one author who was an outspoken novel interceder. As Chapter 3 will show, she argued forcefully for the novel's potential for social analysis. In her view, its intersecting storylines and its organisation of characters in collective formations made it the most appropriate vehicle for writers who aimed to examine the social currents of their time. Although I realise that this assessment of the novel is prejudiced – anyone who has read Robert Browning's *The Ring and the Book* (1869) or comparable narrative poems might raise objections to the propositions made by Bowen – I accept these ideas about the novel as the literary medium with the most fully developed social awareness because it is a viewpoint explicitly conveyed by at least one writer selected for study in *Modernism, Fashion and Interwar Women Writers*. Since the eighteenth century, both of these popular cultural productions, fashion and novels, had been considered by many as invasive forces that threatened to contaminate, if not supersede, the dominion of serious art. As this study acknowledges, at the beginning of the twentieth century, fashion's multiple and conflicting meanings were extensively debated in the novel, the literary form that was its most obvious textual equivalent.

It was on this particular literary terrain that fashion was given the most serious consideration.

I begin with Wharton – a decision that needs, perhaps, some further explanation. Because authorial engagements with the interwar culture industry and with celebrity culture were differently organised on each side of the Atlantic,[39] this study on modernism and fashion generally focuses on analysing the authorial and textual self-stylings performed by interwar female writers that have become associated with the British or Anglo-Irish tradition.[40] Wharton, the grande dame of American realism, clearly stands out in this group. But even if the transatlantic focus of her later novels or her permanent residency in Europe after 1914 are deemed insufficient reasons for putting her side by side with the other women writers in this study, her role as a very determined opponent of fashion demands attention. As Wharton saw it, fashion progressively levelled sartorial and literary styles, creating a market dominated by standardised tastes and forms. But Wharton, Chapter 1 also shows, was an equally fervent critic of modernism's veneration of novelty. In fact, her views about modernism as the conceptual rebound of an entertainment industry committed to constructing an endless line of celebrity authors further explicate my arguments about modernism as a literary fashion that was deliberately constructed in the interwar period. Long before scholars began to be interested in the topic, Wharton, who determinedly self-styled as an author writing in the realist tradition, had perceptively identified modernism's underground links with the contemporary culture industry. For Wharton critics, my argument is therefore significant because it proposes a new way in which to read her renunciation of a younger, presumably more risk-embracing generation of writers and artists. If scholarship to date has tried to excuse her anti-modernist traditionalism as the unfortunate intellectual mood of her later years or found that modernist elements inadvertently crept into her 1920s fiction, my chapter shows that her rejection of modernism was in line with her critical attitude towards an interwar publishing industry that commodified aesthetics. For scholars of modernism, Wharton should matter, I argue here, because she was among the first to note modernism's economic affiliations with those market conditions that many of its main proponents hoped to resist or conceal.

Jean Rhys, who is the subject of Chapter 2, is best described as a marginal modernist of the interwar period. Although she began her writing career under the tutelage of Ford Madox Ford, the thematic radicalness and the stylistic eccentricity of her later interwar work eventually isolated this author from a group of artists with innovative ideas for artistic and political renewal. By the end of the 1930s, Rhys was a little-known author whose name had once been mentioned in the same breath as those of other modernist writers. This narrative about Rhys's self-styling as a trenchant non-conformist is developed in *Modernism, Fashion and Interwar Women Writers* by analysing the role that fashion played in her life and interwar fiction. Through her work as a mannequin, Rhys obviously had insider information about the Parisian fashion industry, and she returned in her writing to explorations of its operational procedures to confirm some of Wharton's views about fashion's tendency to standardise female dress and demeanour. But Rhys, a woman much younger than Wharton, was also the recipient of an extensive advertising campaign that openly capitalised on women's post-war demands for social, political and professional mobility to promote the new look of the Flapper as the symbol of these emancipatory dreams. Although she was herself deeply attracted to fashion's seductive imagery, Rhys, as my chapter argues, saw through this elaborate marketing campaign and realised that the image of the fashionable modern woman, promoted widely as a reservoir for creative image construction, could be adversarial to social change. Because it reaffirmed (and further encouraged) women's position as consumers whose self-esteem relied on a psychological dependence on clothes, it hindered rather than advanced women's demands for political participation and for socio-economic independence. To offset and criticise the prevalent and politically problematic image of feminine energy and competence produced by the contemporary fashion discourse, Rhys created heroines, texts and, above all, an authorial self-image that relied on an overt and extravagant display of (personal and stylistic) difference. If modernism was, due to successful marketing, in the interwar period beginning to be associated with formal idiosyncrasy, Rhys, I suggest in this chapter, significantly extended this request for thematic and stylistic complexity to a degree that could no longer be reconciled with the demands of mainstream culture. As her case illustrates, too much eccentricity gives rise to critical neglect. Had it not been for the spectacular success of her later novel, *Wide Sargasso Sea* (1966), the interwar novels of an author who was as unwilling as she was incapable to effectively self-style as bohemian modernist would be all but forgotten.

The following two chapters focus on the work of two early popularisers of modernism's programmatic concerns: Lehmann and Bowen. Both women, I argue here, fashioned their images as professional writers in response to modernist experimentation in general and to the work of Woolf in particular. Among the two, however, Lehmann must certainly be seen as the author who was more inclined to reverentially imitate aspects of Woolf's work, and this inclination to model herself on the older writer is particularly apparent in the 1932 coming-of-age novel *Invitation to the Waltz*. This text, as I shall show, engages with fashion by discussing women's decisions to follow or to reject preconceived sartorial, social or textual patterns. In the first place, it criticises the 1920s fashion industry, the producer of patterned femininities, for encouraging young women of the interwar period to align themselves with patriarchy's traditional scripts. For Lehmann fashion was the defender of gender orthodoxies rather than the liberator of women demanding political equality for the sexes. But *Invitation to the Waltz*, my chapter proposes, does more than analyse contemporary socio-sartorial protocols. This novel is of further interest to my study because it self-consciously explores its reliance on particular literary patterns that led to its construction. Although it clearly seems indebted to the traditional romance plot, Lehmann explicitly references *To the Lighthouse* in *Invitation to the Waltz*, identifying Woolf's novel as a particularly inviting literary configuration to follow. Her work therefore adopts a form of writing I propose to call modish modernism because it deliberately aimed to combine modernist experimentation with the possibility of popular success. Lehmann herself, I conclude in this chapter, should thus be seen as an author whose complexly formed intellectual and professional aspirations have yet to be acknowledged.

In comparison to the already mentioned novelists, Bowen's outlook on fashion was unperturbed, almost positive. Although she acknowledged that she feared the reality of the mass-produced look, she nonetheless believed that fashion presented the individual with creative possibilities for self-expression. She was a fascinated observer of modern consumer culture, and she enjoyed analysing its impact on the modern subject in those of her novels that are set, like *To the North* (1932), in cosmopolitan centres and contexts. Unsurprisingly, therefore, consumer objects such as dresses and other sartorial items are repeatedly identified as connective devices that bring individuals together in various, sometimes meaningful constellations. But while she clearly welcomed sartorial commodities' ability to generate intersubjective energies, Bowen, who needed to make money from her writing, was nonetheless critical of a marketplace determined to turn her own novels into fashionable commodities. This apprehension encouraged reflections on the commodification of literature. It provoked Bowen's conceptual distinction between the 'imaginative' and the merely 'inventive' writer who seeks publication in order to make money (1952b: 152). And as her business correspondence with publishers and editors shows, it also prompted her to distinguish her fiction from her journalism in the attempt to demarcate her novels as serious works of art. Modernism, I argue in Chapter 4, was particular relevant for Bowen in these attempts to secure a highbrow label for her novels because its insistence on cultural exclusivity provided her with a useful model for artistic self-fashioning, one that allowed her to ostensibly circumvent the demands of a market set on commodifying her work. To realise how much Bowen emphasised her stylistic and thematic idiosyncrasies, I argue, is to acknowledge that she became, like Lehmann, an important populariser of modernist art forms during the interwar period. She might have rejected a modernist insistence on interiority in the development of her characters, but she nonetheless appropriated another one of modernism's programmatic interests when she tried to safeguard her reputation as a serious artist: the insistence on the superior value of a writer's inimitable, individualist style.

Modernism, Fashion and Interwar Women Writers's final chapter turns to the analysis of Woolf's engagement with a particular aspect of modern fashion's conceptual apparatus: uniformity. This topic, I argue, is essential for understanding the political facets of Woolf's later works. These, it needs to be remembered, were produced at a time when totalitarian regimes had begun to manipulate modern identity politics through appropriating modern fashion practices for propagandist purposes. It was in the fascist obsession with uniforms, used deliberately to regiment individuals by incorporating them in synchronised clusters and groups, that the suggestion to emulate prefabricated types found its most ghastly and perverted expression. To Woolf, this submersion of the individual – a concept highly prized in her writing – in such authoritarian constellations bent on enforcing restrictions to personal freedoms through uniformity would have been the logical but also the most frightful outcome of capitalist modernity's investment in producing standardised forms and looks. Unsurprisingly, therefore, a dedication to exploring the cultural meaning of such concepts and signifiers as uniforms and uniformity manifests itself in *The Years* (1937), in *Three Guineas* (1938) and in the three-volume scrapbook of reading notes she collected when writing *Three Guineas* – writing and notes, in which Woolf extensively debated and ultimately critiqued women's reliance on uniform but also on conspicuous dress in the hope of fashioning stable psychological selves and harmonious social relations. But, I show in the second part of the chapter, Woolf's disapproval of fashion as a social force that eradicates individuality through collectivising does not mean that she was categorically opposed to all uniform cultural productions. While she anxiously watched how the political events of the 1930s gave way to another world war, she realised that a partial compliance with a market producing standardised forms and looks was a necessary strategy to bring her feminist and pacifist arguments into wider circulation. My chapter therefore ends by tracing Woolf's voluntary affiliation with an interwar culture industry that favoured the dissemination of standardised and easily marketable literary products and I do this by analysing the Hogarth editors' decision to introduce a Uniform Edition of Woolf's work in the late 1920s. By examining Woolf's different, if not conflicting, views on uniforms and uniformity in this manner, I will show that a surprising willingness to engage with uniformity and with the commercial structures of the literary marketplace distinguished the final years of the career of a writer who had previously made exclusivity and difference important trademarks of her artistic self-conception.

Jointly, these chapters confirm that fashion was a significant presence in the work of the included novelists. All of them noted that it cooperated, in diverse and complex ways, in reinforcing gender hierarchies in a rapidly changing interwar culture that had made the concentration on novelty, diversity and innovation one of its much-lauded inspirations and responsibilities. Fashion, I argue throughout, was a topic of communal interest for these novelists because it gave them the opportunity to examine the workings of modern identity politics. It could be politically appropriated, and it is these appropriations of fashion in the name of contemporary gender politics that they discussed in their writing. But fashion also provided these writers with conceptual vocabulary to analyse the changes brought to their chosen profession. Fashion, they realised, fundamentally changed the commercial and cultural landscape of the early twentieth century, and it affected the ways in which books were written, sold and read. A writer's self-image, reputation and critical reception hinged on what was considered fashionable. To resulting pressures and opportunities women writers responded in different ways. *Modernism, Fashion and Interwar Women Writers* tells the story of five of them, showing how they crafted their literary personas and their novels in response to authoritative cultural guidelines determined by fashion – a cultural force that extended its reach to areas beyond the realm of the sartorial and that directly assisted in the production of artistic tastes at the beginning of the twentieth century. Commercial and aesthetic categories consistently overlapped in debates about literature, culture and taste in the interwar period. This book is about the resulting tensions between economics and art, about the ways in which a select number of women writers of the period used fashion terminology to examine the creation of cultural values and it is also about the possibilities available to women to express difference and individuality in a world that actually seemed to favour standardised products and collective formations.

Notes

1. 'The New Dress' (Woolf 1979a: 61–73) was written as a postscript to *Mrs Dalloway* when Woolf was revising the novel for publication. It deals with the attempt of a middle-aged woman to express difference and originality through dress – a process that backfires, leaving the protagonist to agonise not only about her appearance but also about her personal achievements and lifestyle choices. For a more detailed discussion of this story and of Mabel's sartorial shame, see Celia Marshik (2017: 59–60) and Lisa Cohen (1999: 152–5).
2. Patricia A. Cunningham (2003) offers a detailed account of the changes in women's dress at the turn of the twentieth century.
3. See Vinken 2005; Geczy and Karaminas 2013; Siegle 2011 for representative examples.
4. Dickens's 'experience of celebrity was diagnostic, foundational, premonitory', argues Joss Marsh, who principally relates the author's cultural currency to the emergence of Victorian celebrity photography (102). Lord Byron, whose self-fashioning as diabolic yet seductive rebel figure allowed him, as one critic put it, 'to leap from mere literary fame into modern celebrity' (McDayter 2009: 2).

5. 'By the latter half of the nineteenth century', argues Leo Braudy, 'even before the tremendous expansion of audience and the media sophistication of our own century, both the resources and the public were available to be exploited and appealed to by those aspiring either to construct greater stages or to appear on them' (506).
6. 'Hollywood's most precious products were the stars that it so carefully groomed and created', argue Stephen Gundle and Clino T. Caselli. 'These human commodities were the main object of Hollywood fantasy, and in the 1920s and 1930s vast amounts of effort and money were invested in their creation' (66–7). In 1927, the actress Clara Bow became the most emblematic embodiment of Hollywood's star culture, a phenomenon called the 'It-Effect' by Joseph Roach who identifies it as an actor's 'personality driven mass attraction' that could be manipulated to great effect by Hollywood's directors and producers (3).
7. 'If in a shift of fashion, the cut of a dress has been slightly modified, if clusters of ribbons and curls have been dethroned by rosettes, if bonnets have widened and chignons have come down a little on the nape of the neck, if waist-lines have been raised and skirts become fuller', Baudelaire states, 'you may be sure that from a long way off [the artist's] eagle's eye will have detected it' (401).
8. 'Where, then, is this elusive modernity located, if not merely in "the landscapes of the great city", with their threatening crowds and "pomps and circumstances"? Baudelaire chose to emphasize its location in the fleeing beauty of *fashion*', writes David Frisby (18).
9. Needless to say, this narrative about fashion's absolute preference for the present moment has been challenged by critics who define it as an elaborate system of citationality. 'Despite the fact that fashion is an arena dedicated to novelty, indeed that could be said to fetishise novelty', Caroline Evans argues, 'the present [is] constantly invaded by images of the past that seeped in, settled into the cracks and colonised the terrain of "the new"' (2003: 20).
10. Timothy W. Galow (313–29) examines F. Scott Fitzgerald's later career as a writer in light of these suggestions about the volatility of an author's public appeal.
11. 'Fame shades imperceptibly into fashion, while fashion, in its turn, spawns and then discards an infinite parade of superficial distinctions', Braudy states (4).
12. Felicity Nussbaum (148–68) examines the cultural mechanisms that produced actors and actresses as modern celebrities in the eighteenth century.
13. For further reading on the rise of fashion in the eighteenth century, see 'The Commercialization of Fashion' (McKendrick, Brewer and Plumb 1983: 34–99).

14. Kracauer's pessimistic comments about 'literary hits', which firmly associate artistic productivity with other forms of interwar cultural productions, somewhat contradict Joe Moran's more recent suggestion that literary celebrity 'is not simply an adjunct of mainstream celebrity, but an elaborate system of representations in its own right, produced and circulated across a wide variety of media'. In the views of contemporaries, here represented by Kracauer's observations, literary celebrity was indeed 'a straightforward effect of the commodification of culture' (Moran 2000: 4).

15. Apart from Wharton, Wyndham Lewis can be credited with being one of the first critics who addressed modernism's disavowed collaborations with fashion and mass culture. By uncompromisingly branding their work as intellectually and creatively autonomous, writers such as Woolf and her affiliates, Lewis suggested in 'The Caliph's Design' (1919), strategically advertised themselves as 'superficial corrective' to the dominant taste of the day. Modernism's insistence on its countercultural impulse, he argues, actually confirms the capitalist mechanisms of a market it aims to surpass (162–3). R. S. Koppen further analyses Lewis's critical attitude towards Bloomsbury modernism (92–114).

16. It might have already become apparent how much I am indebted to Faye Hammill's work, which argues that the way in which women writers 'presented themselves, and were presented by publishers and journalists, often relates to the style projected through the language of their texts' (2007: 4). Although Hammill's study does not focus on modernism as such, her pertinent suggestion that the pressure exerted on women writers such as Dorothy Parker, Anita Loos or Stella Gibbons to fashion glamorously distinct authorial personas manifested itself very clearly in their writing has had considerable influence on my arguments. More recently, Hope Howell Hodgkins (2016) has similarly suggested that a select group of twentieth-century women writers aligned their stylistic choices with the descriptions of their characters' clothes.

17. Although they were, no doubt, aware of the problematic cultural associations attached to the image of the woman writer as the producer of commercially successful prose, Bowen and Woolf also noticed that money legitimised their status as working professionals. 'Money dignifies what is frivolous if unpaid for', wrote Woolf in *A Room of One's Own*. 'It might still be well to sneer at "blue stockings with an itch for scribbling", but it could not be denied that they could put money in their purses' (84). Bowen similarly argued in an introduction to a reprint of her first collection of short stories that '[t]here could be but one test of validity: publication. I know I shaped every line in the direction of the unknown arbiter' (1952b: 83–4).

18. As Hammill notes, '[a]ssumptions about gender, popularity, and literary value are also part of the explanation for the marginalization' of women writers whose work is associated with popular culture (2007: 208).
19. It is certainly no coincidence that fashion magazines of the 1920s championed an austere and businesslike look for women who hoped to succeed in the various professional sectors opening up after the end of the First World War. See Chapter 4 for more information on this interwar discourse about women's correct sartorial appearance in the workspace.
20. This cooperative relationship between male modernists and fashion manifested itself in two different ways. In the first instance, these writers could extensively deliberate fashion in their writing. One would only have to think of Joyce's 'Nausicaa' episode to find an example of a high modernist text written by a male author, in which the willingness to discuss fashion's cultural currency is cunningly recalibrated to showcase its producer's ingenuity. In creating a feminine consciousness that constructs itself in response to the rhetoric of contemporary fashion journals, Joyce daringly absorbs an aspect of popular culture into his highbrow novel (Leonard 1998: 98–141; Gibson 2002: 127–49) while still safely assigning the very same discourse to a woman. The result is a hybrid textual construction that challenges established notions of serious literature in the same manner in which it presents Joyce as an artistic rebel figure. But male modernists could also, as was the case with the Futurists, make the invention of a new sartorial apparatus an aspect of their proposition for cultural reconstruction. It is certainly no coincidence that a tradition of exquisite dressing based on flamboyance, which was begun by Oscar Wilde and included Wyndham Lewis, the Futurists and, to a certain extent, even T. S. Eliot, and which would openly fly in the face of Flügel's theory about the great masculine renunciation, established itself among male modernists in Europe. For more information on the Futurist couture see Giacomo Balla, *Il vestito antineutrale* (1914), a short pamphlet that is discussed by Eugenia Paulicelli (2009: 187–207).
21. At this point, my argument departs from that of Loren Glass, who suggests that American male writers such as Jack London, Ernest Hemingway or Norman Mailer deliberately adopted a tradition of 'hypermasculine public posturing' to sidestep derogatory associations with mass culture, celebrity and the marketplace as feminine-coded phenomena and institutions (18).
22. One contemporary reviewer referred to Sitwell as the '"big noise" which is heard above the tinkling rhythms of less original poetry' (Anon. 1927a: 127). Radclyffe Hall, as Laura Doan (2001: *passim*) has shown, was similarly successful in her careful self-styling as celebrity author by appropriating male postures and costumes. And Mina Loy and Djuna Barnes are, as Alex Goody has argued, other examples of modernist

women writers who effectively appropriated fashion to develop their authorial personas (266–82).

23. It is, of course, hardly necessary to point out that the fashion theory canon that includes the work of such writers as Thomas Carlyle, Herbert Spencer, Baudelaire, Georg Simmel, Sombart, Kracauer, Benjamin and Flügel was exceptionally male-dominated at the time when my chosen authors were writing. The tendency to assign the role of fashion critic to a man and that of the scrutinised object to a woman thereby manifests itself most explicitly in Baudelaire, whose 'The Painter of Modern Life' proposes 'an artist, man of the world, man of the crowd' as the critical appreciator of fashion. In fact, 'the soldier' and 'the dandy' are the only masculine types singled out for closer inspection by Baudelaire in an essay that concludes with an extensive discussion of 'woman', whose 'iridescent clouds of draperies in which she envelops herself' are, according to Baudelaire, 'the pedestal of her divinity' and who is identified by the author as 'the object of the most intense admiration and interest that the spectacle of life can offer to man's contemplation' (423; 424).

24. 'In his theorisation of the fields which structure cultural production, Pierre Bourdieu uses terms that resonate particularly strongly with the modernist period', argues Joanne Winning. 'Modernism, with its protean attempts at innovation, its experimental emphasis on form and its reliance on network and coterie culture for dissemination, represents just such a field of restricted production' (127).

25. I am referring here as much to Nicola Humble's pioneering work, *The Feminine Middlebrow Novel, 1920s to 1950s: Class, Domesticity, and Bohemianism* (2001), as to other scholarship following in the wake of her influential study. See, for instance, Erica Brown and Mary Grover (eds), *Middlebrow Literary Cultures: The Battle of the Brows, 1920–1960* (2012) for a recent essay collection that further investigates the possibilities and limitations inherent in using this critical designation for the study of twentieth-century literary culture.

26. A recent collection edited by Maroula Joannou aims to recuperate the work of lesser known, interwar women writers for academic consideration by similarly complicating our understanding of modernism. Joannou here proposes to move towards 'a consideration of a plurality of Modernisms distinguishing between "high Modernism" and low' when studying British women's writing (2013: 4).

27. Tyrus Miller similarly argues that late modernists struggled against but also confirmed 'the apotheosis of form in earlier modernism' by developing 'a repertoire of means for unsettling the signs of formal craft that testified to the modernist writer's discursive mastery' (1999: 19).

28. Bowen's role as an early critic of literary modernism is further evidenced by her other essays on such authors as Forster, Joyce, Lehmann, Rose

Macaulay and Katherine Mansfield (Bowen 2008: 239–47, 272–83, 284–7; Bowen, 1952b: 53–74, 155–8). In 1949, she also reviewed one of the earliest pieces of criticism on Woolf, Bernard Blackstone's *Virginia Woolf: A Commentary* for the *New York Times* (1950: 78–82).

29. Given Simmel's reputation as a theorist of the modern, it is perplexing to see why his work on fashion has been given relatively little attention by scholars working on modernism – especially because his interest in analysing the social responses arising from this apparent interdependency of individuation and assimilation finds such an obvious expression in a literary tradition that is equally invested in the study of the modern individual's responsiveness to multiple, often competing, social impulses. While Simmel's frequently anthologised essay 'The Metropolis and Mental Life' (1903) appears on practically every undergraduate syllabus dealing with modernism, his work on fashion has attracted fewer critical responses. A notable exception is an essay by Ilya Parkins that examines his explorations of fashion from a feminist perspective (2009: 28–49).

30. According to Burstein, the consecration of consciousness and individuality conventionally associated with modernist aesthetics is the outcome of an intellectual debate about a troubled subject-object relationship to which 'hot modernism' responds by producing narratives that 'communicate significance, value, purpose'. Burstein's prime example of 'hot modernism' is D. H. Lawrence's *Women in Love* (1920) – a narrative in which, she asserts, the 'body is resonant with meaning, beating it out like a pulsing heart' (2012: 23–4).

31. Because she insists on 'the importance of style for cold modernism', Burstein considers essential 'the appearance of sartorial fashion' to 'this modernism's contour' (2012: 19). 'Glamour', Brown concurs, 'is cold, indifferent, and deathly; it relies on abstraction, on the thing translated into an idea and therefore the loss of the thing itself, curling away from earthly concerns as if in a whiff of smoke. . . . Here we find another connection to the modernism that favors blankness, the polished surface, the stance of impenetrability (as true in architecture and design as it is in literature), the suspicion of the nothing behind it all . . .' (2009: 5). The conceptual synergies between artificiality and modernism are also drawn out by Faye Hammill in her study of a related concept. She traces sophistication's modern meanings to notions of performance, irony and camp taste and detects impersonality as the motivating force in modern attempts of self-styling (2010: 118).

32. As the editors of a recent collection have argued, fashion 'helps us see everyday life as a site for identity formation through both self-perception and negotiations of the self in relation to others', and it 'provides the ground for an analysis of collectivities as dynamic and dissonant entities

that are composed of individuals – that central category of modernity – whose selfhood is formed through interactions with other people, communities, objects, and ideas' (Parkins and Sheehan 2011: 8).
33. Because I am particularly interested in exploring the representation of fashion's social causalities in modernist fiction, *Modernism, Fashion and Interwar Women Writers* also seeks affiliation with a particular body of scholarship focusing on modernism's depiction of community building. Indicative of this trend are Kate McLoughlin's edited collection *The Modernist Party* (2013) or Jessica Berman, *Modernist Fiction, Cosmopolitanism and the Politics of Community* (2001b).
34. The only critic who has briefly touched upon this subject is Jane Garrity who states in her analysis of Lawrence's *Women in Love* that 'modernist writers used material objects . . . such as clothes and fashion accessories to establish intersubjective relations between characters' (2014: 270).
35. Catherine Clay's analysis of women writers who contributed material to the feminist weekly, *Time and Tide*, comes closest to persuasively suggesting that a close-knit professional community of women writers existed in Britain between the wars. See *British Women Writers 1914–1945: Professional Work and Friendship* (2006).
36. Both words derive their present-day meaning from Middle French terms denoting different components of that which is new. The French nouveauté (innovation, change, character of that which is new) informs the English expression 'novelty', whereas the Middle French nouvelles (news, information) can be identified as the etymological origin of the word 'novel' (*OED*).
37. See, for instance, Samuel Richardson, *The Rambler* 4, Saturday, 31 March 1759 (Johnson 1977: 155–9).
38. 'Fashion is not only a kind of prearticulate anthropology, but the temporal institution prerequisite for the genre of the novel', Mary Campbell argues (2004: 226).
39. Faye Hammill makes this point when noting that the 'systems of literary celebrity culture were on a larger scale in America than elsewhere' (2007: 18).
40. For a comprehensive study of American literary culture and its representation of early twentieth-century fashion, see Lauren S. Cardon, *Fashion and Fiction: Self-Transformation in Twentieth-Century American Literature* (2016). Cardon shows in her readings of canonical American writers such as Wharton, Theodore Dreiser, Anzia Yezierska, Ernest Hemingway, William Faulkner and Nella Larsen that American fashion became increasingly democratic in the early decades of the twentieth century.

Chapter 1

Novelty and the Market: Edith Wharton

The Edith Wharton Collection in the Beinecke Rare Book and Manuscript Library at Yale University contains, among its vast holdings, a torn-out yet carefully preserved newspaper clipping, advertising, in 1913, the imminent publication of *Laddie: A True Blue Story*, sixth novel of the bestselling romance author Gene Stratton-Porter (Figure 1). Natural imagery, birds and thorny branches, frame the ad, while the accompanying blurb ecstatically celebrates the novel's commercial success, calling it 'a wonderful record for a wonderful book'. Indeed, the ad claims that the first printing of *Laddie* – 150,000 copies – had already been sold in the 'two weeks before publication', and the second printing had sold 50,000 copies just 'two weeks after publication'. The literary value of Stratton-Porter's work, at least in this particular newspaper ad, is rendered in numerical terms. Commercial success is explicitly associated with writerly talent.

No doubt, Wharton – who kept this ad and underlined in red pen the phrases 'the three million mark', 'vast reading public because it is true to life' and 'people who love their homes; who figure neither in newspaper nor divorce court; who are the source of the real vitality of the nation' – must have regarded Stratton-Porter as a typical case of an American media-made celebrity author, whose readership might have been vast but whose fame was not necessarily matched by artistic ability.[1] 'Here is a book that every one is talking about', Wharton had noted dryly ten years earlier in her essay 'The Vice of Reading', before concluding that 'the number of its editions is an almost unanswerable proof of its merit' (1996: 102). In all likelihood,

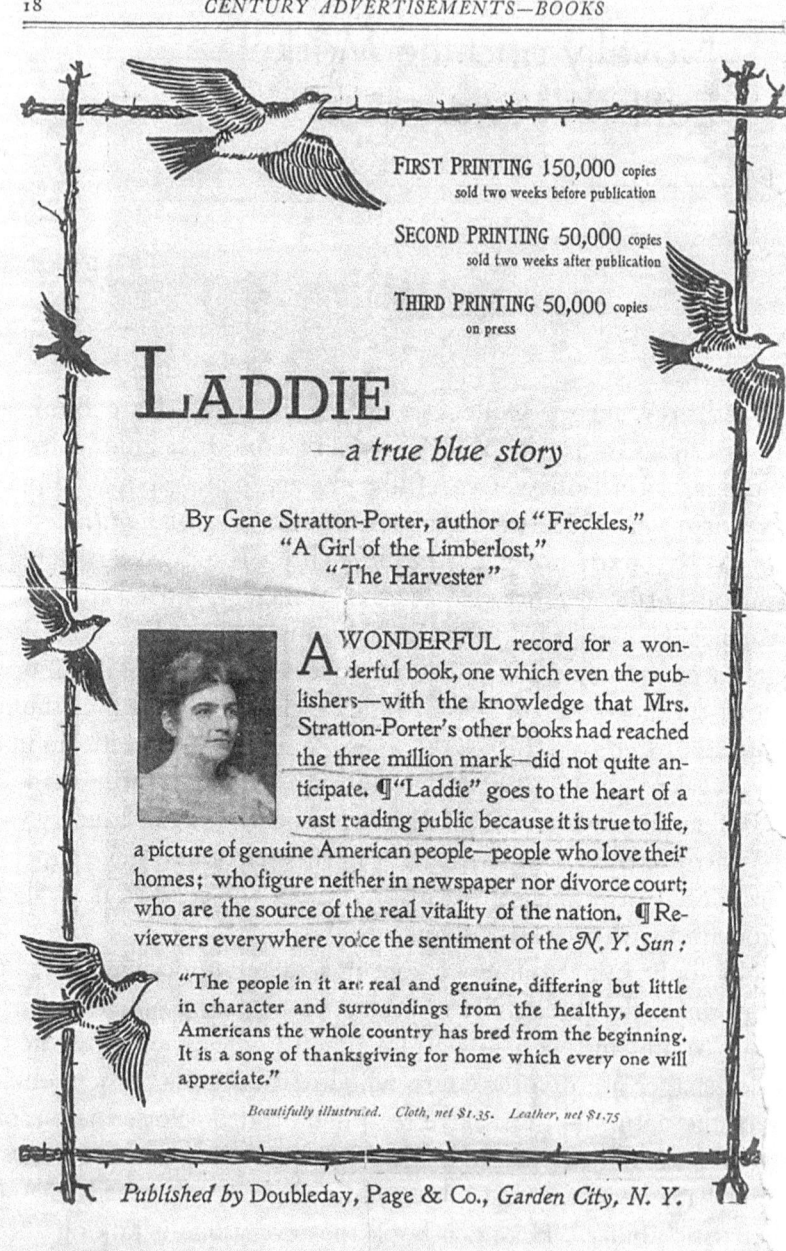

Figure 1 *Century Advertisements: Laddie: A True Blue Story*, 1913, Edith Wharton Collection, 1862–1937, Beinecke Rare Book and Manuscript Library, YCAL MSS 42 1/10/268

the ad for *Laddie* was preserved because it supported Wharton's fear about the decline of artistic standards at the beginning of the twentieth century.[2] If the mass production of literature was responsible for converting readers into unimaginative consumers, blindly following the latest literary trend promoted by publishers' publicity campaigns, this commercialisation of reading habits was synchronised by what Wharton called the 'standardization' of writing practices (1996: 155). In the 1927 essay 'The Great American Novel', Wharton accordingly lamented, in her discussion of standardised American tastes, that '[i]nheriting an old social organization which provided for nicely shaded degrees of culture and conduct, modern America has simplified and Taylorized it out of existence, forgetting that in such matters the process is necessarily one of impoverishment' (1996: 154).[3] In Wharton's view, this trend towards uniformity in literature and the arts amounted to 'cultured mediocrity' and a slow but steady erosion of the intellectual landscape of her time (1996: 178).

Wharton's pessimistic views about a literary marketplace that fetishised novelty while standardising appearances are the focus of this chapter. Throughout, I should say at the outset, I am particularly interested in this author because she was an often perceptive critic of interwar literary culture in general and of modernism in particular – as will become apparent, many of her critical comments about modernist literary aesthetics predate by decades aspects of Aaron Jaffe's conception of the modernist imprimatur. But this chapter also proposes that Wharton's aversion to modernism needs to be read in concert with her equally categorical rejection of fashion. She might have been exceptionally fond of designer dresses, openly acknowledging her 'love of ~~for~~ pretty things – pretty clothes, pretty pictures, pretty sights' in her autobiographical writing (2009, vol.1: 187).[4] But the fact that she patronised Parisian fashion shows throughout her life did not prevent her from determinedly expressing her dislike for fashion, firmly associating it, after she studied the works of the sociologist Herbert Spencer, with common taste, mass culture, even with vulgarity. Indeed, not unlike Sombart, Wharton began to see fashion as a democratising force that produced increasingly uniform looks and forms and that limited – in spite of the often proclaimed veneration of novelty – the subject's ability for creative expression through clothes. The production and reception of interwar literature, she believed, was similarly conditioned by the rules set by modern fashion. In her creative and critical writing, fashion vocabulary therefore surfaces consistently whenever Wharton wanted to criticise literary productions that flourished under the sponsorship of an interwar culture industry that deliberately fashioned celebrity authors and that prioritised artistic creations that conformed to the requirements of serialisation and mass production. Wharton, in other words, would have wholeheartedly endorsed Kracauer's suspicion that literature in the age of industrial modernity was in danger of becoming nothing but a series of 'literary hits whose relevance is limited to their topicality' (1995: 90). In her view, literature had become subjected, like feminine beauty, to the dictates of modern fashion whose perennial search for novelty effectively concealed capitalism's tendency to reduce to a mass standard such cultural productions as books.

Novels such as Stratton-Porter's *Laddie* were representative, Wharton believed, for this observable trend in modern publishing that produced uniformity in writing. But modernism did not score much higher on Wharton's conceptual map of interwar literary culture and it is, once again, her critical attitude to fashion that motivated and that can explain her – perhaps surprising – rejection of a literary movement that fervently insisted on idiosyncrasy and its anti-commercial stance. Fashion, as Sombart had already suggested in 1902, makes change and novelty its organising principles, prescribing a perpetual renewal of last year's models to cover up the drift towards standardisation facilitated by mass production. For Wharton, who seemed to have accepted this perhaps slightly too simplistic reading of fashion as novelty's attendant,[5] an expression of this cultural fixation on the new were the literary efforts of the younger writers of the 1920s. These modernists she censored as harshly as the Stratton-Porters of her time because they remained, she believed, dependent on the commercial conditions of an interwar literary marketplace they ostensibly rejected and hoped to surpass. Because they remained committed to the dictates of modern fashion, neither of these presumably incompatible types of literary productions – mainstream literature or modernist idiosyncrasy – was able, Wharton thought, to check the trend towards 'cultured mediocrity' that she observed with such concern.

Wharton's efforts to carve out her own space as a writer in relation to an interwar culture industry that manufactured a form of patterned originality and that created, as quasi structural inversion, the formal disorder she associated with the work of the modernists were thereby riddled with contradictions. She might have deplored the serialised production of countless Stratton-Porters, but her commercial success in the 1920s made her very dependent on the publishing practices condemned so vehemently in her writing.[6] What is more, her exhaustive criticism of interwar literary culture offered no real solutions to avert or check the much-lamented deterioration of intellectual standards. Although she decisively advocated the importance of an individualist 'style' in writing – an idea suddenly bringing Wharton herself into unexpected conceptual proximity to Aaron Jaffe's notion of the modernist imprimatur – this suggestion is loudly proclaimed rather than clearly defined in her writing.[7] But Wharton, I maintain, nonetheless remains an extremely important critic of fashion and of modernist literary aesthetics. Both, she astutely noted, were cultural phenomena invested in fetishising novelty and distinction. But neither, she believed, liberated the individual from market conditions that made serial renewal of standardised products the prerequisite for commercial success and/ or social approval. For her readers today, I shall suggest in this chapter, the analytical focus on fashion has therefore one particularly important critical payoff: it provides an opportunity to challenge existing readings of Wharton's antagonistic relationship with literary modernism. The work of these younger writers was not rejected, as many scholars have implied, because her novels were used 'to bring out, by contrast, the artistic virtues of her technically adventurous successor' (Wegener 1998: 116-17). Rather, she looked at this particular literary movement with concern because it seemed to vindicate her fears about the commercialisation of culture, taste and literary aesthetics. Fashion, as I shall show in the following pages, is the thematic node that can assist in offering such a critical corrective to existing scholarship on Wharton's relationship with literary modernism.

'The compromise between the fashion book and the law of life': 'fashion', 'dress' and Wharton's views on art, design and taste

This chapter section addresses Wharton's seemingly paradoxical attitude towards such related but nonetheless distinct concepts as 'fashion' and 'dress' by discussing her early work on architecture and interior design that already evidences this author's lifelong interest in art, design and questions of good taste. Once these issues have been established, subsequent passages can then move on to discuss how Wharton's critique of fashion manifested itself in her writing and they can show how she aligned her evaluation of fashion with her work as a literary critic. Before I begin to discuss her views on art and taste or her preoccupation with sartorial concerns, however, I first want to clarify in what ways my reading of fashion in Wharton's work differs from existing criticism on the topic – an area of research that has already attracted significant attention from her critics. Martha Banta, for one, correctly argues:

> It is not frivolous, therefore, to claim that Edith Wharton viewed women's fashions as one of the more important markers by which she traced shifts in the social habitus occupied by her fictional characters in the final decades of the nineteenth century and the first three decades of the twentieth century. (2003: 52)

And nowhere does this issue become more apparent than in *The House of Mirth* (1905), in which Lily Bart's dwindling fiscal power and market value as a desirable socialite in New York's best social circles is rendered visible in her changed status from consumer to producer of fine millinery articles. My contribution to the debate about fashion in Wharton's work departs from such existing critical accounts, however, because, as I shall outline in more detail below, it proposes that Wharton's engagement with fashion exceeded debates about sartorial matters to include such topics as taste and literary culture.

One particularly important distinction that I would suggest as essential for the analysis of Wharton's work is that between 'fashion' and 'dress'. To date, I would also propose, scholars interested in analysing sartorial references in Wharton's work have approached the topic from the critical perspective of dress or design historians. Wharton's philanthropic work in Paris during the First World War has thereby attracted particular attention because the sewing workrooms for unemployed seamstresses and the lace-making school she managed in France provide striking examples of her involvement with the manufacturing side of the early twentieth-century garment industry.[8] Katherine Joslin, in what is certainly the most comprehensive and informative study of sartorial politics in her work to date, similarly focuses on Wharton's responsiveness to contemporary dress culture when she reproduces images of garments worn and referenced by Wharton. It is only in passing, when she discusses Wharton's collection of critical essays, *The Writing of Fiction*

(1925), however, that Joslin acknowledges the author's synchronised reflections on sartorial and literary fashions (2009: 3). For the most part, Joslin is interested in uncovering the complex meanings imparted by the dresses and garments worn by Wharton or by her characters. Although the title of her monograph contains the word 'fashion', this interdisciplinary study ultimately focuses not so much on 'fashion' but rather on Wharton's multifarious connections to the 'dress' culture of her time. A similar reading of sartorial codes in *The House of Mirth* can be found in Clair Hughes's *Dressed in Fiction* (134–56) while Jennifer Shepherd, in drawing attention to dress's function in emphasising and upholding class and race categories in the same novel, also adds valuable facets to the study of Wharton's relationship with contemporary garment culture (2007: 135–58). Thematically related to these three studies is Meredith Goldsmith's article on the significance of clothes in Wharton's *Summer* (1917). Her analysis provides new critical insights by tracing the underlying connection between consumer culture and homosociality that structures Wharton's references to garments in this particular novel (2010: 109–27). But Goldsmith, as Joslin, Hughes and Shepherd before her, sidesteps the debate of fashion as a modern cultural condition criticised so extensively in Wharton's work.

In a sense, 'fashion' and 'dress' are, of course, somewhat related concepts but in order to resolve a possible contradiction in Wharton's attitude towards 'fashion', it is essential to note the differences between these two often interchangeably used terms. 'Fashion', as the art and costume historian Anne Hollander notes, is 'the whole spectrum of desirable ways of looking at any given time. The scope of what everyone wants to be seen wearing in a given society is what is in fashion' (1993: 350). Evident in Hollander's definition is the influence of Roland Barthes who regarded fashion as a 'system' – as 'the "totality" of social relations and activities that are required for fashion to come into existence' (Carter 2003: 145) – and who also distinguished it structurally from 'the garment'.[9] Fashion, in other words, is a generalising term, one that denotes a cultural condition, a mode of collective behaviour or an industry. It understands clothing in relation to broader socio-economic structures. And as this chapter will show, it is this '"totality" of social relations and activities' relating to fashion that Wharton would go on to criticise so severely in her writing. Conversely, 'dress' can refer to the specific clothes and garments worn by individuals. For Wharton, it was a personalised response to the many sartorial possibilities provided by the fashion industry. 'Individuality' and 'conformity' emerge, therefore, once more as the two relational concepts that determine the definition of these sartorial terms, and it is far from surprising that Lady Wilde (Speranza) saw 'dress', as early as 1893, as the 'compromise' between 'the fashion book and the law of life' (between abstract guidelines and individual experience) – albeit one that required, according to Speranza, 'resolute self-assertion and heroic defiance of conventional prejudice' on the part of the wearer (2010: 108).

Wharton's well-documented love of designer clothes and the plethora of references to garments in her fiction, which help to establish characters' socio-economic conditions and which strengthen her writing's affiliation with realist literary conventions, can serve as the most obvious examples of this author's affirmation of 'dress' as an important factor in processes of identity formation. Early on in *The House of Mirth*, Lawrence Seldon unsurprisingly notes that it is due to her exquisite clothes and carefully made-up appearance that Lily Bart was so 'highly specialized' (2008: 6, 7). Individuality rather than conformity to a mass standard is expressed by her skilful use of sartorial articles and beauty products. And shortly before her death, when Lily concludes the review of her remaining 'handsome dresses' with the examination of her white 'Reynolds dress' that is drawn last 'from the bottom of her trunk' (308, 309), the particularity of this and of her other garments is once more evoked. Stating that an 'association lurked in every fold', that 'each fall of lace and gleam of embroidery was like a letter in the record of her past' (308), Wharton's narrator unequivocally reads these garments as material expressions of Lily's personality. They are highly personalised, infused with meaning, and they are therefore far more than fashionable ephemera. For Wharton, garments, that is to say, have the potential to express the individual's 'heroic defiance of conventional prejudice' that Lady Wilde had associated with 'dress' as the manifestation of a possible site of conflict between fashion's idealising guidelines and life's actual requirements. It is understandable, therefore, that existing scholarship has given priority to an analysis of 'dress' in Wharton's writing. What the characters (or Wharton) wore has been the starting point for analysing her thoughts about clothes, identity formation and gender relationships. My chapter acknowledges the importance of these critical debates but also proposes a different approach to reading sartorial references in Wharton's work – one that aims to complement these discussions of individual displays of garments by debating the role that the more comprehensive concept 'fashion' as organising generality played in her reflections about style, taste and literary culture. 'Fashion', as we shall see in more detail below, received, unlike 'dress', a more critical reception from Wharton, the professed lover of designer clothes, who was herself the creator of narrative scenarios in which individuality is repeatedly expressed by characters' strategic use of garments.

In this context, it is worth taking into consideration Allan Hepburn's comments on the economic conditions accountable for a change in the culture of collecting as they are, in some ways, akin to my own thoughts on Wharton and fashion. As Hepburn notes, in a world in which material goods proliferate, it is only the collector, the 'expert', who can separate, thanks to his or her good taste and expertise, 'the authentic from the fake' (1998: 27). At the same time, however, the material circumstances of modern capitalism transform taste and knowledge into economic assets and immerse the collector in the commercial structures of the marketplace. Money, in other words, vulgarises taste and the aesthetic appreciation of art. According to Hepburn, Wharton critically observed this economic appropriation of the art of collecting and discussed it repeatedly in her fiction. In what follows, I suggest a similar approach to reading Wharton's preoccupation with fashion – one that illustrates that she rejected fashion as a vulgar preoccupation with personal appearance for the sake of instant (but short-lived) approval. As much as the culture of collecting was threatened by the invasion of capitalist imperatives, fashion represented, for Wharton, yet another intrusion of economic matters into the world of taste and aesthetics: it represented the most drastic example of the commodification of the life of the mind.

Most problematic in this new cultural commitment to fashionable ephemera was, according to Wharton, the preoccupation with exteriors, surfaces and outward appearances. For someone who believed in the importance of deep-rooted structures, this obsession with surface impressions could only have been offensive. In Wharton's view, art, manners and customs were as much conditioned by 'everlasting laws' as the organisation of the natural environment (Wharton and Codman 1978: 192). Unsurprisingly, therefore, when Wharton co-authored the treatise on interior design, *The Decoration of Houses*, in 1897, she consistently promoted scientific eclecticism in the use of ornaments in interior design. Good architecture and interior decoration, the authors insisted in this work, have to be based on the study of such classical principles as proportion, symmetry, unity and, above all, moderation (Wilson 1988: 155).[10] No doubt, this emphasis placed on structure and, above all, scientific parameters in these early considerations of beauty already explain why Wharton, the literary artist, would be drawn to the realist tradition that would make chronological and causally structured narratives as well as the narrator's quasi-scientific detachment essential aspects of its artistic purview.[11] In *The Decoration of Houses*, the authors likewise emphasised the scientific underpinnings of aesthetic compositions:

> Proportion is the good breeding of architecture. It is that something, indefinable to the unprofessional eye, which gives repose and distinction to a room: in its origin a matter of nice mathematical calculation, of scientific adjustment of voids and masses, but in its effects as intangible as that all-pervading essence which the ancients called the soul. (Wharton and Codman 1978: 33)

'[E]verlasting laws' had to be adhered to because they guaranteed the structural soundness of aesthetic projects. As the writers of *The Decoration of Houses* made clear, the appreciation and the careful study of underlying patterns and mathematical forms are essential in the design of personalised interiors. 'Structure conditions ornament', Wharton and Codman argued, 'not ornament structure' (14). For this reason, the challenging task of designing interiors cannot be left to the uninitiated – those individuals, Wharton noted much later in *The Writing of Fiction*, whose 'reluctance to look deeply enough into a subject leads to the indolent habit of decorating its surface' (1997b: 42–3).

In Wharton's view the commercial structures of modern capitalism that renounced perpetuity for a culture of change and novelty had all but dissolved this essential understanding of the scientific, everlasting principles that condition beautiful things and forms. She believed that the result was a condition of cultural anarchy – a world populated by cheaply produced and expendable artefacts. Modern fashion, she would go on to suggest, encouraged this preoccupation with ephemerality and surface impressions that she viewed with such apprehension. It was also due to its widely spread (and its constantly mounting) influence that literary culture and the arts were, she argued, in such a precarious state in the early decades of the twentieth century. Viewed in this light, some of the contradictions in her considerations of sartorial matters can be easily explained. While she enjoyed the lavish displays of Parisian fashion shows and while she relished the acquisition of beautiful haute couture dresses, she nonetheless regarded fashion disapprovingly as a destructive dynamic that problematically unsettled the relationship between commerce and aesthetics, between deep-seated beauty and cheap originality. It was this issue, fashion's rule over contemporary culture, which she hoped to examine and challenge in her writings. And since she believed that all meaningful cultural productions required a secure scientific underpinning, it is no surprise that she reached out to the sciences – and to Herbert Spencer's evolutionary theories to be more precise – when voicing her most sustained critique of fashion's cultural authority.

'Life à la mode': Herbert Spencer, evolutionary theory and Wharton's critique of fashion

By now it is a critical commonplace to align Wharton's work with Thorstein Veblen's *The Theory of the Leisure Class* (1899). The grande dame of American letters and the socio-economist both noted and examined the changed economic patterns of the moneyed American leisure class at the turn of the twentieth century.[12] What has so far passed unnoticed, however, is how much Wharton, in her assessment of fashion, drew on Spencer's evolutionary theories that she perused with interest during her 'self-education as a cultural analyst' that was meant to serve as one of her most 'determined exit strategies from her parents' society' (Lee 2007: 3). In the following paragraphs, I will discuss Spencer's sociological work and propose that it was here that Wharton found a conceptual framework and the relevant vocabulary to articulate her scepticism about modern fashion's cultural achievements.

Spencer's own interest in fashion came to the fore, most unambiguously in his article 'Fashion and Manners', published in 1854 in the *Westminster Review*. Here, Spencer unreservedly pronounced his verdict on fashionable manners and mannerisms: 'But instead of a continual progress towards greater elegance and convenience, which might be expected to occur did people copy the ways of the really best, or follow their own ideas of propriety, we have', Spencer noted, 'a reign of mere whim, of unreason, of change for the sake of change, of wanton oscillations from either extreme to the other – a reign of usages without meaning, times without fitness, dress without taste. And thus', he continued, 'life *à la mode*, instead of being life conducted in the most rational manner, is life regulated by spendthrifts and idlers, milliners and tailors, dandies and silly women' (199). But why, one might feel compelled to ask, did Spencer criticise fashion, life *à la mode*, so severely? And why did he develop an interest in fashion in the first place? Presumably this was the case because fashion can function as a material index of evolutionary theory by constantly negotiating the relationship between social adaptation and differentiation. According to Spencer, evolutionary progress manifests itself in the transition from (biological and social) homogeneity to heterogeneity. Differentiation and specialisation equal progress. But fashion, which Spencer associated in 1854 with 'copyism', 'imitation' and 'conformity' (199) is, for him at least, indicative of social and evolutionary stasis or impoverishment.

Years later, in his study *Ceremonial Institutions* (1879), Spencer returned to and dealt more comprehensively with fashion as a cultural force. Once more taking a progressivist approach, he expanded his thoughts on the evolution of contemporary society out of 'primitive' origins and on the particular role that garments played in the organisation of modern social institutions. He noted that sartorial markers in primordial societies functioned predominantly as insignia of social (and physical) superiority before stating that clothes, in the industrial age, obtained an important constitutive function in producing democratic structures. In the early days, when social customs established themselves, clothing, in the service of ceremonial practices, 'subordinated the individual' because it unmistakably advertised class distinctions (Spencer 1888: 210). Differences in social rank went hand in hand with differences in dress, which means that ceremonial dress produced and upheld constellations of domination and subjection. As Virginia Woolf would similarly observe in *Three Guineas* (1938), ceremonial dress reinforced authoritarian structures and actively assisted in stabilising social hierarchies. Into these hierarchically organised structures fashion, Spencer argued in *Ceremonial Institutions*, introduced a democratic element. 'Everywhere and always', he explained, 'the tendency of the inferior to assert himself has been in antagonism with the restraints imposed on him; and a prevalent way of asserting himself has been to adopt costumes and appliances and customs like those of his superiors' (1888: 208). Gradually – with the rise of an industrialised, capitalist society – imitation prevails and fashion becomes a means to 'obscure, and eventually to obliterate, the marks of class-distinction' (1888: 210). As Spencer proposed, '[i]mitative, then, from the beginning', fashion 'has ever tended towards equalization' (1888: 210).[13] Paradoxically, therefore, because fashion insists on 'likeness instead of unlikeness' (1888: 205), an increase in personal freedoms is inversely proportional, in Spencer's evolutionary model, to individualised clothing. If Spencer is correct, the more democratic a society becomes, the more uniform its clothing turns out to be.

All this means that 'copyism' and 'imitation' were not necessarily regarded as detrimental cultural practices by Spencer. The problem he claimed to have identified as early as 1854 when writing 'Manners and Fashion' is that the majority of individuals do not copy the behaviour, style and manners of the cultural and social elite. As Spencer explained at this point:

> [I]t must yet be concluded, that as the strong men, the successful men, the men of will, intelligence and originality, who have got to the top, are, on the average, more likely to show judgment in their habits and tastes than the mass, the imitation of such is advantageous. By and by, however, Fashion, corrupting like these other forms of rule, almost wholly ceases to be an imitation of the best, and becomes an imitation of quite other than the best. (199)

While fashion thus deteriorates into 'a reign of mere whim, of unreason, of change for the sake of change', taste remains, in Spencer's opinion, a special privilege of the educated and cultured elite – a point of view strongly endorsed by none other than Wharton, who found in evolutionary theories such as Spencer's a lot to commend.

Wharton's own interest in evolution and sociology has of course been well documented.[14] The theories propagated by Charles Darwin, Alfred Russel Wallace, Thomas Henry Huxley, Herbert Spencer and other evolutionary theorists formed an integral part of her reading diet, and her writing was steeped, at least in its early phase, in the belief in evolution's programmatic manifestations. But it is *The Decoration of Houses* that very explicitly associated, in a manner reminiscent of Spencer, wealth with taste and an ability to impress on others a certain cultural superiority: 'When the rich man demands good architecture his neighbours will get it too . . .', Wharton and Codman explained. 'Once the right precedent is established, it costs less to follow than to oppose it', they claimed (3). Equally Spencerian are the authors' views on fashion, which is explicitly associated with a pointless pursuit of novelty: unfortunately, they proposed, the current 'Athenian thirst for novelty', is 'not always regulated by an Athenian sense of fitness', and it therefore leads to the 'worst defects of the furniture now made in America' (29). 'This quest for artistic novelty would be encouraging', they similarly observed, if it were 'based on the desire for something better, rather than for something merely different'. But the 'tendency to dash from one style to another, without stopping to analyse the intrinsic qualities of any, has defeated', they concluded 'the efforts of those who have tried to teach the true principles of furniture-designing by a return to the best models' (29–30). Although Wharton certainly developed an increasingly critical attitude towards Spencer's view of evolution as 'goal-directed process' as Paul J. Ohler correctly proposes (5), she continued to be influenced by his theories and echoed, as late as 1927, some of his views on the progressive differentiation and specialisation of the species. In 'The Great American Novel', for instance, she asserted that 'all growth, animal, human, social is towards an ever-increasing complexity' (Wharton 1996: 155).

Predictably, Wharton's interest in evolutionary theory resurfaced when she analysed fashion as a modern sociological phenomenon in her fiction. There is, in my view, clearly Spencerian thinking behind the depiction of Undine Spragg, the protagonist of Wharton's 1913 novel *The Custom of the Country*, who is the embodiment of the upwardly mobile, ruthless social climber and whose name is a derivative of a patent beauty merchandise produced by her father's company. Undine is, of course, the incarnation of modern fashion, and she is shown to distinguish herself by her social and psychological malleability. She is able, through her extensive reading of society journals such as 'Boudoir Chat' (Wharton 1995a: 12), to keep abreast of and adapt to the latest fashionable trends:

> Undine was fiercely independent and yet passionately imitative. She wanted to surprise every one by her dash and originality, but she could not help modelling herself on the latest person she met, and the confusion of ideals thus produced caused her much perturbation when she had to choose between two courses. (13)

As Judith Fryer has argued, 'Undine's power lies partly in her ability to perfect imitation into something of an art. We often see her rehearsing – "making up" before a mirror ... and she learns quickly the way to dress, move, posture, gesture, adorn herself' (1986: 103).[15] But while Undine excels in this form of sartorial and behavioural mimicry, Wharton, like Spencer before her, criticised in Undine's depiction fashion's emphasis on imitation for the sake of change and novelty. Although it seems as if imitation or 'cheap originality' as Wharton and Codman called it in *The Decoration of Houses* (19) is the formula for the protagonist's success – Undine *almost* gets what she wants at the end of the novel – the success is one-dimensional. It is economical and it is achieved at the cost of moral standards and other forms of cultural advancement. By fashioning a series of different and desirable selves, Undine actively creates her fortune and facilitates her social ascent but none of her achievements are perceived worthy in the eyes of the novel's narrator. Undine might be fashionable and socially successful, but it is precisely her awareness of what is fashionable at the present moment that prevents her from achieving refinement, true elegance and a discriminating appreciation of what it means to have good taste.

In a key passage from *The Custom of the Country*, Raymond de Chelles, Undine's third (and French) husband, therefore reprimands his wife on her lack of respect for family traditions, cultural heritage and the collector's emotional attachment to the beautiful objects in his possession:

> You come among us speaking our language and not knowing what we mean; wanting the things we want, and not knowing why we want them; aping our weaknesses, exaggerating our follies, ignoring or ridiculing all we are about – you come from hotels as big as towns, and from towns as flimsy as paper, ... and the people are as proud of changing as we are of holding to what we have – and we're fools enough to imagine that because you copy our ways and pick up our slang you understand anything about the things that make life decent and honourable for us! (Wharton 1995a: 341–2)

Undine's proposition to have his ancestral Boucher tapestries priced offends Raymond's belief in tradition and the emotive, not economic, value of art objects. Consequently, as Allan Hepburn notes, he 'condemns', in his wife, 'the American habit of imitating surfaces without understanding traditions' that coincides with a slavish dependence on fashion's imperative for newness. Undine, Hepburn argues, 'translates this fascination for novelty into a habit of donning dresses and decorating houses', and she therefore violates Raymond's desire for tradition and good taste (1998: 30). In this scene in the novel, ruthless American capitalism is juxtaposed with European appreciations of tradition that expose the commercial activities of selling and purchasing art objects as a modern (and particular vulgar) form of cultural imperialism.

The problem with Undine, it transpires, is her lack of character that can guide her in her sartorial, social and emotional choices. Because she has no fixed principles and lacks good taste, she is destined to go after whatever catches her fancy. Realising that writing can be a commercially successful undertaking, she instantly casts her (second) husband (and herself) in the appropriate roles: when 'literature was becoming fashionable', she 'decided that it would be amusing and original if Ralph should owe their prosperity to his talent. She already saw herself', the reader is told, 'as the wife of a celebrated author, wearing "artistic" dresses and doing the drawing-room over with Gothic tapestries and dim lights in altar candle-sticks' (178). Once more, Undine responds to the prospect of reconditioning her lifestyle in the only way she can image: by a change of its surface decoration (dress; drawing room). Unfortunately, however, Undine is likely to abandon everything she acquires on a whim, whenever she gets bored. What drives her is the perpetual desire for something else, something 'better', 'more luxurious, more exciting, more worthy of her' (Wharton 1995a: 35).[16] She is Wharton's case study of an individual who has become a cultural inevitability in a capitalist market economy. Instead of copying the dress and behaviour of those who are culturally superior as demanded by Spencer, Undine is unmasked as one of his 'silly women' whose imitations have become unguided and directionless. Fashion and a perpetual desire for 'change for the sake of change' have become the controlling influences in her life.

Undine's is an individualised case study. But Wharton, in taking the logic of her own thinking about fashion as a general social phenomenon to its obvious conclusion, broadened the scope of her analysis in one of her later novels, thereby evidencing that her critique of fashion was durable as well as harsh. Rather than observing one person's response to fashion's cultural demands as in *The Custom of the Country*, in other words, she introduced into her novel, *The Children* (1928), a barely concealed disapproval of fashion's tendency to submerge all individuals in increasingly undifferentiated groups. 'Oh, Martin, won't it be too awful if beauty ends by being standardised too?', exclaims her character Rose Sellars after spotting a 'girl in peach-colour', who is 'lovely', but has been seen, as Mrs Sellars notes, 'a thousand times, in all the "Vogues" and "Tatlers"' (Wharton 2006a: 105). Here, fashionable dress and conduct are seen to be detrimental to the development of personal distinctiveness, and it is no wonder that Wharton's protagonist, Martin Boyne, when contemplating 'Mrs Sellars's deepest attraction', explains her desirability by relating it to the fact that she 'belong[ed] to a day when women still wore their charm with a difference'. As for 'these new beauties', Martin explains, he 'shouldn't always be able to pick her out in a crowd', if he ever 'owned' one (105). Conformity to recognisable patterns and standards rather than the development of a personalised style are identified as the outcome of fashion's ascent to cultural hegemony. In *The Children*, these modern social phenomena are referred to as 'mechanical terror' by Boyne:

> Every one of the women in the vast crowded restaurant seemed to be of the same age, to be dressed by the same dress-makers, loved by the same lovers, adorned by the same jewellers, and massaged and manipulated by the same Beauty doctors. (154)

For these individuals, Boyne concludes, it 'would have been unfashionable to be different' (154).

In view of Boyne's slightly inappropriate infatuation with the adolescent Judith Wheater, which will become responsible, in the course of the novel, for dissolving his engagement to the mature and very appropriate Rose Sellars, his comments on feminine conformity and male ownership of women are of course nothing if not challenging. While he certainly cannot be accused of social conformity in his particular choice of love object, Martin ultimately revolts from making his desires explicit. Although he produces an ill-articulated marriage proposal towards the end of the novel, Judith, in her (feigned) 'simplicity' (311) interprets his proposition mistakenly as adoption – of herself and of the rest of the Wheater children – and silences Wharton's middle-aged protagonist. If Martin had previously condemned the standardisation of looks, taste and social practices in the name of fashion, his unsuitable desire is equally, if not more offensive to his sensibility and results in a self-inflicted exile to 'the other end of the world' (323). In a further twist, the novel's final pages see Martin three years later observing, from a distance, a now grown-up Judith during an exclusive ball in 'the newest and most fashionable hotel in Biarritz' (338). Before he is able to detect her, his eyes wander 'in vain from one slender bare-armed shape to another' (345), afraid that he might not identify Judith in a crowd of seemingly interchangeable young women. Boyne clearly fears that the young girl who used to be Judith has become part of the fashionable social apparatus rejected in the novel's earlier scenes. Three years after their last encounter, she might appear – at least to an unconcerned observer – as a member of an army of featureless young women who go to fashionable balls and who rejoice in the purchase of 'a new dress for the dance' (344). But when he finally sees her, Boyne instantly perceives the singularity of her 'fitful beauty' (347) among all the other elegantly ornamented young women. In fact, the novel's antepenultimate paragraph details Judith's apparel, zooming in, for instance, on 'the rich stuff' and 'double tier of flounces' in her 'silk dress' that 'was of that peculiar carnation-pink which takes a sliver glaze like the bloom on a nectarine' (346). In the novel's last scenes Wharton, in presenting Judith as she is seen through Martin's love-struck eyes, therefore seems to complicate Boyne's (and her own) disapproving judgment of sartorial conformity. As these paragraphs illustrate, desire and subjective impressions recognise, in the standardised look, glimpses of individuality. Very likely, however, it takes a perceptive observer such as Boyne to see through surface ornamentation to the essence of Judith's personality. He is drawn to her not because but rather in spite of her fashionable clothes, finding it almost 'impossible to believe' in 'her being Judith, her being herself' (347) in the stylish ballroom scenario he observes. Fashion adorns. But for Wharton, fashion subdues expressions of personality. As these pages from *The Children* demonstrate, she was worried about the trend 'toward equalization' facilitated, according to such cultural theorists as

Spencer, by modern fashion. At the same time, she acknowledged that beauty might be in the eye of the beholder – that is if good taste, an individualised appreciation or discriminating judgment are able to discern, underneath its fashionable surface decoration, traces of its peculiar characteristics. It is in such moments that fashionable outfits can be transformed into 'dress', into garments that clearly express the individuality of the wearer.

'Fashions in the arts come and go': Wharton's literary criticism

If Wharton's attitude towards fashionable dress styles was laden with criticism, it has to be noted that she synchronised, throughout her work, comments on clothes and garments with the assessment of literary composition and writerly techniques. Sartorial and literary fashions, that is to say, were closely aligned and associatively connected in Wharton's thinking. For instance, in her unfinished novel *Disintegration* – a text later to be rewritten and published in 1925 as *The Mother's Recompense* – a conceptual translation turns a character's 'gowns' into 'poems' and 'her bonnets' into 'sonnets' (Wharton 2009, vol. 1: 87). Likewise, in one of her notebooks, written between 1910 and 1914, Wharton compared 'a lovely book, all cover, margins & fly leaves' to 'a beautifully dressed girl with very little to say' (YCAL MSS 42 1/21/700). Humorously exploited is the same motif also in the description of the lately deceased writer Mrs Aubyn, a character in Wharton's 1900 novella 'The Touchstone'. 'Her dress', the narrator here claims, 'never seemed part of her; all her clothes had an impersonal air, as though they had belonged to someone else and been borrowed in an emergency that had somehow become chronic.' Although Mrs Aubyn 'was conscious enough of her deficiencies to try to amend them by rash imitations of the most approved models', her 'plagiarism', as the narrator, 'borrow[ing] a metaphor of her trade', explains, 'somehow never seemed to be incorporated with the text' (Wharton 1995b: 30). Wharton's prose, it seems, consistently invites the reader to associate the composition of one's personal outfit with that of a literary text. Indeed, this conceptual fusion of sartorial and literary composition vocabulary becomes very apparent when Wharton opens one of her essays on literary criticism with the confident pronouncement that '[f]ashions in criticism change almost as rapidly as fashions in dress' (Wharton 1996: 293). In Wharton's view, novelty, ephemerality and obsolescence – precisely those of its features that, she believed, sustain the fashion industry's cultural authority – have begun to dictate the ways in which modern literature is conceptualised, produced and critically assessed. And predictably, Wharton's verdict on fashionable literary culture was as harsh as her judgment and condemnation of sartorial fashion as one of the social forces responsible for standardising feminine beauty. It is at this point that Wharton glanced, nostalgically, back to times when '[t]raditional society with its old-established distinctions of class, its pass-words, exclusions, delicate shades of language and behaviour' formed 'one of man's oldest works of art' (Wharton 1996: 155).

Most explicitly expressed are Wharton's coordinated thoughts on fashion and literary composition in her already mentioned 1925 collection of critical essays *The Writing of Fiction*. This text, which is characterised, as Frederick Wegener argues, by 'its anti-modernism, its traditional emphasis, its weariness of technical novelty' (1995: 72), also represents one of Wharton's most outspoken critiques of literary productions in a culture dominated by what she called the 'machine made "magazine story"' (Wharton 1997b: 39).[17] It is in this text, for instance, that Wharton dismissively states: 'Fashion in the arts come and go, and it is of little interest to try to analyse the work of any artist who does not give one the sense of being in some sort above them' (111). A few years later, she would address the same topic with similar acerbity in her novel *Hudson River Bracketed* (1929) – the text that is, in many ways, the novelistic counterpart of *The Writing of Fiction*. This story, which graphically details the pressures of writing and submitting commissioned material to literary magazines according to a pre-arranged schedule – producing 'machine made "magazine stories"' – presents its protagonist, the talented but inexperienced young writer Vance Weston, as one of the many casualties of the world of capricious, profit-driven publishing. After reaching the heights of fame and experiencing what it feels like 'to be It' (Wharton 2006c: 279),[18] his career continues to unfold erratically. Ultimately, he fails as a bestselling author. But *Hudson River Bracketed* sides with Weston in prioritising the integrity of his creative vision, the 'real stuff' that 'is way down, not on the surface' (Wharton 2006c: 320), over the monetary rewards that come with being a widely acclaimed and commercially successful author. As in her critical writing, Wharton, in this late novel, therefore condemned the quasi-industrial production of literature and authorship that destroys the singularity she associated with the artist's creative vision.

This singularity of vision, 'the most personal ingredient in the combination of things out of which any work of art is made' (Wharton 1997b: 21), is defined in *The Writing of Fiction* as the author's 'style'. Personal, distinctive, individualistic, it is, according to Wharton, 'the way in which [the incidents of the narrative] are presented, not only in the narrower sense of language, but also, and rather, as they are grasped and coloured by their medium, the narrator's mind, and given back in his word' (21). Interestingly, as I have already suggested in passing, in proposing that an author's singular 'style' is incompatible with the aping of current literary trends that force writers to abandon their vision and commit to literary templates demanded by the market, Wharton develops a theory of stylistic fingerprinting that would become, as Aaron Jaffe has argued, central to the modernist conception of the inimitable genius. Wharton, however, was not aware or unwilling to notice this obvious resemblance between her own theory of artistic composition and modernism's literary productions – for reasons that will become very apparent in a moment. For her, this theoretical abstract she referred to as 'style' was synonymous with an essential antidote to fashion's influence on interwar literary culture. As she observed in her fictional and non-fictional writing, fashion, producing a cultural environment that values perishability and standardisation, had extended its reach far beyond sartorial matters. As much as it was associated by Wharton with the seasonal change of clothes and garments, fashion made its presence felt in her own professional sphere by demanding a continuous production of bestselling material that promised to saturate, temporarily at least, the market's unquenchable hunger for new reading material.

Wharton herself proposed that cultural, aesthetic and social progress was contingent on the adaptation of established forms and traditions to modern settings, and it is for this reason that she routinely chastised, in the 1920s and 1930s, younger writers for their lack of historical mindfulness. In her 1934 essay 'Tendencies in Modern Fiction', she therefore bemoaned 'the initial mistake of most of the younger novelists, especially in England and America', to decide 'that the old forms were incapable of producing new ones' – a tendency in modern prose writing that has, according to Wharton, 'definitely impoverished the present' (Wharton 1996: 179). According to Wharton, a rather 'unsettling element in modern art', which she defined as 'that common symptom of immaturity', is 'the dread of doing what has been done before' (1997b: 17). Although she acknowledged that 'imitation' is 'one of the instincts of youth', 'another, equally imperious, is that of fiercely guarding against it' (1997b: 17). And many writers who aim to satisfy publishers with an 'insatiable demand for quick production' are kept in 'a state of perpetual immaturity', unable to link, as she suggested, an engagement with the themes, techniques and values of the past with the task of answering to the demands and opportunities of the present (Wharton 1997b: 17). '[O]riginality', Wharton and Codman had already asserted in *The Decoration of Houses*, 'is never a willful rejection of what has been accepted as the necessary laws of the various forms of art. Thus, in reasoning', they continued:

> Originality lies not in discarding the necessary laws of thought, but in using them to express new intellectual conceptions; in poetry, originality consists not in discarding the necessary laws of rhythm, but in finding new rhythms within the limits of those laws. (11)

Hence, 'the supposed conflict between originality and tradition is', in their view, 'no conflict at all' (11). Taking her cue from evolutionary theories, which similarly saw culture evolving out of previous settings, Wharton thus advocated an ongoing reliance on rather than rupture with time-honoured values and customs as a formula for cultural growth or improvement. Within this context, she also declared, as we have already seen, that a writer's foremost duty was the cultivation of a distinctive voice or 'style' that has the ability to contend with a literary culture moving towards the marketing of mass-produced, homogenous ephemera for the sole purpose of generating profit. Akin to T. S. Eliot's 'Tradition and the Individual Talent' (1919),[19] her *The Writing of Fiction* therefore proposed:

> True originality consists not in a new manner but in a new vision. That new, that personal, vision is attained only by looking long enough at the object represented to make it the writer's own; and the mind which would bring this secret germ to fruition must be able to nourish it with an accumulated wealth of knowledge and experience. (17–18)

Maturity and an appreciative commitment to imaginatively engage with past (literary) traditions are, according to Wharton, the ingredients of personal 'style' and of originality in writing.

At this point it must be noted that Wharton published her most comprehensive work of literary criticism, *The Writing of Fiction*, only three years after the publication of such seminal works as Eliot's *The Waste Land* and Joyce's *Ulysses*. Wharton's piece therefore represents a debate with an avant-garde movement that had started to dominate the literary scene in Paris (and elsewhere) and that threatened to eclipse the achievements of mature writers such as Wharton herself. Although there can be no doubt that very obvious intellectual continuities existed between her work and that of some modernist authors, Wharton's comments on the literary efforts of the younger generation were obviously very unforgiving. Perhaps Robin Peel is right in suggesting that this was the case because this new generation of writers 'had taken experiment and subject matter too far' for her liking (2005: 89). But as I want to suggest at this juncture, it is much more likely that Wharton's condemnation of these 'younger writers' and their work was motivated by her suspicion that an underground relationship between modernism and mainstream culture existed that many of modernism's principal proponents were vehemently disavowing. In Paris in the 1920s, modernism was becoming a dominant (fashionable) art form that represented, for Wharton, mainstream literature's highbrow counterpart: work authored by a group of artists that was, due to its creators' obsession with novelty and innovation, as contingent on modern fashion's cultural dictates as that produced by commercially minded writers. The modernists' 'fear of being unoriginal' as well as their tendency to regard 'formlessness' as 'the first condition of form' are judged severely by Wharton and provoked, in *The Writing of Fiction*, her judgmental classification of modernism as 'anarchy in fiction' (15).[20]

Equally harsh is Wharton's critique of these 'fishers in the turbid stream-of-consciousness' in *The Gods Arrive* (1932), the sequel to *Hudson River Bracketed*. Modernism's 'microscopic analysis of the minute in man' is here rejected by Vance Weston, who suspects that this 'new technique' 'substituted pathology for invention'. 'Man was man by virtue of the integration of his atoms, not of their dispersal', Vance argues, and it 'was not when you had taken him apart that you could realise him, but when you had built him up' (Wharton 2006b:

115–16). Wharton, as this passage from *The Gods Arrive* suggests, favoured a holistic approach to character development and criticised modernist narratives because, in her view, they resembled analytical, quasi-medical case studies that examined human nature like vivisectionists dissected their victims.[21] Elsewhere, the novel delivers an even more explicit rejection of modernism marketed by many as the latest fashion in the arts. As the story of Vance Weston progresses, he finds himself in Paris surrounded by an arty crowd that enjoys the patronage of the wealthy Mrs Glaisher – a patroness, whose artistic preferences, the reader is told, change as frequently as the content of her wardrobe. Once she had realised 'that the Grand Opera, *pâté de foie gras*, terrapin and Rolls-Royce were no longer the crowning attributes of her class', this unrelenting supporter of the arts had turned her attentions elsewhere and she 'had begun to buy Picassos and Modiglianis, to invite her friends to hear Stravinsky and Darius Milhaud, to patronize exotic dancers, and labour privately (it was the hardest part of her task) over the pages of "Ulysses"' (Wharton 2006b: 127–8). The full extent of Wharton's sarcasm materialises when one of her protégés, Lorry Spear, lectures Mrs Glaisher (and the rest of his party guests) on the essence of modern art – remarks that identify 'destruction' as 'the artist's instinct'. 'Just picture to yourself the lack of imagination there is in putting up with the old things', Lorry declares. 'Things made to please somebody else, long before we were born, to please people who would have bored us to death if we'd known them. Why should we be saddled with all that old dead masonry?' he asks laconically before uttering the Futurist war cry: '"Ruins are what we want – more ruins. . . . If only the lucky people who have the means to pull down and build up again had the imagination to do it . . ." "Ah, that's it: we *must* have imagination"', his patroness agrees 'in the same decisive tone in which, thirty years ago, she might have declared: "We *must* have central heating"' (131).

In these and similar sarcastic representations, modernism's brokers are unmasked by Wharton as playing into the hands of a public with an insatiable appetite for newness and temporary distractions – in spite of the modernist insistence on intellectual autonomy and independence from the literary marketplace. Although the work of Woolf or Joyce might have been poles apart in stylistic terms from that of the Gene Stratton-Porters of her time, Wharton nonetheless associated the bestselling author of literary trivia with modernism's intellectually exclusive agenda. Both were literary productions that she saw as inevitable consequences of an interwar culture industry that had made fashion its ruling principle. For Wharton modernism was therefore not simply a literary movement. It was a symptom. Because of its self-proclaimed desire to be 'new' or 'different', it was a highbrow expression of contemporary culture's fascination with fashion. It is for this particular reason that I suggest reconsidering Wharton's alleged aversion to modernist writing. Rather than interpreting it exclusively as a mature writer's fear of being superseded, her forceful rejection of modernism's conceptual apparatus is in agreement with her critique of a mercurial publishing industry that facilitated the manufacturing of celebrity authors and produced, as quasi-intellectual rebound, a literary culture that prioritised unintelligibility and formlessness as revolutionary modes of artistic expression.

However, Wharton's own professional entanglement with a literary market so vehemently condemned in her writing is far from straightforward. In one of her letters from 1913 to her former governess, Anna Bahlmann, for instance, Wharton reports that she 'just had a big unexpected dividend from Macmillian', before stating that 'the Custom will be a gold-mine' (Goldman-Price 2012: 239). Suddenly, commercial success with its desirable monetary benefits is no longer intolerable. Indeed, it must be noted that Wharton's own novels, at the time she was writing her most sardonic evaluations of commercialised literature, were being released to considerable acclaim – especially after the publication of the Pulitzer Prize-winning *The Age of Innocence* (1920). Moreover, not only did writing become a very profitable occupation for Wharton after the First World War, but she was also extremely adept, as Frederick Wegener has pointed out, in 'taking advantage of newer additional sources of literary income (film rights, book-club selections, mass-circulation magazines, etc.)' (1995: 60). In 1934 she also complained in a letter to her editor at Appleton about the publisher's 'principle of non-advertising'. 'As every other publisher old and new, American and English, seems to be advertising more than ever', Wharton observed, 'this policy surprises me.' But, as she tersely concluded:

> You are entitled to your own views, and authors who disagree with them can only change their publishers. I may as well tell you frankly that I intend to do this for the simple reason that I cannot afford to neglect any chance of selling my book. (Wharton 1988: 580)

In an ironic development, Wharton, in the 1930s, seemed to have demanded from her publisher exactly the kind of publicity that she had rebuked twenty years earlier by underlining passages in the advertisement of Stratton-Porter's *Laddie*.

Given Wharton's considerable entrepreneurial talents, it is by no means surprising that she soon became 'one of the leading money-makers among the writers of her time' by taking advantage of the contractual offers made by publishers and magazine editors vying for her work (Lewis 1975: 422). To illustrate this point, her biographer R. W. B. Lewis discusses the publication history of *The Age of Innocence*. For the serial rights *Pictorial Review* offered $18,000 while Wharton's publisher paid another $15,000 as an advance. Accordingly, *The Age of Innocence* 'came into being', Lewis notes, 'as a result of a shrewd estimate of the literary market by both the editor of a slick picture magazine and the representative of an up-and-coming firm of publisher' (1975: 423). Maximising her profit in these and similar negotiations, Wharton distinguished herself as a sharp-witted business woman who knew very well how to negotiate the commercial challenges of her chosen profession.[22] All this means that Wharton – although she viciously attacked the commercialisation of literary work in *Hudson River Bracketed* – had nonetheless become deeply entangled, in the decade in which she published this novel, in the commercial structures of the literary marketplace. In an age in which the novelist's work had been restructured to become a cultural commodity, Wharton enjoyed the benefits of this particular trade-off while she anxiously guarded her reputation as a writer of highbrow fiction.

It is of course tempting to suggest that Wharton – in spite of becoming a bestselling novelist in her later years – managed to preserve, in this particular contest between commercial success and artistic integrity, the kind of idiosyncrasy and distinctiveness of literary 'style' that she had referred to repeatedly in *The Writing of Fiction*. Unfortunately, however, the critical reception of her late work suggests otherwise. While *The Glimpses of the Moon* (1922), *The Mother's Recompense*, *Twilight Sleep* (1927) and *The Children* were commercially successful (Lewis 1975: 444, 466, 473, 484), these novels failed to excite critics who unfavourably compared Wharton's latest efforts with her earlier novels. 'By the time she wrote *Hudson River Bracketed*', Jennifer Haytock observes, 'Wharton found herself a little put out at the disparity between her sales record and the critics' regard for her work' (2008: 160).²³ However, this is not the place, I want to suggest in response to these critical observations, to engage in detail with debates about the literary merit of Wharton's late prose. If anything, the commercial success of these novels evidences that Wharton had learned her trade and was able to negotiate the relationship between economic imperatives and artistic independence in the way that pleased *her*. There is little or no evidence that she was dissatisfied with her work. On the contrary, she seemed to have liked what she wrote in the final years of her life and *Hudson River Bracketed*, in particular, seemed to have been an authorial favourite. In 1930 Wharton wrote that she would 'rather hear [praise] of this than of any other I have written' because it dealt with:

> [A] theme that I have carried in my mind for years, & that Walter [Berry] was always urging me to use; indeed I had begun it before the war, but in our own milieu, & the setting of my own youth. After the war it took me long to re-think it & transpose it into the crude terms of modern America. (Wharton 1988: 525)

For Wharton, her efforts seemed to have paid off and she considered herself 'happy to find that my readers think I have succeeded (Wharton 1988: 525).²⁴

But what needs to be said at this point is that Wharton's conceptualisation of 'style' remained frustratingly vague: nowhere did she explain in detail how she understood and turned into practice this notion of an author's formal or stylistic signature. Her intellectual affiliation with literary realism suggests, of course, that she regarded as essential representational techniques that relied on linear plots, scientific detachment and verisimilitude for harmonious novelistic compositions.²⁵ While she explained in *The Writing of Fiction* that '[v]erisimilitude is the truth of art, and any convention which hinders the illusion is obviously in the wrong place' (65), her writing is certainly invested in displaying a balanced relationship between the characters' psychological compositions and their exterior surroundings. The detailed description of the fashionable interior of the Hotel Stentorian described at the beginning of *The Custom of the Country*, for instance, effectively communicates to the reader the tastes and inclinations of the Spragg family – and of Undine in particular. By the same token, Wharton acknowledged in *The Writing of Fiction* that the 'creative imagination' is distinguished by the ability to combine 'with the power of penetrating into other minds' the 'standing far enough aloof from them to see beyond, and relate them to the whole stuff of life out of which they but partially emerge' (15). Once more, *The Custom of the Country* with its detached, analytical narrative perspective – an extension of the sociological observations provided by the novel's character Charles Bowen – provides an example of the kind of quasi-scientific viewpoint that appears with regularity in Wharton's prose writing. Finally, Wharton also suggested in *The Writing of Fiction* that a 'conscious ordering and selecting' of material is required 'to produce on the reader the effect of the passage of time' (16),[26] an indication that for her an essential technical detail of a narrative that aspired to 'the Latin tradition' was a measured, linear development of the events narrated (Wharton 1997b: 28).

But even if these authorial guidelines must be deemed insufficient in defining Wharton's understanding of her own novelistic 'style', the existence of these and countless similar remarks on artistic composition and the modern writer's work obviously illustrates how extensively and self-reflexively this author thought about the technicalities of fiction writing and how critically responsive she was to those market conditions that had, she believed, undercut contemporary writers' attempts to develop formally balanced, technically mindful and individualist work. My suggestion, then, now that I am coming to the conclusion of this chapter, is not to seek fault with possible inconsistencies in Wharton's theoretical model of fiction writing but to read her first and foremost as an important cultural critic of fashion and of interwar literary culture – a writer who thoughtfully aligned her critique of fashion with an analysis of the contemporary literary field and who clearly saw and eagerly discussed fashion's various inroads into debates about taste and artistic standards. It is also worth re-emphasising at this point that Wharton herself considered the results of her literary work worthy of her own, very high, standards. She was convinced that she had remained faithful, in spite of the obvious commercial success, to her 'style' in novel writing. For that particular reason, she must have been extremely pleased when she was praised, on the occasion of being awarded her honorary degree from Yale University in 1923, for her 'sincerity in art', for her 'beauty in construction' and, most importantly, her 'distinction in style' (YCAL MSS 42 5/50/1519).[27]

Wharton, interwar women writers and fashion: a few common threads?

In 1928 Wharton was urged to read Woolf's recently published fictional biography *Orlando*. Disinclined she responded that the author's 'photograph in the advertisements "made me quite ill. I can't believe"', she declared, '"that where there is exhibitionism of that order there can be real creative gift"' (Lewis 1975: 483). Given Woolf's reservations about the rise of 'middlebrow' literary culture in the early 1930s (Woolf 2011: 470–9) and given her attempts, in the early days of her career, to separate her artistic endeavours from the professional practices of a profit-driven publishing industry, Wharton's verdict on what she read as the younger novelist's intellectual prostitution can only surprise. But the fact that Woolf had decided to use her image for marketing purposes in this manner must have confirmed Wharton's suspicion that modernism was, as an art form, deeply immersed in the commercial structures of a market that valued this particular literary movement because its emphasis on artistic distinction nurtured contemporary culture's demand for novelty and turned it into a commodity that could be effectively marketed and successfully sold. If anything, the example of Woolf's publicity photographs would have strengthened Wharton's opinions about an interwar literary culture susceptible to economic imperatives. If Gene Stratton-Porter was an author who represented, for Wharton, a new type of producer of 'machine made "magazine stories"' who throve in a cultural environment that rewarded writers whose gift for imitation pleased a risk-averse reading public with an appetite for patterned stories, modernism, in its most extreme abstraction, was seen by Wharton as the other expression of an interwar literary field that was guided by the rules and laws of modern fashion. Modernism's mantra 'make it new', which seemed incompatible with Wharton's insistence on a writer's historical consciousness, was for her synonymous with one of fashion's variables: its emphasis on change, difference and novelty. For Wharton, modernist art therefore remained connected to mainstream literature and its predisposition to cater for common or standardised literary tastes. Paradoxically, perhaps, she regarded literary bestsellers and avant-garde art as the two inevitable symptoms of a materialist culture that commodified literature, that produced literary expendables and that encouraged momentary stardom.

What might have biased Wharton towards this younger generation of writers could have been their wholesale rejection of established authors, one that paid little tribute to individual efforts and achievements. When Woolf made her now famous, categorical distinction between 'Georgian' and 'Edwardian' writers in 1924 (Woolf 1988: 421),[28] she indiscriminately dismissed the novelists of Wharton's generation as outdated relics. While it was, no doubt, imperative for Woolf to champion her own work and that of like-minded contemporaries by establishing this particular distinction between literary fossils and risk-taking innovators, it was a juxtaposition that someone like Wharton must have regarded as extremely problematic. As a taxonomic system Woolf's model left little, if any room for considering those individual nuances between writers that Wharton had singled out as mandatory in the formation of an author's 'style'. However, if Wharton retaliated by establishing another taxonomic system for assessing fiction writing, it was not only because her work was 'uncharitably compared with Woolf's' (Wegner 1998: 116–17). What clearly concerned her, I have suggested in this chapter, was the covert link she detected between modernism's desire to be 'original' and a contemporary fascination with fashion that had begun to dominate the production and the marketing of literature and art. It was her critical stance towards a culture ruled by literary fashions, in other words, that underpinned Wharton's dismissal of other people's artistic practices.[29]

As a practising writer, Wharton had of course much more in common than she was willing to acknowledge with some of these much-censored modernists. The example of Woolf can serve as an obvious case in point. Both women, Wharton and Woolf, expressed critique of the interwar literary marketplace at some point during their careers. But both of them also made considerable concessions to the very same marketplace in the hope of promoting and selling their work. Both of them, that is, resembled each other in the attempt to emphasise the highbrow nature of their work while their occasional, tactical compliance with the commercial realities of modern publishing suggests a grudging acceptance that writing had become a salaried profession in the interwar period. Subsequent chapters of *Modernism, Fashion and Interwar Women Writers* will unearth further resemblances between Wharton's work and that of the other included women writers who have often been associated with modernism's literary innovations. In doing so, they will also make the critical suggestion that the two literary formations that, according to Wharton, divisively structured debates about artistic standards in the interwar period were of immense relevance to these other novelists. The question of how to develop literary aesthetics that were accessible to many but managed to remain somewhat independent from mainstream culture clearly preoccupied them all. Wharton, as the case of Bowen will show, was certainly not the only woman writer of the interwar period who was concerned about the commercial transactions involved in being a successful writer, who promoted the notion of an author's individualist 'style' but who still wanted to distinguish herself conceptually from modernism's formal innovations. And there are other similarities between this vociferous critic of modernism and the women writers selected for study in the next chapters. With Rhys, for example, Wharton shared a love of designer dresses and of Parisian haute couture. But would Rhys's eccentric and idiosyncratic writing have satisfied Wharton's demand for an author's inimitable 'style'? The next chapter will analyse how the producer of numerous 'Left Bank' stories developed her self-conception as a woman writer in response to a literary culture ruled by fashion's demand for novelty and change.

Notes

1. In her 1927 essay 'The Great American Novel', Wharton grieved over the modern novel's focus on the 'average individual'. Here, she states that in the eyes of the reading public the 'great American novel must always be about Main Street, geographically, socially, and intellectually'. 'Main Street', Wharton explained, 'stands for everything which does not rise above a very low average in culture, situation, or intrinsic human interest; and also for every style of depicting this dead level of existence, from the photographic to the pornographic.' It is synonymous with a gradual levelling of tastes and a cumulative depletion of intellectual standards (1996: 152–3).
2. Here, I depart from Pamela Knights's suggestion that Wharton kept this advertisement simply because the relationship between Wharton and Stratton-Porter was one of fierce competition. 'At the peak of their fame, from the early 1900s into the 1920s, Mrs. Porter and Mrs. Wharton were rival names in the best-selling charts, commanding voices that made an impact', Knights notes (6).

3. The Edith Wharton Collection in the Beinecke Rare Book and Manuscript Library also contains a newspaper article entitled 'American Fiction', published probably in 1901, which addresses the same topic. Here, the reader is told that for many critics 'the test of [a book's] success is commercial'. They believe 'that a novel which by dint of advertising and the use of all the resources of the publishing art, and by the help of an uninformed public taste, sells enormously is a better novel than another which sells moderately'. Moreover, the writer asserts that nowadays, every 'book must be new, like a dress-pattern, if it is to sell, and there seem to be no limits to the possibilities of advertising' before celebrating Wharton as 'good an example as need be of the writer whose aim is literary and not commercial', whose 'felicity of diction' will not 'win over the multitude' but is 'likely to win immortality'. The writer thus distinguished Wharton's work from the mass-produced novels of her time (YCAL MSS 42 5/50/1503).

4. Katherine Joslin suggests that Wharton 'would measure sartorial splendor by what she saw at the House of Worth and Doucet in the 1870s' (2009: 8). Surviving photographs of Wharton as a young woman certainly illustrate that she was deeply attracted to beautiful clothes and that she eagerly awaited the 'annual arrival of the "trunk from Paris"' (Wharton 1934: 20). Moreover, Wharton's extensive correspondence with her governess Anna Bahlmann, which is interspersed with news about the acquisition of fabrics and dresses – for both Wharton and Bahlmann – also reveals how extensively Wharton thought about clothes (Goldman-Price 2012: 163–4). Writing from Paris on 18 April 1891, for instance, Wharton reported that she is 'much less hurried this year than usual, having got so many dresses in Cannes', before informing Bahlmann that she bought her 'a brown serge dress, & a dark blue clothes mantle' (YCAL MSS 361 1/2/27).

5. Needless to say, fashion's emphasis on novelty is by no means as uncompromising as Sombart or Wharton assumed. In practice, I should repeat here, its designs work by elaborately citing and referencing a host of earlier styles. Ulrich Lehmann is one critic who argues this point when he states that 'fashion, even in its most contemporary form, quotes from the past' so that 'in fashion, *quotation is sartorial remembrance*' (2001: 164).

6. Amy Kaplan, who has written on Wharton's apprenticeship as a professional writer, notes the 'unresolved conflict' between 'the apparent freedom of the literary marketplace' and 'her own class's disdain for and fear of work, which was treated as a dirty word – akin to sex or money' in Wharton's attitude towards professional authorship (1988: 67–8).

7. 'Edith Wharton does not in *The Writing of Fiction* or elsewhere analyse in any detail the elements of style', writes Penelope Vita-Finzi (1990: 39).
8. Alan Price discusses the organisation and management of Wharton's Parisian *ouvroir* in *The End of the Age of Innocence: Edith Wharton and the First World War* (1988: 23–6).
9. As Michael Carter explains, in his structuralist analysis of the fashion system Barthes distinguished between 'the real garment', 'the represented garment' and 'the used garment' – definitions that correspond to the 'different modalities that clothes assume in their journey across the fashion system' (production, dissemination and consumption) (2003: 145).
10. According to Wilson, 'scientific eclecticism' in architecture as practised by Ogden Codman relied on the systematic study and recording of a wide range of past models. Subsequently, these past styles are arranged according to group or category prior to being replicated side by side in modern houses. Both the precision with which these past models are studied and classified as well as the accuracy of their replication justify the use of the term 'scientific' in the description of this particular school of thought. It is the unscientific, disorderly appropriation of past styles and ornaments that Wharton and Codman criticise in *The Decoration of Houses*.
11. Liisa Stephenson (2010: 1096–104) analyses Wharton's concerted views on fiction writing and architecture in more detail.
12. How closely Wharton's thinking resembled that of Veblen can be seen in a passage in 'The Great American Novel'. When she states that '[l]eisure, itself the creation of wealth, is incessantly engaged in transmuting wealth into beauty by secreting the surplus energy, which flowers in great architecture, great painting, and great literature' (1996: 156), Wharton seems to parrot the sociologist's theory on 'conspicuous leisure' (Veblen 1994: 75).
13. The fashion critic Barbara Vinken argues that the point at which clothes' ability to mark class distinction diminished, is when they acquired their new role of marking the distinction between the sexes (2005: 7–12).
14. One of Wharton's biographers discusses, as early as 1975, her engagement with 'the extraordinary world of Darwin and Spencer, Huxley and Haeckel' (Lewis 1975: 56). Recently, two studies on Wharton's interest in evolutionary theory have appeared: Paul J. Ohler, *Edith Wharton's 'Evolutionary Conception': Darwinian Allegory in Her Major Novels* (2006) and Judith P. Saunders, *Reading Edith Wharton through a Darwinian Lens* (2009). Although Ohler, who identifies Undine's 'training in mass culture' (108) correctly as Wharton's critique of its 'message that change is progress whether it takes the form of new fashion or new identity'

(109), refers to fashion in passing when discussing *The Custom of the Country*, it is not the focus of his study.

15. Elsewhere, Fryer notes explicitly that 'Undine is an *imitation*' (109).
16. A few years later, in *Twilight Sleep* (1927), Wharton created with her character Lita Wyant another young woman with a 'perpetual craving for new "thrills"' (Wharton 1997a: 18).
17. The irony in Wharton's dismissal of the 'machine made' story is apparent since her essays, in setting up and then explaining critical parameters for writing, participate in the process of categorising fiction for marketing purposes. 'Most novels', Wharton proposed, 'may be grouped under one or the other of the three types: manners, character (or psychology) and adventure' (Wharton 1997b: 51). In proposing this critical terminology, Wharton inadvertently committed herself to contributing to a literary culture of collectivising criticised elsewhere.
18. Naturally, this reference to the 1927 Hollywood film that spurred Clara Bow's career as 'It Girl', is indicative of Wharton's own complicity with contemporary mass culture. She was obviously familiar with the film adaptation of Elinor Glyn's novel of the same title. That one of Wharton's guilty pleasures was the consumption of mainstream and popular literature is also evidenced by a 1926 letter from *Vanity Fair* editor Frank Crowninshield who thanks her for expressing approval of *Gentlemen Prefer Blondes*, Anita Loos's 1925 satire of American popular culture. According to R. W. B. Lewis (1975: 468), Wharton publicly called *Gentlemen* '*the* great American novel'. The letter from Frank Crowninshield is in the Edith Wharton Collection in the Beinecke Rare Book and Manuscript Library at Yale (YCAL MSS 42 7/60/1716). Chapter 2 will include a brief discussion of Clarence G. Badger's film adaptation of Glyn's novel.
19. Eliot, although he clearly stated that 'novelty is better than repetition', also insisted in 'Tradition and the Individual Talent' that aspiring artists needed a well-developed 'historical sense' in order to be able to create meaningful work: 'No poet, no artist of any art', Eliot claimed, 'has his complete meaning alone. His significance, his appreciation is the appreciation of his relation to the dead poets and artists' (Eliot 1951: 14, 15).
20. Wharton's aversion to modernist literary aesthetics also becomes apparent in her essay 'Tendencies in Modern Fiction', in which she lamented that if 'the new novelists may be said to have any theory of art, it seems to be that every new creation can issue only from the annihilation of what preceded it' (Wharton 1996: 170).
21. Among Wharton's own writings, *Ethan Frome* (1911) is often regarded as a text that engages with, and even anticipates, some of literary modernism's stylistic concerns. The novella's frame narrative and its

unreliable narrator are certainly unusual for Wharton. For a detailed discussion of *Ethan Frome*'s modernist inflections see Linda Costanzo Cahir (2003: 20–3); Robin Peel (2005: 123–54); Vike Martina Plock (2010: 184–203). This early experiment with modernist literary conventions shows that Wharton was open to these particular stylistic innovations at an earlier stage in her career as a writer. Ultimately, however, this experiment remained an isolated one. Her later work with its linear plots and exterior-focused narratives returns to a more obvious realist framework.

22. For a comprehensive review of Wharton's involvement in marketing and selling her work, see Gary Totten (2012: 127–36) and Jamie Barlow (2007: 44–62). One particular case, the packaging of the serialised *The Mother's Recompense* with its accompanying illustrations in *Pictorial Review* is perceptively discussed by Edie Thornton (2001: 29–59).

23. Indeed, it is only in recent years that scholars have started to stress the literary merit of these later, bestselling Wharton novels, that are, according to Avril Horner and Janet Beer, 'hybrid and experimental works, intellectually ambitious in both form and content' (2011: 2). According to Melissa M. Pennell, Edmund Wilson's opinion 'that 1905 to 1917 marked the period of her best work' was responsible for this polarised perception of Wharton's writing (2012: 94–5). Wharton herself, it needs to be said, was certainly perplexed by the palpable incomprehension with which some readers – and critics in particular – welcomed her novels of the 1920s. The reception of *The Children* is one particular case in point. This was a novel (and theme) to which Wharton had 'become passionately attached' and she understandably lamented 'the uncomprehending drivel (laudatory or not)' it provoked. 'To have had such a vision', she noted, '& be able to convey only *that* of it', before deploring, once more, consumerist attitudes affecting the assessment of contemporary literary productions: 'I know nothing more depressing than to see a book selling & selling, & feel that nobody knows what they're buying' (Wharton 1988: 525).

24. In a 1920 letter to Bernard Berenson, Wharton also expressed pleasure that he and 'the few people whose opinion I care about' have understood her efforts to create with *The Age of Innocence* 'a "simple & grave" story of two people trying to live up to something that was still "felt in the blood" at that time' (Wharton 1988: 433).

25. The 'early French "*realists*," that group of brilliant writers who invented the once famous tranche de vie, the exact photographic reproduction of a situation or an episode, with all its sounds, smells, aspects realistically rendered', are 'still readable', Wharton accordingly acknowledged in *The Writing of Fiction* (11–12).

26. Penelope Vita-Finzi accordingly notes that the 'focus on point of view and the effect of the passage of time' are Wharton's 'central technical concerns' (1990: 40).
27. Met with less approval by the author were no doubt those early reviews of her novels that assigned them a 'ready-to-wear quality' and conformity to the 'fashions of the times' (quoted in Shepherd 2007: 156).
28. It should be noted that the young Virginia Stephen wrote a very supportive review of *The House of Mirth* in 1905 (Woolf 1986: 67–8).
29. At this point, it is important to remember that Wharton's stance towards modernism was by no means as uncompromising as her critical writing would let us believe: she was known to have savoured an eclectic mix of modernist artworks ranging from writers (Colette, W. B. Yeats, Evelyn Waugh, Rainer Maria Rilke) to composers, painters and dancers (Igor Stravinsky, Isadora Duncan, Paul Cézanne). For the full list see Wegener (1998: 119). Very likely, this periodic intake of modernist art indicates a particular form of critical engagement with the artistic practices of Wharton's successors, one that is best compared to a selective harvesting. In all likelihood, Wharton regarded herself as a discerning reader and appreciator who was able to identify, among the bulk of modernist productions, those works that satisfied her demand for 'style'.

Chapter 2

Conformity and Idiosyncrasy: Jean Rhys

Although aspects of this chapter assess, like the previous one, fashion's impact on female identity formation through standardisation and typecasting, its focus is different in that Jean Rhys was, unlike Wharton, not only a consumer but through her work as a fashion model in several Parisian couture houses also a participatory agent in an emerging industry that brought into circulation images of desirable femininity. Surviving photographs of the young Rhys depict a woman who is exceptionally conscious of her good looks, who poses comfortably for the camera and who seems happy to accept the necessity to conform to contemporary beauty standards in exchange for social approval.[1] To claim that she had a critical attitude towards fashion might therefore sound controversial. On the face of it, this young, bohemian woman, who regarded exquisite clothes, fashionable accessories and make-up as constitutive for female identity formation, is positioned – more than any of the other women writers discussed in this study – in a very obvious psychological and professional proximity to the fashionable circuits of her time. Moreover, in terms of her development as a writer, Rhys's willingness to publish her short story cycle *The Left Bank* (1927) and her first novel *Quartet* (1928) under the patronage of Ford Madox Ford associated her, right from the beginning of her career, with those literary circles that would eventually become known as the modernist avant-garde. Personally and professionally, Rhys, at the end of the 1920s, seemed to have embodied the image of fashionable femininity and of modernist authorship as it was constructed by contemporaries.

Yet, it is precisely this suggestion – that Rhys's fiction contains a far from subtle critique of the modern fashion industry and its impact on young women who had to earn their living – that I intend to develop in this chapter. Although her writing resonates with images of alluring garments and fashionably dressed women, I will suggest that it also unmasks as prohibitive illusions some of fashion's instructive propositions on how to cultivate images of modern, successful and desirable femininity in the interwar years. On closer scrutiny, it becomes obvious that Rhys's 'Left Bank' fiction of the 1920s and 1930s registers the complications and sacrifices involved in living up to the beauty standards devised and disseminated by contemporary fashion lore. If being fashionable implies accepting and conforming to mainstream notions of female loveliness, Rhys's heroines fail in their desire to become absorbed into an expanding crowd of young, modish women, produced in a conveyer-belt manner, in interwar Paris. Although all of these women have aspirations that have been roused and fuelled, at least in part, by modern fashion, Rhys's 'Left Bank' fiction shows how these ambitions (romantic, social, materialist and professional) become thwarted by economic restrictions, naiveté and, sometimes, sheer bad luck. Fashion is so exceptionally seductive for the Rhys heroine because it promises narratives of advancement, transformation and improvement. But in *Quartet, After Leaving Mr Mackenzie* (1930), *Good Morning, Midnight* (1939) and some of Rhys's short stories, the glittering success stories of personal and social progress that fashion indirectly nourishes become explicitly tied, as I shall explain, to a particular psychological economy that paralyses and defeats.[2] Fashion is therefore exposed as the producer of social fantasies that are accessible for some but by no means all women in the interwar years. There are always those individuals for whom, to paraphrase one of Rhys's own expressions, the disparity between your actual self and the one you hope to be – the desire to be fashionable and socially successful – remained unfulfilled.[3] It is these stories that Rhys's fiction prioritises.

This aspect of Rhys's work has already received considerable critical attention. In fact, for many Rhys scholars, her fiction elicits critical approval because of its powerful depiction of women's economic and, above all, sexual exploitation in a hostile patriarchal world. Even more disturbing is the fact that the Rhys heroine seems masochistically complicit in her own victimisation.[4] The line-up of abused, mistreated women in Rhys's interwar novels, which makes for a very depressive reading, provides a pessimistic counterpoint to narratives about women's emancipation in the 1920s and 1930s. Here is depicted a world of women on the margins of society, who are constantly in danger of slipping into poverty, prostitution and oblivion. Although they might come from a relatively stable family background, like *After Leaving Mr Mackenzie*'s Julia, '"[m]iddle class, no money"' (2000a: 53), they are predestined to follow, as Celia Marshik suggests, the 'downward paths' sketched by contemporary purity pamphlets with an equal amount of fervour and creativity (2006: 170). Predetermined and conditioned by biology, psychology and milieu, the women in Rhys's fiction resemble female characters in Émile Zola, Stephen Crane or other writers belonging to the naturalist tradition.[5] Stripped of authority and free will, they wander aimlessly from one café and lover to the next. As a chorus girl, one 'can drift like that for a long time', the narrator in *Quartet* comments, lining up a 'vague procession of towns all exactly alike, a vague procession of men also exactly alike' even if 'this wasn't what one had expected of life. Not in the very least' (2000c: 15). It is for this reason – because Rhys's women emblematically represent female apathy and helplessness that has become a chronic condition – that many critics associate her fiction with that of her naturalist precursors. There is literally no way out for the Rhys woman.

Recently, however, Sean Latham has argued for a different reading of Rhys's *roman-à-clef*, *Quartet* – one that acknowledges the paralysis of the heroine while simultaneously locating, in the writing itself, a subversive energy that defies the novelistic depiction of vulnerability and emotional exhaustion. Latham asserts that the novel takes revenge on Rhys's one-time lover and benefactor Ford by exposing him, through his novelistic counterpart Heidler, 'as a brutal and abusive misogynist whose bohemian ideals are merely a hypocritical pose' (2009: 164). And while Latham is certainly correct in proposing that the public exposure of the older man's vices and personal flaws ultimately empowers the woman writer, this analysis of reciprocal aggression hardly moves beyond uncovering a cycle of mutually constitutive exploitation in which textually embedded violence has taken the place of emotional abuse. There is no doubt that anger and frustration are significant undercurrents in all of Rhys's writing. But emphasising these textual strands is hardly productive for critical attempts that aim to free Rhys from the victim status that so persistently attaches to her person and her fiction. What I shall propose in response, then, is a reading that uses fashion as a trope to assess how Rhys's interwar writing became progressively autonomous from external influences. It is worth remembering at this point that fashion constantly invokes the dialectic relationship between conformity and idiosyncrasy, between adaptation and difference. In this chapter's final pages, I will therefore suggest that Rhys underwent a process of intellectual growth in the interwar years that is rendered explicit in the increasingly experimental nature of her novelistic prose. The fragmented, impressionistic tableaux encountered in *Good Morning, Midnight* are the result of an apprenticeship in writing that began with the more conventional prose of *Quartet* and *After Leaving Mr Mackenzie*. By the time she published the last of her interwar novels, Rhys had developed a mode of writing that openly defied the conventions of traditional composition still somewhat heeded in earlier novelistic attempts. While her protagonists encounter social alienation rather than the liberating autonomy suggested by optimistic narratives about self-empowerment through fashion, Rhys's novels therefore translate marginality into a productive impetus for artistic self-fashioning. Even if the lives of Rhys and her heroines provide disturbing biographies of women whose desire for social integration through sartorial conformity has horribly gone awry,[6] her prose nonetheless offers a potentially more hopeful view of nonconformity because it purposefully turned the articulation of difference into a strategy for novelistic accomplishment.

Fashion, I argue in this chapter, provides a particularly productive concept for analysing Rhys's professional trajectory and her relationship with literary modernism in the interwar years: its conflicting but mutually constitutive tractions (conformity versus idiosyncrasy) throw into sharp relief the various pressures encountered by a woman who hoped to succeed as a writer – a woman novelist who longed for popular recognition, who ascended to intellectual maturity during the interwar years but whose personal and writerly idiosyncrasies simultaneously exiled her from adjacent literary communities and rendered difficult any attempt to effectively promote and disseminate her work.[7] If modernism began to be known for its formal experiments at the time Rhys was writing, an apparent irony would be that her work was not firmly absorbed at that time by an avant-garde movement that prized the kind of thematic and formal riskiness she was embracing. Had it not been for the popular success of *Wide Sargasso Sea* (1966), Rhys's interwar writing, characterised by its heightened subjectivity and its aesthetics of failure, would have been permanently obscured from critical view. Only the commercial success of her later novel, in other words, retrospectively secured Rhys a place among the 'dissident modernists' of the interwar period. As Peter J. Kallinay has recently suggested, this 'accomplished-but-forgotten white modernist' suddenly succeeded in 'reinvent[ing] herself as a postcolonial intellectual in the 1960s' and therefore managed to renew critical interest in her long-forgotten interwar fiction (2013: 222).[8] In *Modernism, Fashion and Interwar Women Writers* Rhys emerges as the example of a writer who built her early career on the principles of nonconformity and eccentricity but who failed or who refused to affiliate with an artistic formation that had begun to dominate critical discussions in the interwar period by making exactly this kind of rebelliousness its actual trademark. For the present project, her work is such a productive site for analysis because it is distinguished by a countercultural current but resisted appropriation by an ascendant artistic formation (modernism) that had found effective mechanisms, as Aaron Jaffe has suggested, to accommodate its own countercultural impulses within existing commercial and institutional structures of a market that relied on the production of literary celebrities. Rhys and her 'Left Bank' fiction could not be subjected to this profile-raising makeover process: there was no way her eccentric work could be turned into a commercially viable fashion before a sudden critical interest in (post)colonial topics provided this writer with a new and immensely popular authorial persona decades after she debuted as a 'Left Bank' modernist.[9]

Styling modern womanhood: Coco Chanel and the allure of fashionable femininity

In order to analyse Rhys's views on fashion, sartorial practices and female identity formation, I begin this chapter by looking at another influential modernist heroine: Coco Chanel, who became one of the most authoritative style guides for young women such as Rhys who turned to fashion columns and display windows of metropolitan department stores of the interwar period for advice on what to wear.

Although Chanel was by no means the only couturier who revolutionised the design and perception of women's clothing from the mid-teens onwards – Madeleine Vionnet, Elsa Schiaparelli and Jean Patou were others who created similarly radical sartorial designs – she was exceptional, as Rhonda K. Garelick argues, in that she 'embodied and publicized a concomitant lifestyle and growing personal celebrity, which echoed and underscored the social message of this new silhouette' (2014: 85). Born in 1883 as a contemporary of such writers as Joyce and Woolf, Chanel's shrewd manipulation of the market – she created the look of functional chic in a time of deprivation when fabrics were sparse – and her careful self-styling as a haute couture designer clearly ensured her triumphant professional success and helped to advance her celebrity status. In a sense, Chanel not only sold but also embodied the myth of modern womanhood at the time when Rhys was starting to write her 'Left Bank' fiction in the 1920s. Unlike any other turn-of-the-century star couturier, that is, she personified the success story of female emancipation through hard work that was also advocated by her sartorial designs. It is this aspect of the Chanel myth – her ability to effectively manipulate her public image as a professionally successful woman for the purpose of advertising her creations – that had immense cultural resonances and that made other women believe that the purchase of the Chanel couture was synonymous with access to emancipatory opportunities. The Chanel myth also serves, I shall argue in the following pages, as an important cultural intertext in Rhys's 'Left Bank' fiction, in which fashion's involvement in creating such inviting and irresistible illusions about women's emotional, social and professional freedoms is critically examined.

Chanel, as many critics have pointed out, built her professional empire on the promise of assisting in women's struggle for political, social and economic independence. 'I gave women a sense of freedom; I gave them back their bodies' (De La Haye and Tobin 2001: 19), Coco famously claimed when promoting her *garçonne* look as a seductive image of slim, youthful, modern femininity. In fact, her simple and classical style redefined more than just women's wardrobes. Like many other contemporary designers, she engineered clothes that facilitated ease of movement by liberating women from the confining and restricting, tight-laced garments that had marked the silhouette of the Gibson Girl. Instead, Chanel's Flapper designs, which emphasised practicality, flexibility and adaptability to a modern, active lifestyle, represented the increased emancipation of women in the post-war years. As Catherine Driscoll explains, Chanel's 'little black dress', 'her use of men's fabrics and reference to men's tailoring translated into some mobility between gender norms' (2010: 121). Women's social mobility, their political progress and their autonomy were thus expressed in sartorial patterns that marketed comfort, simplicity and locomotive freedom.

Paradoxically, though, Coco's fitting methods were 'a test of endurance for her mannequins who had to stand for an exhausting six to seven hours' (De La Haye and Tobin 2001: 19), unable to move or stir. One of Chanel's biographer notes that:

> The *mannequins* were the ones who suffered her scalding tongue, hair-trigger wit, and the pricks of her pins. . . . 'Stand straight, girl,' Coco would hiss through her pins in her mouth while the individual dresses were being created and re-created and the effects viewed and alterations contemplated. (Madsen 1990: 161)[10]

In Jean Rhys's short story 'Mannequin', published in the 1927 collection of stories *The Left Bank*, the protagonist Anna has to remain similarly motionless 'for an hour to have a dress draped on her'. 'About five o'clock', the narrator states, 'Anna became exhausted' 'fighting an intense desire to rush away' from the confining walls of the couture house (1972: 154–5).[11] In this manner, Chanel's case indicates that mobility and freedom of movement (or the lack thereof) were central aspects of the sartorial reform that took place in Paris in the 1920s. Her sartorial designs energetically advertised women's socially progressive itineraries. At the same time, her treatment of other working women such as mannequins, shopworkers and seamstresses was often derogative if not exploitative. While she paid her models a monthly salary that amounted to roughly one-tenth of the price of one of her dresses, notorious statements such as – 'A woman's education consists of two lessons: never to leave the house without stockings, never to go out without a hat' – illustrate the full complexity of Chanel's stance towards women's professional and social ascent or advancement (Madsen 1990: 160).[12]

In Rhys's writing, mobility, stasis and locomotive flexibility or restrictions also surface as conceptual configurations and are connected, I argue later in this chapter, to her understanding of fashion as an inspirational yet ultimately disabling cultural script. As many critics have noted, Rhys's female ex-pat characters are constantly on the move. They find themselves in transition 'between spaces' (Thacker 2003: 193) while these 'social and psychical places' are, paradoxically, 'oppressively constant and claustrophobic' (Bowlby 1992: 34). Early on in *Quartet*, a merry-go-round symbolically registers the protagonist's aimless, circular movements that force her into a series of repetitive and increasingly degrading emotional routines. Marya's weekly trip to Fresnes to see her imprisoned husband is flanked by Lois's Thursday evening parties that provide the Heidlers with occasions to display Marya, like a prize trophy, in front of their bohemian friends. '"She must be chic", . . . "She must do us credit"', Lois tells her husband as if 'discussing the dressing of a doll' when Marya becomes his mistress.[13] Eventually, the humiliating business of tagging along as the object of the Heidlers' unsound patronage is translated into the language of fairground attractions. '"Let's go to Luna-park after dinner"', Lois suggests. '"We'll put Mado on the joy wheel, and watch her being banged about a bit. Well, she ought to amuse us sometimes; she ought to sing for her supper; that's what she's here for, isn't it?"' (2000c: 67). Here, the funfair machine, devised to entertain and divert, is sinisterly manipulated by Heidler's jealous wife to take revenge on the financially dependent resident/mistress. It pointedly illustrates the complex emotional transactions constituting a triangular relationship that is by no means amusing for any of the parties involved. At the same time, it captures Marya's precarious social status, her entrapment and psychological paralysis, generated by interpersonal dynamics that have significantly diminished her ability to take control of her own life.

Not surprisingly, Andrew Thacker notes that the 'perception of a voyage that goes adrift from its final destination might be taken as a dominant trope for all of Rhys's work' (2003: 192). Rachel Bowlby similarly identifies the lack of narrative and personal progress as one of the most distinctive features of Rhys's protagonists and texts: '*Good Morning, Midnight* begins where it ends', Bowlby notes, 'ends where it begins: in the same room, outside a street which is "what they call an impasse"' (1992: 36). Earlier on in her career, in *Quartet*, Rhys had already depicted this condition of apathy and confinement in an image of a restless 'young fox' in 'a cage perhaps three yards long at the end of the zoo' (124). Eliciting an emphatic response from the protagonist Marya, the young woman who feels equally trapped and victimised by the gawping, pleasure-seeking crowds she encounters in Parisian cafés, the captured animal becomes representative as the victim of a lurid, materialistic culture, the 'organized society' to use the words of another Rhys heroine (2000a: 17), in which the trafficking and the commodification of living creatures have become routine practices. Cafés and cages, Rhys seems to suggest, are the two corresponding spaces where animals and women end up performing monotonous, repetitive tasks in service of public entertainment and distraction. Fashion, as I intend to show below, brings to the fore the problematic dynamics attached to fictions about female empowerment through clothes. Although they energetically promote the image of female liberation, emancipation and progress, the fashionable tableaux of the 1920s and 1930s in some ways exacerbate the plight of some women. Put simply, those glamorous images of feminine desirability and prestige seduce and captivate but they also draw attention to the difference between idealising fantasy and the grim reality faced by women such as those encountered in Rhys's fiction. Shop windows and department store displays consistently accentuate, Anna Snaith notes, the juxtaposition between 'the actual and desired position' of Rhys's protagonists (2014: 144). Access to the economic and social benefits implicit in the image of female perfection remained restricted. Rhys's narratives explicitly address this problem and expose the interwar fashion narrative for what it was: a tempting fantasy and illusion that compelled many women to plunder their physical, emotional and material resources. Fashion, in other words, is often indirectly responsible for heightening the Rhys heroine's paralytic condition.

'I'll do anything for good clothes. Anything – anything for clothes': fashioning the female self in Jean Rhys's 'Left Bank' fiction

As her readers will note at first glance, Rhys's 'Left Bank' fiction is interlaced with references to fashion, clothes and garments.[14] Several of her short stories, such as the already mentioned 'Mannequin' and its thematic counterpart 'Illusion', as well as three of her interwar novels, *Quartet*, *After Leaving Mr Mackenzie* and *Good Morning, Midnight*, are set in 1920s and 1930s Paris, the heart of the fashion industry that is setting the standards for sartorial innovations and revolutions at the beginning of the twentieth century. Moreover, all of Rhys's protagonists seem exceptionally cognisant of and receptive to the allure of modish, modern femininity. In *Quartet*, Marya, for instance, expertly notes another woman's 'figure and coiffure of the nineties', the silhouette of the Gibson Girl: 'her waist goes in, her hips come out, her long black hair is coiled into a smooth bun on the top of her round head' (11). And both Julia in *After Leaving Mr Mackenzie* and Sasha in *Good Morning, Midnight* have experience of working (like Rhys herself) as a mannequin in one of Paris's numerous fashion houses (Rhys 2000a: 20; Rhys 2000b: 18).[15]

Needless to say, this proximity to the French fashion industry conditions Rhys's protagonists and their sense of self. Self-esteem is repeatedly measured by the success or the failure of a particular outfit. After Sasha, in *Good Morning, Midnight*, completes her 'transformation act' (53) – the acquisition of a new hat, dress and hair dye – she is understandably alarmed to note that her attire attracts the attention of a young gigolo. 'Oh Lord, is that what I look like? Do I really look like a wealthy dame trotting round Montparnasse in the hope of–? After all the trouble I've gone to, is that what I look like?' (61), she panics while she also critically assesses another woman's accomplished sartorial display:

> A girl came into the café and sat down at the next table. She was wearing a grey suit, the skirt short and tight and the blouse very fresh and clean. And a cocky black hat like a Scots soldier's glengarry. Her handbag was lying on the table near her – patent leather to match her shoes. . . . And she walked so straight and quick on her high-heeled shoes. Tap, tap, tap, her heels . . . (103)

Instinctively, Sasha contemplates emulating aspects of this successful performance, of which clothes and fashion accessories are the most significant indicators: '(Handbag. . . . What a lot of things I've got to get! Would a suit like that be a good thing to get? No, I think I had better get. . . .)' (103). Elsewhere in Rhys's fiction, in the short story 'Illusion', the protagonist is constantly in motion to look 'for *the* dress, the perfect Dress' (1972: 143) that will beautify her and that can provide the exhilarating feeling of perfection. 'I'll do anything for good clothes. Anything – anything for clothes', similarly states Anna Morgan in *Voyage in the Dark* (1934) when describing 'the shop windows sneering and smiling in your face' (Rhys 2000d: 22).

Seductive and enticing, these fashionable displays function like instruction manuals on personal adornment. But they also advertise more than the clothes displayed on department store dummies. Implicit in the mounted garments and accessories is the abstract promise of obtaining perfection that exceeds the realm of corporeal enhancement. Access to better and more elegant clothes is tantamount to and indicative of social prestige and betterment. At the beginning of the twentieth century, an increased instability of formerly clear social structures meant that someone's clothes could no longer be seen as a definite index of affluence or status.[16] People could easily be misguided when judging other people's social position or financial power by reading their clothes. This mistake is made by characters in Cicely Hamilton's 1908 play *Diana of Dobson's*. The elegant setting of a Swiss hotel in Pontresina forms the backdrop for two marriage proposals made to a former shop girl who has spent all of her recently inherited money on the acquisition of stylish dresses and a one-month pleasure trip abroad. Neither of the proposals is accepted, but the play strikingly illustrates the social possibilities inherent in dressing well.[17] It is for that reason, for the assistance of clothes in (temporarily) transcending class structures, that Julia Martin bitterly regrets selling 'the fur coat she had once possessed. The sort that lasts for ever, astrakhan, with a huge skunk collar.' A status symbol more than a fashionable ornament, the fur coat guarantees social approval. 'People thought twice', Julia notes, 'before they were rude to anybody wearing a good fur coat; it was protective colouring, as it were' (Rhys 2000a: 57). Fashion, Celia Marshik explains in relation to Rhys's protagonists, is in service of 'signal[ing] a woman's worth' (2006: 183).

This apparent transformative power of clothes is described by Rhys as something she experienced herself at a particularly formative time of her life. Invited to a fancy-dress party as a young girl, she is being congratulated on her choice of frock. 'I went home, I suppose, somewhere between twelve and one and looking at myself in the glass', she states in her autobiography, concluding: 'I knew that

that night had changed me. I was a different girl, I told myself that I would be just as happy the next day, now I would always be happy' (1979: 91). Even though this adolescent memoir lacks the complexity of later, fictional depictions of clothes' socio-economic meanings, it nonetheless describes their quasi-magical power to secure well-being and happiness. In Sasha's case, the garments most explicitly connected to such liberating fantasies of self-fashioning are the 'Cossack cap and the imitation astrakhan coat' that her husband Enno bought for her 'in 1923 or 1924' (Rhys 2000b: 11).[18] Not only do these opulent accessories display images of desirable femininity, but they are also responsible for the wearer's self-styled rebirth. It is due to these exotic clothes that Sasha appropriates her foreign-sounding name in the hope that it will bring her luck. Anna, the mannequin-protagonist of Rhys's story of the same title, feels similarly enchanted once she leaves the oppressive and stifling environment of the couture house 'in her beautifully cut tailor-made and beret' (Rhys 1972: 155). Very likely, one of the reasons why the career as a mannequin must have been exceptionally attractive to young women such as Rhys was the promised proximity to the couturier's latest designs. Although Caroline Evans notes that the 'model garment' shown to clients in French couture houses at the turn of the century 'was rarely the elaborately finished garment that the private client received', resembling 'a canvas toile, made up in inferior fabric' (2013: 15–16), the thought of wearing haute couture dresses for a living must have been seductive for many young women who had a vested interested in nice clothes. The end of Rhys's short story 'Mannequin', which compares the mannequins 'coming out of the shops' to 'gay and beautiful . . . beds of flowers' (Rhys 1972: 155), captures some of those feelings of excitement associated with the thought of wearing designer dresses. These seem to have the power to transform a little shop girl into the radiant image of feminine perfection and therefore invite attempts of sartorial mimicry. It is also for this reason, for fashion's ability to disseminate seductive images of accomplishment, that Sasha understands her present-day purchase of a new dress less as an economic transaction but more as another complex makeover ritual. As *Good Morning, Midnight* insists, new accessories are purchased in the hope of assembling a new self. Its protagonist has wholeheartedly absorbed the main tenets of contemporary fashion lore.

However, if Rhys's fiction circulates the seductive narrative of fashion's transformative power, it also notes the apparent instability of this ostensibly energising plot. In 'Illusion', read by Jane Garrity as a story about closeted homosexual desire (2014: 274–5),[19] the middle-aged Miss Bruce's hunt for '*the* dress' exemplifies 'a craving, almost a vice' (Rhys 1972: 143) for idealising fantasies of selfhood represented by the beautiful and tucked away frocks. A (hitherto disappointed) desire, the 'love of beautiful clothes', which Maroula Joannou associates with women's 'visceral needs' (2012: 469), motivates repeated acts of consumption and produces a wardrobe that 'when one opened it was a glow of colours, a riot of soft silks . . . everything that one did not expect' beneath Miss Bruce's 'cool sensible, tidy English outside' (Rhys 1972: 141–2). Of course, as Miss Bruce is hasty to admit in a conversation with the story's narrator, '"I should never make such a fool of myself as to wear them . . ."' (144). Expectations about age, demeanour and nationality, Rhys's story suggests, form a set of prohibitive social codes that prevent its character from living out her ravishing sartorial dreams. None of 'the beautiful things' condemned to 'life in the dark' (143–4) will ever be worn by Miss Bruce who faithfully sticks to her 'neat serge dress', her 'tweet costume' and her 'black gown of crêpe de chine' (141) – clothes that suitably express her status as an ex-pat Montparnasse portrait painter of advanced years. And although Miss Bruce is clearly unusual as a Rhys heroine in that she has the financial means to purchase a superfluous collection of expensive designer dresses, 'Illusion' nonetheless illustrates that she is as excluded as many other women in Rhys's fiction from the liberating fantasy simulated by Chanel's exquisite costumes. What the story alludes to, therefore, is the universality of 'the perpetual hunger to be beautiful and that thirst to be loved which is the real curse of Eve' (Rhys 1972: 143). Independent of age, social position or physical characteristics, practically all women, 'Illusion' implies, are seduced by fashion's suggestive images that associate the display of sartorial splendour with social prestige, prosperity and desirability. Because it is mainly economical, in Miss Bruce's case the damage to the protagonist's welfare is, by comparison, relatively insignificant. But here as elsewhere in Rhys's fiction, the limitations of fashion's remedial power are concretely underlined. The story's title as well as its narrator's perceptive analysis of Miss Bruce's unfulfilled desire point to the futility in committing oneself to a success story that is built, in spite of its universal appeal, on exclusion as one of its organising principles.

Indeed, the extent of fashion's reliance on discrimination through effective typecasting can be gleaned by analysing the operational practices of French couture houses in the interwar years. In her study on the early fashion shows in France and America, Caroline Evans notes that Fordist aesthetics and Taylorist management routines had started to affect work in the French fashion industry since the beginning of the twentieth century (2013: 147–8). According to Evans, these new business procedures were also responsible for developing a reformed, and more ritualised, approach to modelling designer clothes. Foregrounded in the choice of fashion mannequins from now on were, above all, uniformity and the models' conformity to a particular type. For example, in 1924 the French couturier Jean Patou contracted a number of American mannequins for the exclusive purpose of representing on European catwalks the American physique, the so-called 'greyhound silhouette': slender, athletic, Amazonian (Evans 2013: 126). To maximise sales figures, these American imports were entrepreneurially juxtaposed to 'the rounded French Venus' prevalent at home (Patou quoted in Evans 2013: 125). This categorisation of particular feminine physiques according to national types is probably the most extreme example of a new business attitude dominating the French haute couture houses of the interwar years. But the drift to displaying increasingly standardised images of feminine beauty in the showrooms was pervasive at the time. It was, as Siegfried Kracauer noted in 1927, a prevailing feature of contemporary mass entertainment, 'a process that began with the Tiller Girls' whose industrialised aesthetics relied on producing 'no longer individual girls, but indissoluble girl clusters whose movements are demonstrations of mathematics' (1995: 75–6). Increasingly, the line-up of particular female types, mimicking the aesthetics of the chorus line, became an accepted (and expected) feature of French fashion shows.

Rhys expertly illustrates the standardisation of female looks in the 1920s fashion industry. In the story 'Mannequin', for instance, the protagonist Anna is confronted with a particular line-up of different but characteristic feminine types prevalent in Parisian couture houses:

> Round the austere table were now seated Babette, the gamine, the traditional blond enfant: Mona, tall and darkly beautiful, the femme

fatale, the wearer of sumptuous evening gowns. Georgette was the garçonne: Simone with her green eyes Anna knew instantly for a cat whom men would and did adore, a sleek, white, purring, long-lashed creature. (Rhys 1972: 152)

Eliane, the reader is told, 'was the star of the collection' (Rhys 1972: 152), the term 'collection' thereby explicitly drawing attention to the commercial viability and commodification of the young women's bodies.[20] Anna herself, it is noted, 'was to wear the jeune fille dress' and she spends her first day at work learning 'the way to wear the innocent and springlike air and garb of the jeune fille' (150). In Rhys's fiction, the mannequin's body thus becomes a site that renders problematical such binaries as distinction and conformity, consumer object and subjective identity, while Rhys, with astuteness and insight, comments on the typecasting and commercialisation of women's appearances and physiques in French couture houses of the 1920s.[21]

From this catalogue of desirable feminine types someone like Miss Bruce is, very obviously, excluded. She is one of many women in Rhys's fiction whose aspirations to be beautiful are unmasked as unattainable illusion. If she has the financial means to purchase the desired dresses, she is restricted by age and social position to wear them. Other characters in Rhys's fiction face different sets of restrictions that thwart their desires for beautiful dresses – and associated dreams of socio-economic improvement. While the enhancing garments worn at least occasionally by Rhys's protagonists support enabling fantasies of feminine assertiveness, these liberating glimpses of prospects and potential are erratically dispersed and temporary in nature. Predictably, they also become inversely proportional to the protagonists' increasing age. Julia, in *After Leaving Mr Mackenzie*, can still think 'of new clothes with passion, with voluptuousness'. The sensation of 'a new dress on her body and the scent of it, and her hands emerging from long, black sleeves' (15) provokes physical pleasure and excitement and generates sudden bursts of activity. It is certainly significant that her most obvious act of rebellion against an exploitative patriarchal coterie – striking Mr Mackenzie's cheek with her glove 'so lightly that he did not even blink' – involves a sartorial object. Having failed to provoke Mr Mackenzie's sympathy by putting 'her hand on his', she uses her glove to hit him in the face in a stylised gesture that could almost be interpreted – by disinterested observers – as flirtatious or playful (26).

Haptically recalling or reviving former intimacy is obviously futile. Mr Mackenzie remains untouched when Julia laments that she has 'been pretty unhappy' (25). The glove – paid for, of course, by money from Mr Mackenzie's subsistence check – becomes a retaliating agent and indicates that clothes and fashionable accessories remain, for Rhys's younger protagonist, psychologically related to fantasies of non-compliance if not active rebellion.

Conversely, in *Good Morning, Midnight* this appealing fantasy has lost much of its persuasive force. Although Sasha is in Paris for two weeks in order 'to buy a lot of clothes to startle my friends' (40), aspiration has been replaced with anxiety. The selection and purchase of new clothes is no longer eagerly anticipated but purposefully delayed by observing other women in the process of consumption. Increasingly, Sasha becomes obsessed with age and with the inability to mask the signs of her advanced years with clothes, while a woman with 'dishevelled' 'half-dyed, half-grey' hair who tries on hats and 'makes faces at herself in the glass' that become increasingly 'hungry, despairing, hopeful, quite crazy' (57) turns into a grotesque vision of what the future might hold in store for Sasha. 'Watching her, am I watching myself as I shall become', 'in five years' time, in six years' time', Rhys's protagonist uneasily inquires (58). No wonder, then, that the act of buying a new hat for herself – an activity with regenerative potential in earlier years – becomes an emotionally charged, unsettling experience. After spending 'nearly two hours' in the hat shop's 'cruel, crude light' (58), Sasha finally resolves to put her trust in the salesgirl to make the choice on her behalf. The result is the purchase of a hat that is scarcely desired but one that has the explicit approval of the younger woman. It also shields its wearer from unwanted attention. 'Nobody stares at me', Sasha states matter-of-factly, 'which I think is a good sign' (60). Clothes, in Rhys's later fiction, no longer function as agents of embellishment or enhancement. Rather, they conceal and disguise those aspects of the self – age, worry and other imperfections – the wearer wishes to ignore. Even now, their assistance in identity management is acknowledged. What has changed, however, are the symbolic overtones of the very same sartorial markers. If clothes remain, at certain times, connected to narratives of personal growth and empowerment for Rhys's younger protagonists, their ability to enhance has vanished alongside the subject's sense of self-worth. Attracting attention is no longer the desired outcome of Sasha's sartorial purchases. In her case, clothes can only assist in delaying or obscuring the inevitable disintegration of the formerly attractive self.

At this point it is useful to consider, as J. C. Flügel does in *The Psychology of Clothes*, the dialectic relationship between modesty and decoration that conditions individual choices of dress:

> The essential purpose of decoration is to beautify the bodily appearance, so as to attract the admiring glances of others and fortify one's self-esteem. The essential purpose of modesty is, if not indeed the exact contrary, at least utterly opposed to this. Modesty tends to make us hide such bodily exellencies as we may have and generally refrain from drawing the attention of others to ourselves. (Flügel 1966: 20)

Sasha has clearly lost her younger self's desire for elaborate sartorial decoration. And although her present behaviour is by no means motivated by modesty in Flügel's sense – there is no evidence that Sasha thinks of any of her physical attributes as assets – the former need to advertise personal distinction through stylish clothes has given way to self-effacement and camouflage that invert clothes' ability to decorate. Paradoxically, exactly those sartorial agents that formerly assisted in the process of adorning the self are now used to conceal and disguise – those social practices associated by Flügel with decoration's psychological counterpart: modesty. Sasha's 'transformation act' is thus unmasked by Rhys as a complex, yet ultimately futile experiment, a repetitive, almost mechanically practised routine that has lost all of its former significance. Sasha has ceased to believe in the regenerative potential of clothing but she continues to invest, as Cynthia Port observes, 'in clothes and appearance in order to sustain [her] status as increasingly devalued commodity' (2001: 207). They can no longer help her in building confidence. Nonetheless, little else remains to be done. Without any other way of achieving self-esteem, Sasha continues to buy and don new clothes in the hope that they will assist in generating a new self. Hers is yet another unsettling story of a woman's psychological reliance on haute couture and sartorial designs – fashion's 'games of appearance' as Alissa G. Karl calls it in her perceptive analysis of literary modernism's relationship to early twentieth-century consumer capitalism (2009: 16).[22]

In this manner, by focusing on the lives and experiences of the marginalised, Rhys's fiction consistently disrobes optimistic notions associating female empowerment with displays of sartorial perfection. Good clothes simply cannot make the woman. Moreover, as I will show in the next section of this chapter, Rhys also unmasked a more specific ideological aspect dominating the symbolic infrastructure of the Flapper couture. What I show in the next paragraphs is that Rhys repeatedly engaged with the seductive story that aligned women's professional opportunities with the new, loose-fitting clothes created by Chanel and other designers of the early twentieth century. What Rhys criticises is not so much women's choice of a particular type of modish femininity. Instead she debunks the ideology of choice itself – an illusion carefully created, nourished and yet never explicitly delivered by contemporary fashion rhetoric. As I indicated above, promoted explicitly as heralds of women's invasion of male-dominated public spheres (work, leisure, travel), Chanel's unrestricting garments (and her own professional success) offered visions of the modern woman whose sense of self-esteem had ceased to depend on the display of sexual availability. Here was the fantastic promise of a new avenue to happiness, one that replaced male approval with female success in the workspace as one, and as the preferred, way for women to legitimise their existence. Not only desirability but modernity was signalled by these post-war sartorial designs. As Chanel's case illustrates, implicit in the radically modern garments was the image of potential. Achieving economic independence through hard work and professional progress was one option available for aspirational women. Suddenly, all this was in reach for young women of Rhys and Chanel's generation whose clothes represented this new culture of choice.

Rhys's fiction, however, articulates a profound scepticism about the achievability of these and similar utopian visions. In her texts, an insistence on women's upward and progressive trajectories, so ubiquitous in contemporary stories of women's professional progress, is replaced by psychological panoramas in which paralysis and stasis emerge as dominant sensations. As such, Rhys acknowledged that women's social roles were exceptionally ill-defined in a post-war world in which social, economic and professional relations had become increasingly fluid, unstable and unpredictable. Although there can be no doubt that this was a time of progressive change, of mobility and transformation that was beneficial to women and that created room for their demands for gender equality and personal freedoms, Rhys's fiction nonetheless shows that the relative insecurity marking this culture of upheaval left many women in a state of emotional and perceptual confusion. Registered and rendered visible is this sense of psychological disorientation in the spatial imagery of Rhys's fiction that I have already discussed – the impasse faced by virtually all of her protagonists at least temporarily in so many of her 'Left Bank' stories. Particularly evident, however, becomes the psychological dislocation experienced by Rhys's protagonists in those text passages that deal with their professional experiences (past and present). It is to these key sections in her texts that I shall turn next to show the full extent of Rhys's criticism of fashion as the producer and disseminator of appealing yet ultimately inaccessible stories about women's socio-economic progress and emancipation.

'Thinking of my jobs. . . .': Rhys and the salaried-bohemians of the modern metropolis

Before turning to Rhys's texts, it is worth noting that narratives about women's socio-economic progress had a lot of cultural currency in the interwar period. And interestingly, in many of these accounts, professional aspirations are identified as a set of opportunities for women to obtain social approval, a feeling of self-worth and a stable sense of self. Work, political and social responsibilities as well as other, similar achievements, in other words, began to be seen as equally, if not more beneficial, for happiness and positive identity formation, and it is my contention in this chapter that Rhys's texts responded critically to these optimistic stories about women's upward mobility that made regular appearances in contemporary literature, film, drama and music-hall performances. As Catherine Driscoll notes, 'on screen working girls were portrayed in a set of stories about personal transformation and escape from the banal difficulty of modern life' (2010: 105), and the ubiquity with which this story about women's social progress was dramatically rehashed by the interwar culture industry in no way diminished the audience's eagerness to emulate, off-screen, the sartorial codes that represented this alluring possibility of women's professional and personal success.[23] Representative, in this context, is the 1927 Hollywood classic *It*, the silent romance responsible for the meteoric career of its female lead, Clara Bow. As the 'It-Girl', Bow gained global celebrity status and became, in the silent movie era, the quintessential image of glamorous, sexy and attractive femininity. The film itself, as Marsha Orgeron argues, 'enacts a fantastic narrative of female sexual aggression and class transcendence' (2003: 82). It focuses on an episode in the life of its protagonist, Betty Lou Spence, a plucky shop girl who manages to capture her boss's attention and – at the end of the film – his hand in marriage. Central to their budding romance is the department store setting with Betty Lou's dress counter and the owner's office-table featuring prominently in some of the movie's key scenes. The workspace is therefore explicitly designated as a social backdrop for a young woman's ascent. Work brings Betty Lou in contact with men from different socio-economic backgrounds. Given the fluidity inherent in modern professional spaces, it is entirely possible, the film seems to suggest, to move, with a little ingenuity and determination, from fling to ring in no time at all.

While Clara Bow's stardom provides one, extremely impressive, account of one woman's professional rise, the film, in spite of its emphasis on class transcendence, opts for a conservative image of female progress by following the conventional romance plot that prioritises matrimony over economic independence through work. A different account of female achievement and success is presented in Dorothy Whipple's 1930 bestselling novel *High Wages*. Its protagonist, Jane Carter, who starts her career as a sales assistant in a small-town drapery store in Lancashire, eventually becomes the owner of a retail shop specialising in ready-to-wear garments. Although there is romance in her life – Jane has a passionate love affair with a married man – plans for elopement, love and a new start in South Africa are ultimately frustrated. At the end of the novel, the reader sees Jane embark on a new business venture. She sells her shop and moves to London in the hope of opening another retail enterprise, even bigger and more prosperous than her small-town store. In *High Wages*, Whipple, who was to become an extremely successful writer of popular fiction in the interwar years – the kind of writer Rhys failed to or was reluctant to become – accordingly identifies self-sufficiency and economic independence as essential trademarks of women's social ascent in the interwar years. Although romantic love is clearly desirable, it is by no means the only way by which young women of Jane's calibre can access prosperity and social status.

These are two representative examples of stories about women's socio-economic progress, about women who were able to embark, in the interwar period, on different courses for economic improvement than the one prescribed by the ideology of the two separate spheres dominating social conventions in the nineteenth century. No longer tethered to the sartorial and social paraphernalia essential in the construction of charismatic yet submissive femininity, women moved resolutely into previously male-dominated spaces and took on new professional and social responsibilities. And the prevalence of such and similar tales about new feminine confidence in popular accounts between the wars certainly strengthened propositions that the results of this great emancipation were, ultimately, much more satisfying for women than a careful cultivation of their physical appearance in the hope of attracting a wealthy husband. But what this positive narrative about women's economic progress through work fails to acknowledge is how much these two things, the cult of beauty and the notion of women's social and professional opportunities, remained associatively connected in the fashion rhetoric of the interwar period. Chanel and her competitors advocated images of fashionable, modern femininity that incorporated the promise of social, professional and economic transformation and success. At the same time, the professional, modern woman was, of course, always well dressed and strategically used her clothes to advertise her newly gained social status.[24] Unsurprisingly, therefore, Whipple's young protagonist resolves to buy a new collar with the first commission she is due in her new job as sales assistant – a symbolic transaction that promises to advertise her newly acquired professional status.[25]

This straightforward story of upward mobility that coordinates women's professional success with their sartorial accomplishments is somewhat more complicated in Rhys's 'Left Bank' novels and short stories. Although most of her protagonists long for new clothes to advertise their assets, it seems as if none of them can see work as a means to achieve economic prosperity. It is rarely, if ever, fulfilling. At best it is a means to an end – to secure subsistence in times when other (male-sponsored) forms of economic support are unavailable. In *After Leaving Mr Mackenzie*, Julia's half-hearted attempts to obtain a post as lady companion or governess are instantly aborted when Mr Horsfield's unexpected cheque arrives. 'Besides, getting that job is all a bluff. What chance have I really?' (131), Julia asks herself before spending all the recently received money on new clothes. Here and elsewhere, Rhys dismantles aspects of the appealing fantasy of female liberation through employment and hard work. In describing their failed career paths and their reluctance to work, she directs attention to those women who have invested too much in a contiguous illusion: that the display of sartorial and physical perfection alone suffices to prompt economic and emotional stability.

In fact, Rhys's protagonists might be best considered members of the so-called 'salaried-bohemians', a social group that Siegfried Kracauer described in his study *The Salaried Masses* (*Die Angestellten*) in 1930. These are young (sometimes middle-class) women, who arrive in big cities looking for adventures and the thrills of a cosmopolitan lifestyle with its added benefits of sexual and personal liberation. Although the trajectory of their career is uncertain, leading variously towards 'the street or the marriage bed', women such as Julia, Sasha or Marya gather, Kracauer claims, in the interim as employees in the various workplaces on offer in the big, bright city (1998: 73).[26] To escape the tedium and monotony of the workplace these 'salaried-bohemians' then haunt, after business hours, the fashionable cafés and surround themselves with artists, students, and the intellectual elite of the metropolis. These escapist outings are temporary, however, and the adventurers ultimately have to return to the dreariness of the workplace. Nothing substantial has been gained by their short forays into the world of bohemian cosmopolitanism. Furthermore, since each of them is a member of an increasing crowd of young, aspirational girls – all of them in search of entertainment, distractions and social advancement – Kracauer's 'salaried-bohemians' unavoidably confound individual desire with collective practices. What is carried out in the service of self-fulfilment becomes – in analogy to the standardisation of female labour in the workplace – ubiquitous and interchangeable. All these young women (and their personal and professional goals) are so much alike that they blend into a uniform group of self-improving fortune hunters. Theirs remains a routinised performance that traps these young women in a world that, paradoxically, forfeits individuality by stressing the value of subjective characteristics and aspirations.[27] Like T. S. Eliot's 'typist' with her gramophone, her 'combinations' and her short, meaningless sexual encounter with 'the young man carbuncular' (Eliot 1974: 71–2),

Rhys's quasi-interchangeable heroines who only work to finance their escapist fantasies and who flitter from one job and café to the next are manifestations of this restless female army on the lookout for something different, something new. It is this 'risky' business, a life that 'swayed regularly, even monotonously, between two extremes, avoiding the soul-destroying middle' that Marya in *Quartet* values in her married life to Stephan Zelli, the 'secretive' 'liar' and 'expert lover' who treats her like a 'petted, cherished child, the desired mistress, the worshipped, perfumed goddess' (Rhys 2000c: 20).

Unfortunately for Rhys's protagonists, however, (men's) expectations of women had dramatically changed after the First World War. It was no longer enough to model oneself on Victorian images of beauty and female submissiveness. What Mr Mackenzie criticises in Julia Martin is, above all, her 'softness'. In his eyes, 'she was a female without the instinct of self-preservation. And it was against Mr Mackenzie's code to believe that any female existed without a sense of self-preservation' (Rhys 2000a: 19–20). Julia attracts him, but she lacks the resolve, ambition and audaciousness advertised in all places as essential attributes of modern, desirable femininity. One of the reasons why Julia and Rhys's other protagonists fail and are adrift, aimlessly promenading the streets of the French capital, is that they don the garb of modern femininity without living up to attendant cultural expectations.[28] They lack Betty Lou's boldness, Jane Carter's resourcefulness. Julia, for instance, is seen 'walking along blindly', 'bump[ing] every now and again into somebody coming in the opposite direction' (Rhys 2000a: 16). It is in passages such as these that the already discussed lack of direction, orientation and spatial or social progress that marks the lives of Rhys's protagonists comes to the fore most prominently.

Moreover, when Sasha, in *Good Morning, Midnight*, reviews her working life – 'Thinking of my jobs. . . .' (Rhys 2000b: 26) – the image of a labyrinth is explicitly evoked to emphasise her sense of confusion in view of the many professional dead ends she has encountered. To date, Sasha has worked as a shop assistant, a tourist guide and a mannequin, and she comments despondently, 'I try, but they always see through me. The passages will never lead anywhere, the doors will always be shut. I know. . . .' (28), while Anna, in the story 'Mannequin', also experiences a lack of social and professional definition in her work environment, the couture house, which is, in turn, identified as 'a rabbit warren and a labyrinth' with 'countless puzzling corridors and staircases' (Rhys 1972: 150). In both cases, an apparent lack of vocational stability and structure reads like an ironic comment on the professional versatility and flexibility indexed by the sartorial designs of interwar haute couture. My suggestion is, therefore, that while Rhys's fiction offers detailed reflections of women's opportunities at the beginning of the twentieth century, it also emphasises that this abundance of social, professional and emotional choices could in some cases generate feelings of paralysis, apathy and helplessness. Ironically, the so-called freedom of movement advocated by both suffragettes and fashion designers creates, Rhys's fiction suggests, psychological impasses for women. In the post-war world, the absence of constraining customs, which were symbolised by the Edwardian corset, placed women into an indeterminate psychological realm. Although the majority of them 'enjoyed' as Celia Marshik has rightly argued, 'the fruits of modernity, such as independence and the ability to travel', others were left in limbo without explicitly defined social responsibilities (2006: 182). With traditional structures gone and no clear and stable markers of identity to draw on, sexual exploitation and social decline are shown by Rhys to be two, and probably rather common, inevitabilities for some women who possessed little money and only half-hearted emancipatory ambitions.

It is these particular social and psychological impasses that Rhys's fiction everywhere addresses. Her protagonists simply do not know which script to follow.[29] They are seduced by contemporary sartorial designs and the desirable image of progressive and liberated femininity that the clothes in question evoke but they respond to the excess of available social itineraries with a sense of disorientation and confusion that is often described in spatial terms.[30] For instance, in *Good Morning, Midnight* Sasha's inability to deal with overpowering occupational pressures is translated into experiences of spatial dislocation. Unable to understand the instructions given to her by her employer, Sasha aims to trace the addressee of a letter she is supposed to deliver. But her passage through the couture house becomes increasingly confused:

> This is a very old house – two old houses. The first floor, the shop proper, is modernised. The showrooms, the fitting-rooms, the mannequins' room. . . . But on the ground floor are the workrooms and

offices and dozens of small rooms, passages that don't lead anywhere, steps going up and steps going down. . . . Somewhere in this building is a Monsieur L. Grousset. I have got to take this letter to him. Easy. Somebody will tell me where his room is. . . . After this it becomes a nightmare. I walk up stairs, past doors, along passages – all different, all exactly alike. There is something very urgent that I must do. But I don't meet a soul and all the doors are shut. (22–3)

In Sasha's case, the lack of comprehension of her professional location and her inability to successfully navigate the labyrinthine life of working women in interwar Paris manifest themselves in her failure to negotiate her way through the complexly organised couture house. This 'claustrophobic interior space' therefore becomes, as Chris GoGwilt has argued, 'a metaphor for [Sasha's] exclusion from employment' (2005: 68) and Rhys's 'Left Bank' fiction reveals that the apparent revolution in vocations and vestments, which took place at the beginning of the twentieth century, produced ill-defined social and professional roles for women.[31] If fashion designers sold the illusion of female liberation and women's political progress, Rhys conversely illustrated the flaws in this new social design and fantasy. Although her protagonists try very hard to conform to the normative sartorial protocols of their time, Rhys indicated, in writing about their failed attempts to secure social success through such acts of sartorial imitation, that the radically modern couture of the early twentieth century might have been the '"marker" but certainly not the "maker" of social change' and women's political modernity (Roberts 2003: 69). The sartorial grammar of the interwar period may frequently have been life-sustaining. But in the majority of cases depicted in Rhys's fiction it rarely assisted in fashioning a new – and better – life.

'Until my work ceases being "sordid and depressing" I haven't much chance of selling': Rhys, nonconformity and 'dissident modernism'

Fashion, it can be inferred from previous remarks, was considered by Rhys as a seductive yet problematic intervention in women's lives. Her characters, who cyclically try to escape their outsider position by buying new clothes, are shown to mistakenly believe that donning fashionable outfits will inevitably secure social approval.

For this group of women who feel increasingly alienated from their environment, fashion functions like a barometer with which to measure degrees of social integration. And Rhys very clearly resembled her protagonists in excessively thinking about her ability to blend in, to form socially and emotionally stable relationships, while she similarly and somewhat inconsistently noted her desire for social seclusion.[32] In her interwar writing, exclusion is thus the perpetual theme in stories dealing with itinerant, marginalised women, who use fashionable accessories to conform to sartorial and social protocols in the hope of forming meaningful connections with other individuals. Across her texts, moreover, an expanding pessimism is, as I have indicated above, relational to the protagonist's advancing age. While Marya's fate is, of course, left undecided at the end of *Quartet*, the final passages of *After Leaving Mr Mackenzie* identify Julia's detached request for money from her former lover as a convenient and obvious method to secure some further income. Clearly mindful of his guilt, Julia, it seems, has learned to adapt to circumstances and can exploit the situation to her economic advantage. Although this change in behaviour hardly makes her a better person, there is at least the hint that she has now developed that 'instinct of self-preservation' formerly identified by Mr Mackenzie as essential in the modern woman's strategy for survival. By comparison, Sasha's sexual submission to the repulsive commis at the end of *Good Morning, Midnight* has a clear sense of finality. It is the disheartening culmination of a sequence of degrading acts involving alcoholism and attempted prostitution.

If things get progressively worse for Rhys's fictional incarnations, the story about her own development as an intellectually autonomous artist might offer an optimistic counterpoint to this depressing story of socio-economic decline, and it is the purpose of these concluding paragraphs to examine how Rhys's interwar novels attempted to turn nonconformity into a potentially productive incentive for artistic self-fashioning. Unconventionality, eccentricity and idiosyncrasy, I want to suggest at this point, are textually indexed in the gradually increasing formal experimentation characterising these novels. Although there are, of course, thematic as well as stylistic continuities among these texts, the intersecting but discontinuous narrative fragments in *Good Morning, Midnight* make this final interwar novel the most explicit expression of Rhys's compulsion to convey the experience of being different. What follows here, therefore, are some brief attempts to read *Good Morning, Midnight* as the culmination of a significant section of Rhys's career as a writer. Although her 1930s novels were far from well received,[33] they nonetheless project, as a collection, the image of successful authorial formation – albeit one that defies programmatic notions of resolution and synthesis in favour of a late style characterised by Edward Said as a 'deliberately unproductive productiveness going *against* . . .', the 'moment when an artist who is fully in command of his medium nevertheless abandons communication with the established social order of which he is a part and achieves a contradictory, alienated relationship with it' (2007: 7, 8). The Rhys of the interwar period, Said would in all likelihood have concurred, can offer us an example of an artist whose 'late works constitute a form of exile' (2007: 8).

The most obvious stylistic development observable in Rhys's fiction of the interwar years is, of course, a change in narrative perspective. *Quartet*'s third-person, omniscient narrator who relates the events of Marya's failed romantic adventure with Hugh Heidler in a chronological manner reappears in *After Leaving Mr Mackenzie*. But here, the narrative mode is complicated by interpolations, in which the second person dominates as narrative construct. 'When you were nineteen, and it was the first time you had been let down, you did not make scenes', the narrator comments. 'You felt as if your back was broken, as if you would never move again. But you did not make scenes' (Rhys 2000a: 78). The effect of this sudden change in narrative perspective is the reader's increased intimacy with the protagonist. By the same token, the text's invitation to feel included in these statements about one woman's disappointments in love identifies Julia's story as the individual expression of broader, more universal patterns. Julia, you, me, the narrator seems to intimate, all of us have to deal with these unpleasant, unfortunate circumstances. Then, with the appearance of the first-person, stream-of-consciousness narrative in *Good Morning, Midnight*, used already in *Voyage in the Dark*, Rhys completed the move from detachment to intimacy that organises the development of her novelistic form in the 1930s. For many readers, the final novel's compelling power is related to this change to a narrative perspective that directly discloses, seemingly without narratorial intervention, the protagonist's emotional vulnerability.

However, although this shift from exteriority to introspection is already indicative of Rhys's mastery of the novelistic form, what interests me in particular is *Good Morning, Midnight*'s discursivity. Alissa G. Karl has argued that the novel's impressionistic, elliptical and non-sequential fragments formally express its preoccupation with 'shopping' and consumption (2009: 28). Linear narrative progress is abandoned in favour of a perspective that emulates the indecisive shopper's habit of looking around. As much as department store displays invite customers to browse, *Good Morning, Midnight*'s fragmented appearance simulates the possibility of unsystematic, non-linear perusal. Karl's is an intriguing suggestion since it locates, on the novel's formal level, the presence of modern consumerism criticised as overwhelming ideological influence in the text. Stylistically, that is, *Good Morning, Midnight* still adheres to the consumerist logic that conditions its protagonist. To this persuasive reading, I would like to add another trope for consideration, that of the ill-assorted outfit that ostracises its wearer in the same manner in which Sasha's incongruous clothes – the 'last idiocy' being that 'damn old fur coat slung on top of everything else' (Rhys 2000b: 14) – attract the disapproving attention of a hotel patron. This image is, in my view, particularly fitting for Rhys's final interwar text since it identifies the co-existence of incompatible styles as a possibility for novelistic composition. The consumerist logic is, of course, only one among many cultural influences that affect the text. In this context it is worth remembering, as Christina Britzolakis does, that surrealist dream aesthetics condition the 'spatial disjunction' and 'syncopated temporality' of *Good Morning, Midnight* (2007: 457, 460). Comfortably accommodating elements of mass and avant-garde culture, the novel assembles an eclectic mix of narrative fragments that resist synthesis or aggregation.

To this image of heterogeneity and discord should be added the text's linguistic polyvocality. Rhys is certainly unusual among English-speaking female novelists of the interwar period for systematically including foreign-language elements into her final interwar text. Although her earlier novels incorporate references to foreign-language songs and represent conversations conducted in languages other than English, it is only with *Good Morning, Midnight* that these foreign-language elements are seamlessly integrated into the first-person narrative to increase the complexity of Rhys's verbally economic prose. For instance, in one of its retrospective sections, Sasha's jumbled recollection groups idioms and expressions inflected by different European languages. As the text imaginarily moves to London and Paris from Sasha and Enno's actual location in The Hague ('Haagse Bosch'), French and Germanic language elements infiltrate the prose that relies on English as the dominant linguistic structure. 'The war is over. No more war – never, never, never. Après la guerre, there'll be a good time everywhere . . . But no more money? Nix?' (Rhys 2000b: 96). In this passage, the post-war spirit of reconciliation and international collaboration that resulted in the founding of such institutions as the League of Nations (1919) is acknowledged in Rhys's recourse to the French language in this multilingual sentence. But while the nuptial couple's hopeful plans for a new start in Paris are rapidly thwarted by financial constraints, 'no more money', the unexpected intrusion of the German expression 'nix' ('nichts') also counteracts the earlier sentence's reconciliatory note that was struck by democratically aligning French and English language expressions. Rhys is obviously writing this section in the late 1930s when a second war with Germany was imminent. In that sense, this particular passage in *Good Morning, Midnight* has a certain proleptic quality – rendered visible by a strategic use of foreign-language elements in her linguistically idiosyncratic text.

Because of the stylistic complexities of Rhys's novelistic mosaics in *Good Morning, Midnight*, the sartorial image of the ill-assorted outfit has significant figurative potential. Whereas its protagonist desires coherence and stability in lieu of disintegration as the dominant tenor of her subjective experiences, I propose that Rhys's final interwar novel relies and thrives on fragmentation and on re-assembling mismatched ornaments and styles. This formal eccentricity clearly sets *Good Morning, Midnight* apart from similarly themed (and often commercially successful) fiction of its time that deal, like Dorothy Whipple's *High Wages*, with women's emotional and professional experiences in the interwar years. And it also separates this novel from Rhys's earlier interwar works that more rigorously adhere to the pattern of the chronologically organised anti-*Bildungsroman*.[34] Tracing an augmentation in stylistic complexity in her interwar fiction in this manner therefore suggests a possible reversal of the downward path that is such a dominant critical concept in Rhys scholarship. Although the biographical trajectories of her protagonists are as unpredictable as her own, Rhys's ascent to writerly maturity in the 1930s – represented by stylistic idiosyncrasy rather than sensational commercial success – individualises this writer who started her career under the patronage (and editorial supervision) of one of the most influential male modernist writers of the previous decade.[35]

If, as I suggested in the introduction to this study, we read modernism and commercially successful prose as the two formations dominating the literary field of the interwar period, Rhys's work would certainly have to be affiliated, initially at least, with those stylistic experimentations that began to be associated with the writing of the modernists with whom she shared technical preferences as well as geographical locales. However, her last 1930s novel, which showcases with even more uncompromising directness than her earlier work the sexual and emotional exploitation of women and which packages this story about subjection and neglect into the format of a first-person narrative, clearly threatened this partial affiliation with other 'dissident modernists' of the interwar years (Kallinay 2013: 224). In this particular case, the heightened sense of subjective suffering and the solipsism expressed in her final interwar *roman-à-clef* sequestered Rhys's work from that of her modernist contemporaries.[36] By the same token, the experience of this writer as 'an outsider among outsiders', to use Shari Benstock's words, who was 'neither part of the cafe crowd nor an occasional visitor to Sylvia Beach's bookshop' further emphasises that modernism was a collective but exclusive literary movement that became associated with particular individuals, coteries and places (1986: 448). Although she certainly shared with these other artistic innovators the desire to unsettle literary and social conventions and did this by addressing with frankness women's social and economic marginalisation in the time between the wars, Rhys never became part of this literary crowd whose members were able to turn the eccentricity characterising their prose and personalities into effective strategies for authorial self-promotion. As she noted in a 1931 letter, 'I am always being told that until my work ceases being "sordid and depressing" I haven't much chance of selling' (Rhys 1984: 21). In Rhys's case, then, the increasing nonconformity (sartorial, social and textual) that distinguished her biography, as well as the novelistic scripts of her later modernist years, led to critical neglect and marginalisation until the reinvention as a (post)colonial documentarian brought a much-desired but belated fame.

Fashion's repeated citations in her writings, I have suggested in this chapter, can yield a useful critical vocabulary with which to assess the early work of this writer who was by no means averse to commercial success but whose aesthetics of trenchant non-compliance that progressively surfaced in her interwar fiction could not be turned into the kind of symbolic value necessary for popular recognition. Unlike Rosamond Lehmann, who will be the subject of the next chapter, Rhys could not or would not translate her desire for admiration into textual forms that conformed to any of the recognisable literary standards of the 1930s. But as we will see shortly, it was precisely because of its daring and idiosyncratic elements that Rhys's work would become an important reference point for another writer who was very much amenable to the suggestion that imitation could generate commercial success and critical approval. As I will show in the concluding passages of the next chapter, it is in the adaptations of another novelist who was very skilled in rendering challenging textual details palatable for widespread consumption that Rhys's pioneering status as an interwar woman writer was indirectly confirmed.

Notes

1. Famous or rather notorious is the anecdote about Rhys's demand for her 'eye shadow' when she was taken to hospital in an ambulance shortly before she died. To the last, she was aware, as Thomas F. Staley put it, that 'women's small vanities are sometimes their only defence' (1979: 131).
2. Although I refer to Rhys's *Voyage in the Dark* (1934) in passing, its composition history as well as its setting places this novel outside this chapter's focus on her interwar 'Left Bank' fiction. It was published in the 1930s but was originally begun in 1911 in a series of black exercise notebooks (Rhys 1979: 128–30). It is also exclusively set in England whereas the present investigation prioritises Rhys's Paris-based prose. Moreover, the colonial intertext – Anna, the protagonist grows up in the West Indies – makes sartorial practices other than those considered in the present chapter significant influences in the text. Anna's recollection of Caribbean carnival scenes clearly points to the experience of dress codes unavailable to Rhys's other interwar protagonists. For a comprehensive analysis of these Caribbean culture references in Rhys's work see Mary Lou Emery, *Jean Rhys at 'World's End': Novels of Colonial and Sexual Exile* (1990).

3. It has not been possible to secure permission from the Jean Rhys Estate to quote unpublished material from her archive. I have therefore paraphrased relevant sections throughout this monograph. In this particular case, interested readers can find Rhys's exact words in her unpublished autobiographical fragment 'Down Along' (JRA1/1/14).
4. Elaine Savory's suggestion that the Rhys woman is 'in rebellion against conventions of acceptable femininity' but 'tolerates a degree of masochism in her relations with men', is representative (1998: 38). Helen Carr is extending the scope of the analysis by tracing broader power dynamics in Rhys's work, arguing that 'the power structures of organized society depend on a complex interaction of economic, class, racial, national and gender privilege, if there is a faultline in society it runs not between men and women as such, but between the haves and have-nots, the secure and the unacceptable' (1996: 60).
5. Critics have, of course, commented on the irony that Anna Morgan in *Voyage in the Dark* reads *Nana* (1880) without heeding the warning about a woman's social downfall that is chronicled in Zola's novel. For a detailed discussion of the correspondences between Zola and Rhys see Rizzuto (2001: 383–401).
6. Rhys's sense of not fitting in is detailed in the unpublished, autobiographical fragment 'Fears' (1938) where she states that she feared and disliked other people and that she was unable to act in the expected manner (JRA1/1/16). I will return to the topic of Rhys's difficulties in dealing with social protocols in the next chapter on Rosamond Lehmann.
7. In her detailed analysis of cosmetics and make-up in Rhys's fiction, Rishona Zimring has already made a good case for reading her work as negotiating the relational concepts 'individualism' and 'imitation'. But while Zimring notes that Rhys's novels include a critique of the industry that disseminated idealised (and unachievable) images of feminine beauty, her argument ultimately diverts from the present one because she suggests that Rhys still saw in this cultural narrative articulations of a 'new independence and liberatory promise' (2000: 215, 229).
8. The term 'dissident modernism' used in the previous sentence is Kallinay's (224).
9. Sophie Oliver (2016: 312–30) analyses the relationship between Rhys's late fame and the post-war revival of her interwar work in more detail.
10. In her recent study *The Mechanical Smile: Modernism and the Early Fashion Shows in France and America, 1900–1929* (2013), Caroline Evans similarly notes the dichotomy between stasis and mobility that conditioned working patterns in French couture houses in the late nineteenth and early twentieth centuries. While the first mannequins' perceived 'automatism and lack of life' (19) were observed with concern by

contemporary commentators, Evans argues that adaptation to a modern lifestyle meant that clothes had to be fitted on mannequins in motion. Lucien Lelong's 'kinetic designs' are just one example of this changed perception of women's clothes – one that required 'the mannequin intermittently to move around during a fitting to see how the garment worked in motion' (133). At the same time, the fashion show itself became mobile as couturiers opened branches outside of Paris and took fashion shows (and their mannequins) to the Riviera or abroad (117).

11. Another biographer comments on this apparent contradiction in Chanel's attitude towards women's social and locomotive freedoms. He comments on the apparent irony that Coco's notorious fashion statements such as '"no beauty without freedom of the body"' were only heard by 'young women weak with fatigue, whose bodies her dissatisfied hands seemed to be clawing for nights on end' (Charles-Roux 1976: 234).

12. Madsen also describes the following exchange that captures Chanel's lack of concern for female emancipation and her endorsement of women's economic dependence on men: when asked to increase her models' salaries, she allegedly snapped: '"Increase their salaries, are you out of your mind? [. . .] They are gorgeous girls, why don't they find lovers. They should have no trouble finding rich men to support them"' (160). In line with the financial regulations determining business practices in 1920s fashion houses, Anna in Rhys's story 'Mannequin', is engaged by the imperious Madame Veron 'at an exceedingly small salary' (Rhys 1972: 149). Interestingly, although she patronised her workers in this manner, Chanel was nevertheless 'mortally wounded' when the 1936 'sit-in' strike hit her premises with workers turning against her in the aim to negotiate better working conditions (Madsen 1990: 216).

13. In analogy to Hans Bellmer's surrealist artworks, the figure of the doll functions in Rhys as a powerful trope to illustrate the commodification of women's bodies in early twentieth-century art and commodity culture. In *Quartet*, for instance, a doll 'dressed as eighteenth-century lady' that 'smirked conceitedly on the divan' (41) is one of the first things Marya notices when entering the Heidlers' studio – perhaps an uncanny glimpse into Marya's not-so-distant future. Even more explicit is the critique of cultural codes that associate ideal femininity with passivity in *Good Morning, Midnight*. Here, Sasha, in her role as dress-house receptionist, states that the 'beautifully dressed' fashion dolls with their 'charming and malicious oval faces' would make 'a success' 'of their lives if they had been women. Satin skin, silk hair, velvet eyes, sawdust heart – all complete' (2000b: 16). Rishona Zimring has already noted the similarities between the women in Rhys and 'Hans Bellmer's twisted mannequins' (2000: 229).

14. Even a cursory glance at Rhys's biography shows that her upbringing and young adulthood were similarly conditioned by the fashion codes of her time. She read books 'warning us of the dangers of make-up', for instance, commenting that they 'described vividly your horrible and lingering death from lead-poisoning if you used face powder. And other sorts of deaths, equally horrible, if you rouged or painted your lips. Years afterwards', she describes, 'as I slap make-up on regardless, I think I am still defying those books' (1979: 37).

15. Carole Angier comments on Rhys's experience of working as a mannequin: 'She was proud of her body: and as long as she was young, wearing a beautiful dress, and didn't have to speak, she was happy, even eager, to be looked at.' But Angier also records that Rhys was conscious of 'the reality of her powerlessness, her being a plaything, bought for money' in her role as fashion model (1990: 126–7).

16. In fact, how intimately ideas about fashion and social mobility are connected is shown by J. C. Flügel who seems to be parroting Herbert Spencer when arguing in *The Psychology of Clothes* that 'fashion implies a certain fluidity of the social structures of a community. There must be differences of social position, but it must seem possible and desirable to bridge these differences; in a rigid hierarchy fashion is impossible' (140).

17. 'She's quite an acquisition here. Talks well and dresses well and has a style of her own. I like her.' This is the assessment of Diana, formerly of Dobson's Drapery Store, provided by one of the other hotel guests (Hamilton 2003: 97). The play is discussed in more detail by Jane Garrity (2014: 267–9).

18. A garment with similar metaphoric significance is the 'black dress with wide sleeves embroidered in vivid colours' (Rhys 2000b: 25), a display dress worn by mannequins in the couture house in which Sasha works as a receptionist. 'It is my dress', Sasha claims, '[i]f I had been wearing it I should never have stammered or been stupid' (25). The protagonist of Rhys's unfinished, unpublished novel *Triple Sec* also notes clothes' ability to empower, stating that she is certain that a low-cut evening gown and properly styled hair would be remedies for her awkwardness and shyness (JRA1/5/11).

19. Celia Marshik similarly notes that Miss Bruce is 'established as a queer character' but then goes on to read the story as a comment about Britain's secret sartorial life (2017: 50, 52).

20. Jane Garrity analyses this trend towards 'standardization of female appearance' (2003: 61) in relation to race ideology and the desire to conform to images of white, British superiority.

21. A similar note on the increased standardisation of female types in the entertainment industry is included in the section of Rhys's autobiography that deals with her experiences of working as a chorus girl. 'People

talk about chorus girls as if they were all exactly alike, all immoral, all silly, all on the make', she states. 'As a matter of fact', she continues, 'far from being alike they were rather a strange mixture.' Among its members was 'the daughter of a well-known Labour leader', who cheers the loudest whenever her father's party faces an electoral defeat, there was 'the daughter of a woman who stood up for Oscar Wilde', there were 'chorus girls of sixteen and chorus girls of nearly forty' in this eclectic mix of ostensibly identical performing women (1979: 109). What is interesting in this case is the transition from draft to published text. In an unpublished, earlier version, entitled 'Chorus Girls', Rhys talked about these women using the collective expression 'they' much more liberally (JRA1/4/6). In rewriting this passage for publication, Rhys obviously felt compelled to individualise the characters she was describing – possibly in response to the predominant view about the mechanical aesthetics dominating the chorus line and the selection of its performers.

22. 'Rhys's heroines live for the idealized selves proffered by fashion', Karl argues, they 'seek refuge in its supposedly transformative promises' (22). Although Karl's analysis focuses on discussing patriarchy's subjection of women through modern consumer culture, she also notes in passing 'that only certain women can purchase and own many products' (20) – that modern capitalism fashions fictions of exclusivity that are unobtainable for such women as Rhys's 'liminal heroines' (18).
23. The historical and institutional circumstances that led to the emergence of a movie fan culture that enticed many female viewers to sartorially emulate the stars observed on the screen are discussed in Lisa Stead, *Off to the Pictures: Cinemagoing, Women's Writing and Movie Culture in Interwar Britain* (2016).
24. The fashion press's construction and dissemination of images of professional femininity will be discussed in more detail in Chapter 4 in relation to Elizabeth Bowen's *To the North*.
25. This scene in the novel also records women's economic exploitation in the interwar retail industry. Jane, the shop girl, is powerless when her boss withholds the money she is owed for a successful sale (Whipple 2009: 47–50).
26. The German expression used by Kracauer is 'Angestellten-Bohème' (1971: 72).
27. The pressures associated with this culture of standardised norms and collective routines are referenced in *Quartet*. Although her career and personality differ in some ways from those of Kracauer's 'salaried-bohemians', Marya's 'early adventurousness', the text notes, is gradually replaced by 'passivity'. 'She learned, after long and painstaking effort, to talk like a chorus girl, to dress like a chorus girl and to think

like a chorus girl.' From then on, we are told, Marya lives her 'monotonous life very mechanically and listlessly' (Rhys 2000c: 15).
28. Women's 'failure' as a theme in Rhys has recently been addressed by Anne Cunningham, who suggests to read Rhys's depiction of female passivity and 'failure' as a deliberate strategy to reject 'that normalized mode of success' that is the essential by-product of a patriarchal and capitalist logic (2013: 375).
29. In her comments on *Good Morning, Midnight*'s description of Sasha's final sexual violation, Celia Marshik notes that 'the commis offers her a plot to enact. If she can't be a romantic subject in a new relationship, she can be a sexual object and victim' (2006: 197). Marshik is right in proposing that the Rhys heroine aims to write herself into one of the scripts circulated by mass and consumer culture at the turn of the century.
30. In a recent article Terri Mullholland – although she does not relate her arguments to fashion in any way – has commented on the lack of clearly defined personal and professional scripts that Rhys's protagonists can follow. 'For Rhys's characters', Mullholland accordingly argues, 'living alone in the city in the liminal spaces between the private family home and the public streets, the range of socially acceptable identities available to them is severely limited' (2012: 454).
31. In *The Mechanical Smile*, Caroline Evans has also described the complex organisation of French couture houses, especially the function and symbolic import of mirrors. My suggestion is that Rhys captures this sense of dislocation, 'spatial complexity' and 'confusion or elision of images and identifications' as Evans calls it (157), in the fiction she was writing during the interwar period.
32. In her *Green Exercise Book* (JRA1/1/2) Rhys noted that she desired both love and solitude.
33. Celia Marshik recalls Rhys's problems with publishing *Voyage in the Dark*. The manuscript was rejected by publishers, Marshik notes, 'in part on *Voyage* itself, but they were also concerned about the poor sale of the first two novels, neither of which went into a second edition' (2006: 177). As Markshik also details, the 'commercial failure of *Good Morning, Midnight*, along with difficult personal circumstances, relegated Rhys to silence and neglect for the next decade' (2006: 199).
34. Rishona Zimring's suggestion that '[n]one of her novels, and this has been one of their challenges to feminist readers, allows a triumphant genesis of female agency and transformation' offers one very accurate description of Rhys's reversal of the classic *Bildungsroman* (2000: 226).

35. Elaine Savory describes Ford's tutelage of Rhys in detail (1998: 39–42). In his preface to *The Left Bank*, Ford himself would, of course, dismiss the suggestion that he was able to impress Rhys or interfere in any way with her writing. As the following quote illustrates, he felt that he failed in the attempt to suggest the introduction of descriptive passages in Rhys's prose for the purpose of creating a firmer sense of place: 'I tried – for I am forever meddling with the young! – very hard to induce the author of *The Left Bank* to introduce some sort of topography of that region, bit by bit, into her sketches – in the cunning way in which it would have been done by Flaubert or Maupassant, or by Mr Conrad "getting in" the East in innumerable short stories from *Almayer* to *Rescue* . . . But would she do it? No!' (Rhys 1972: 139).

36. 'The pained story of me (the story of lost innocence, lost family, and little money) that drives her 1930s novels', Andrea Zemgulys pointedly states, 'pulls on her style, making something tricky, discordant, and surreal easily seem "monotonous" and overblown with self-pity.' It is for this reason, Zemgulys argues, that Rhys became 'an also-ran in the story of literary modernism between the wars' (2013: 21).

Chapter 3

Patterns: Rosamond Lehmann

Although her genteel upbringing and socio-economic background differed significantly from the outsider existence taken up and embodied by Rhys,[1] Rosamond Lehmann shared her contemporary's fascination with the modern couture of the interwar period. Her novels as well as her correspondence and autobiographical writing testify to the allure that nice clothes and fashion magazines had for this middle-class British woman with literary aspirations.[2] What distinguished Lehmann from Rhys, however, was the former's interest in using her writing to represent and emphasise the shared components in women's emotional experiences. Where Rhys's fiction focused on social outcasts in her explorations of women's engagements with contemporary sartorial politics, Lehmann's texts attempted to differently negotiate the tension between adaptation and difference brought into play by fashion. Even though her representation of modern fashion is by no means uncritical, this chapter will show that Lehmann's heroines – and her novels – try harder to live up to expectations. They are less interested in stylistic originality and individuality than Rhys's eccentric counterparts. Rather, they are more inclined, as will become apparent, to take up invitations to follow various textile, social and textual patterns available to women at the time Lehmann was writing. Critics of her work might therefore argue that Lehmann's fiction is in danger of being intellectually compromised – that the author's desire to fit in rendered her too susceptible to the pressures of the literary marketplace and made her produce a number of novels too inclined to follow established literary paradigms. And as we shall see, Lehmann's correspondence is certainly supportive of such statements. This writer, who 'dreamed complacently about poetic fame' in her youth, never concealed the fact that she hoped to become a successful writer.[3] However, rather than reading her work as its author's obvious submission to market demands, I want to suggest that Lehmann's awareness of, and partial compromise with, existing (sartorial and literary) patterns and her willingness to consider publishing commercially successful work were motivated by her desire to represent communality and solidarity among women as desirable social dynamics. If Rhys could not see beyond stylistic independence and its inevitable concomitants, solitude and social exclusion, Lehmann's complex negotiations with the practices of sartorial, social and textual affiliation and adaptation therefore mark a different understanding of female experiences and authorship in the interwar period. She realised that the representation of collective social practices, a shared cultural vocabulary and an appreciation of recognisable forms was, for her at least, preferable to accentuating radical difference as a mode of thinking and writing. As a consequence, her fiction might have been more commercially successful than Rhys's. But Lehmann's strategy of writing appealingly about and for other women about such topics as romantic love and its various drawbacks gave her the ability to first articulate and then broadcast her views on women's often compromised social positions in the interwar period. Located here, in the ability to speak for women collectively, is the political relevance of her fiction. And fashion, I argue in this chapter, allowed Lehmann to develop her thoughts about women's social and professional roles in a time of significant cultural upheaval.

In what follows, I propose a reading of her 1932 novel *Invitation to the Waltz* that shows how much Lehmann's text engages with images of modern femininity that were disseminated in such 1920s women's magazines as *Vogue* – the fashion journal explicitly referenced in the novel. Although modernity and novelty were apparent reference points in many of the magazine's editorials, my reading demonstrates that Lehmann resembled Wharton and Rhys in her awareness that 1920s fashion consistently emphasised the importance of following preconceived (dress) patterns in the successful construction of the modern feminine self. As we shall see, *Invitation to the Waltz* is extremely responsive to these suggestive cultural codes. Throughout the text, feminine appearance is consistently assessed in comparative readings that apply the standards of contemporary fashion rhetoric. But *Invitation to the Waltz* also criticises, in crucial scenes, the production of such standardised types. More than once, sartorial difference and social disobedience are approvingly considered. The protagonist's academic ambitions clearly set her apart from programmatic patriarchal scripts that associate feminine perfection with sartorial accomplishment.

But the conceptual affiliation between Lehmann's novel and modern fashion lore does by no means end here. While the text certainly appreciates feminine nonconformity brought about by education and intellectual determination, its own appearance inconsistently relies on the very same reproduction of patterned standards it sets out to interrogate. By absorbing aspects of a particular literary model – Virginia Woolf's *To the Lighthouse* (1927) – *Invitation to the Waltz* eagerly recycles modernist textual elements and makes adaptation the source of creative production. In this particular case, imitation emerges as an important feature in Lehmann's mode of textual composition. If fashion as a sociological phenomenon is characterised by the incompatibility of conflicting desires – to imitate and to divert from existing patterns and prototypes – Lehmann's novel formally exhibits the fierce negotiation of this apparent contradiction. The dialectic between adaptation and differentiation, in other words, is one of *Invitation to the Waltz*'s most significant conceptual inspirations.

Moreover, as I will propose in the concluding passages of this chapter, *Invitation to the Waltz*'s intertextual dialogue with Woolf is indicative of Lehmann's wish for developing cooperative relationships with other women (novelists). The various social and literary affiliations she sought at the time of writing *Invitation to the Waltz* and its sequel *The Weather in the Streets* were translated into a composition practice that is intentionally citational, combining an acknowledgment of modernist experimentation with commercial marketability. Lehmann's mode of writing is therefore best described as one I here call modish modernism. She wanted to be recognised by the intellectual elite of her time as a highbrow woman novelist and therefore responded enthusiastically when the prestigious publisher Chatto & Windus accepted her first novel for publication – 'the very publisher', Lehmann noted much later, 'whose list I would, had I dared, have most aspired to join' (1953: 514).[4] At the same time, she hoped to represent the realities of women's experiences in the interwar years and write novels that would appeal to many women readers. *Invitation to the Waltz*, her last novel to be released under the imprint of Chatto & Windus, is a text in which this ostensible conflict manifested itself very clearly: a reliance on particular modernist particles is carefully brought into dialogue with the use of thematic components usually found in the pages of a coming-of-age romance novel about a young girl attending her first ball. Lehmann's case therefore illustrates how imitation and adaptation as compositional practices fashioned the career of a writer who was pulled in opposite directions by what she perceived to be the dominant literary standards of the interwar years. Fashion, I shall show in the following pages, can be identified as a determining influence in the career of this writer, a writer who sought affiliation with the modernist groups surrounding Woolf but who would also willingly seek commercial success to bring into wide circulation her political views on women's opportunities and restrictions in the two decades after the First World War. Fashion, that is, emerges as a particularly useful concept for a reading of Lehmann's work that sets out to complicate the critical consensus that she catered exclusively for a readership with middlebrow taste and horizons.[5]

'Oh, d – – – – clothes!': Lehmann and fashion

Lehmann herself had a complex relationship with fashion and with fashioning an appealing feminine persona. In 1967 she would comment in her autobiographical sketch, *The Swan in the Evening*, on the prevailing gender ideology that dominated women's lives in her formative years: 'Girls should be pretty, modest, cultivated, home-loving, spirited but also docile; they should chastely await the coming of the right man, and then return his love and marry him and live as faithful, happy wives and mothers, ever after' (Lehmann 1998: 68).[6] Her biographer Selina Hastings correspondingly notes that a 'leitmotif in Rosamond's correspondence [during her time as a student at Girton College] was the constant need for money and new clothes' (50). With an allowance strictly controlled by her parsimonious mother, Lehmann frequently worried about dressing appropriately for the various occasions marking a Cambridge student's busy social calendar. On 26 May 1920, for instance, she imploringly wrote to her mother that 'I've sent back the pink dress with a real pang', although 'I *do* need a frock of that kind' because 'Helen & I have been asked to the big tennis match on the 8th, to the races on the 10th & 11th, & I can't imagine what to wear.' Considering different outfits, she complained that the 'pink voile doesn't look nice any more' 'but could, I s'pose be made to do', before exclaiming exasperatedly, 'Oh, d – – – clothes!' (RNL2/341/16/1). On discussing her sister's upcoming wedding, she similarly reminded her mother on 1 November 1920:

> Tell Helen: Any of her discarded clothes MOST gratefully received, particularly a few underclothes, her brown taffeta dress, her fawn-coloured coat with the fur collar, her grey fur, (!), all her stockings & her rust-coloured straw hat for next spring. (RNL2/341/16/1)

Whether recycled, repeatedly patched up or new – clothes and her appearance were constantly on Lehmann's mind.

This preoccupation with suitable attire (as well as with the inevitable wear and tear of garments) that structured Lehmann's correspondence during her Cambridge years, points to the short-lived nature of sartorial fabrics. Money was tight and since the thought of appearing twice in the same frock was inconceivable, clothes had to be creatively amended to satisfy the ever-increasing demand. Image cultivation, Lehmann's letters reveal, was hard work and required versatility and attentiveness to modish trends. Yet while fabrics became rapidly threadbare and clothes were not supposed to outlive one summer, ephemerality at the same time regulated shifts and changes in sartorial styles, which, in turn, strongly influenced behavioural patterns of women such as Lehmann, who were determined to cut a good figure. All these complex associations with fashion's social protocols are debated extensively in the Girton letters, which clearly illustrate how much the young Lehmann associated fashionable clothes with the kind of feminine identity to which she aspired.

Useful guidance on how to negotiate the complex socio-sartorial landscape of the 1920s could thereby be obtained from countless fashion magazines in circulation in the interwar period – and British *Vogue*, founded in 1916, would have been one particularly important compendium for women such as Lehmann who would have turned to its glossy pages for advice on what to wear, how to accessorise and how to conduct themselves in particular social situations.[7] As existing scholarship on interwar British women's magazines has shown, this particular journal aimed at middle-class female readers rose to prominence as the decisive authority on women's fashions in the years after the First World War (Buckley and Fawcett 2001: 11).[8] It is no wonder, then, that *Vogue* is explicitly referenced in *Invitation to the Waltz* – a novel that uses the magazine's assertive instructions on women's sartorial and social performances as a starting point to critically examine fashion's influence on 1920s femininity constructions. In real life, the young Lehmann might have felt that she had no choice but to follow some of its persuasive suggestions. In her third novel, however, she challenged contemporary socio-sartorial protocols by dexterously packaging her critique of *Vogue* as the ambassador of the 1920s fashion industry into the appealing story about a debutante's first romantic encounters.

'You look like the girl on the cover of a special spring number': sartorial, social and textual patterns in *Invitation to the Waltz*

Like all of her books, Lehmann's *Invitation to the Waltz* (set in 1920) explores modern female conduct and psychology. With its loose formal affiliation to the *Bildungsroman*, it is an account of adolescent character formation – a powerful description of an awakening feminine consciousness following the classic plot structure contemporary readers could expect to find in a popular (and sentimental) romance novel.[9] Olivia Curtis – who will also be the protagonist of the novel's sequel, *The Weather in the Streets* – finds herself, on the morning of her seventeenth birthday, at the threshold of womanhood, eagerly (and not a little anxiously) awaiting her first dance and nervously reflecting on a range of femininity constructions on offer in 1920s Britain. Possibly because of its deceptive resemblance to the conventional romance plot, *Invitation to the Waltz* was greeted warmly by critics and became a commercial success a few years after a disappointing critical reception had met Lehmann's second novel, *A Note in Music*. In 1933 *Invitation to the Waltz* was shortlisted for several literary prizes, and it also made the NAME OF THE MONTH selection of the American Book of the Month Club (Pollard 2004: 83). But it was also for this reason – because its romantic elements made it a popular success on first publication – that *Invitation to the Waltz* has often been regarded as a '*divertissement*, almost a side-step out of Rosamond Lehmann's essential world' (Lehmann 1981: xiv). The 'proportion is so perfect and the development so exquisitely modulated' (quoted in Pollard 2004: 76), Lehmann's publisher Harold Raymond at Chatto & Windus excitedly commented, anticipating in this short comment the general tenor of the novel's enthusiastic early reception that preferred to see it as a 'little book' and that overlooked its interest in stylistic experimentation of which a self-conscious awareness of its own design is, as I will show in due course, the most notable feature.[10] As Judy Simons suggests, the novel has been read as standing 'alone among Lehmann's fictions' because 'its darker elements' were 'kept to the margins' (1992: 60). If not openly trivialised, *Invitation to the Waltz* has invited interpretations that tended to downplay its political arguments and interest in modernist experimentation, branding it instead as light-hearted distraction dealing with topics suitable for exploration by a high-society lady-novelist.

However, even if its early critics chose to disregard it, social and cultural change with its numerous instabilities and casualties remains an important topic in *Invitation to the Waltz*: the absence of young men at the dance (fatalities of a recent war), the rise of an energetic capitalist middle class that is about to replace the leisured aristocratic class of the Spencers – not to speak of gender reform crucially affecting young women such as the novel's protagonist.[11] One aim of this chapter is to show that this obvious interest in social commentary is indexed by the novel's complex dialogue with a particular cultural force whose presence is felt everywhere in the scenarios described by Lehmann in this seemingly light-hearted story: the fashion industry here represented by *Vogue* – the magazine designed to '[h]old, as 't were, the Mirror Up to Fashion'; or to use the more ornate and fanciful language of one of its 1923 articles, to reflect 'the figures of Fashion as they passed, with all their confidence and colour, their fluttering ribands, their preposterous flounces, their bendings and bowings, their pretty ways or their bold ones, their charm and their arrogance' (Anon. 1923a: 81). *Invitation to the Waltz* with its scattered references to sartorial patterns, garments and fashionable designs, that is to say, enters into a conceptual flirtation with the vagaries of modern fashion, producer of idealised images of womanhood and determined advocate of change, alteration and variation in post-war Britain.

Early on in the novel, for instance, the reader becomes aware that Olivia's adolescent self-image is yet undefined, inconsistent and subject to unpredictable changes and 'blottings-out and blurrings': 'Nowadays a peculiar emotion accompanied the moment of looking in the mirror: fitfully, rarely a stranger might emerge: a new self' (Lehmann 1981: 11). However, in Olivia's case, particular clothes and garments assist in the creation of a clearly defined, feminine reflection. 'Was it the frock that did it?' (11) inquires Olivia when 'a portrait of a young girl in pink' (12) miraculously emerges in the mirror.[12] Given her relationship to clothes, Olivia falls into the category that J. C. Flügel called the 'supported type': individuals who 'feel pleasurably strengthened and supported by their clothes, especially by tight or stiff clothes' (1966: 99). One of Olivia's most venerated accessories is a 'broad scarlet patent-leather belt' (Lehmann 1981: 10) that is more dependable than her 'thin nigger-brown one of suède' (11) because '[w]ithin its compass she felt a certainty of individuality' (10).[13] If Olivia's self-image is volatile and loose-fitting, clothes provide the outline for its silhouette and mould it into existence by supplying support or a particular structural pattern. Only on special occasions, her birthday, for instance, can Olivia 'suit her clothes, provide the glow, fill out the shape, warm up texture and colouring' (10) and choose a jumper in an inconspicuous colour such as fawn.[14]

Unlike her sibling, Olivia's sister Kate has what *Vogue* calls a 'clothes-sense': 'that inner vision by which you know instantly, unerringly, whether or not a thing is smart'; 'that latest and most exquisite of civilisation's acquired instincts' (Anon. 1923b: 18). Well versed in the art of smart and practical dressmaking – 'I just took it straight from *Vogue*' (Lehmann 1981: 100) – Kate materialises, in her apple-green frock, like 'the girl on the cover of a Special Spring Number' (100). A devoted *Vogue* reader, she has chosen the design for her ballgown from the magazine's 'Pattern Service' (Figure 2), supplier of models distinguished by the 'scientific knowledge which is spent on their smart and careful cut', 'sufficient to stamp them as things apart' (Anon. 1920: 79). By comparison, Olivia's gown is a misfit, a haphazard construction engineered by the dreamy village dressmaker Miss Robinson, whose love for colours that 'revived her spirit' and for textures that 'soothed her' (Lehmann 1981: 43) unfortunately does not translate into technical competence. Although disaster is held at bay by the skilful Kate – who notices Olivia's mistake in putting on her

Late February

VOGUE PATTERN SERVICE

THE patterns on Vogue pattern pages are in sizes 34 to 40 inches bust measure, 24 to 30 inches waist measure, and 35 to 41 inches hip measure, unless otherwise specified.

Vogue patterns are 2/- for each blouse, suit coat, skirt, child's, smock, or lingerie pattern; 4/- for complete costumes, one-piece dresses, separate coats, and long négligées. An illustration and material requirements are given with each pattern.

Though Vogue patterns may be more expensive than the usual pattern on this market, true economy is proved by their purchase. Their distinction is obvious. The scientific knowledge which is spent on their smart and careful cut is sufficient to stamp them as things apart.

There is no reason why, with intelligent handling, any gown or tailor suit should have the slightest "Home-made" air when it is cut from a Vogue pattern. The clever woman may feel doubly satisfied, as she sees her reflection in the street and in her mirror, that she has achieved the smartness of Paris, aided by Vogue, with her own deft fingers.

The hang and balance of skirts, the spring of sleeves, and the ease of corsages are given every consideration in the Vogue pattern, and no untoward complications need be feared by the wearer of the completed garment.

Patterns can be ordered only by post. When writing please mention size, and address communications to

ROLLS HOUSE, BREAM'S BUILDINGS, LONDON, E.C. 4.

Frock No. C5169. A new surplice closing and panel sections simulating pleats are novel touches on a frock of silk ratine trimmed with motifs

Frock No. C5167. A front panel buttoning to the neck-line, kimono sleeves, and hip draperies distinguish this frock of beaver coloured satin

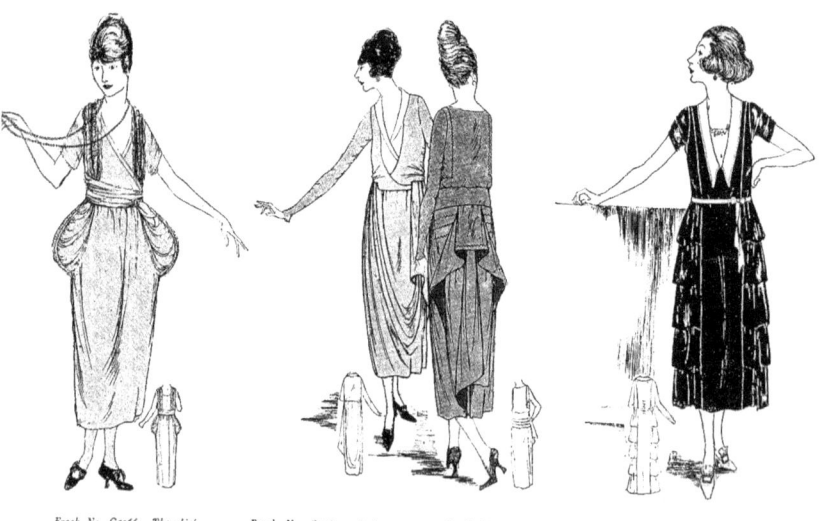

Frock No. C5166. The chief features of this frock are lace shoulder-straps and quaintly puffed panniers

Frock No. C5164. A long-waisted surplice blouse tops the gracefully draped skirt of this frock of satin

Frock No. C5165. This satin frock is chiefly distinguished by unique drapery and a blouse of panel effect

Frock No. C5162. A youthful chemise frock with much-ruffled sides has straight panels back and front

Figure 2 *Vogue* Pattern Service, *Vogue*, 55:4 (1920): 79, Vogue © The Condé Nast Publications Ltd

frock back to front and who 'hooked, tweaked, patted her into shape' (99) – the result is less than satisfactory. 'Why on earth couldn't you *force* her to cut them properly?' (99), exclaims Kate when the arms of Olivia's dress continue to catch. Kate knows, of course, that a good cut or pattern is the prerequisite for a triumphantly fitting textile composition. As *Vogue's Book of Practical Dressmaking*, published in 1926, advised its readers: 'The success of a frock depends not on the colour, the fabric, or even the idea – important as all these things must be. *It depends on the accuracy of the pattern from which the dressmaker works*' (Anon. 1926b: 1; italics in original). Something has gone awry with the design of Olivia's gown, and she is now cutting an eccentric and lopsided figure next to Kate whose 'every feature' was 'the right size' (Lehmann 1981: 13).

Lehmann's novel resembles Kate in having a particularly well-developed sense of colour, design and pattern. *Invitation to the Waltz*, that is, is preoccupied throughout with sartorial ensembles, measurements and with questions of appropriate shapes and forms. Olivia, for instance, mimics the rhetoric of fashion magazines when contemplating Kate and her own reflection in the mirror: 'The younger girl, with her gypsy colouring, afforded a rich foil to her sister's fair beauty' (100). Elsewhere, Miss Robinson notices, with satisfaction and almost simultaneously, Mrs Uniack's '[u]gly shape' and the shape of Olivia's new hat (42). And whereas 'patches of colour' stand out among the 'plain, neat, subdued, unbecoming' clothes in Olivia's wardrobe (35), Lehmann's novel skilfully uses colours in its composition. Throughout the text, both Kate and Olivia are often framed by the shades (red and green) they have chosen for their ballgowns. Back home in the schoolroom after tea, the 'red curtains were drawn', while Kate 'sewed, her crammed basket on the hairy green tablecloth beside her. Olivia read' (70–1). The same colours mark the opening scene of the novel: the representation of the sisters' home village, Little Compton, with its 'red brick' houses and the 'pump on the green' – a setting that has, according to the novel's narrator, 'more atmosphere than form, than outline' (3). Likewise, the Curtis's home is described, in the novel's first pages, as a 'pre-war residence of attractive design' (5).

This obvious emphasis on outline, colour composition and design identifies *Invitation to the Waltz* as an exceptionally self-conscious text, and it is therefore hardly surprising that we find Olivia immersed in a world of sartorial and social patterns. On returning home from her first fitting with Miss Robinson, she contemplates her future and concludes: 'For all young girls should be fitted for a career' (46). If Rhys had already noticed that sartorial and professional competence were essential components in empowering narratives about female desirability in the interwar period, *Invitation to the Waltz* similarly registers women's compulsion to write themselves into dominant cultural scripts about social success that incorporated the imperative to be physically attractive. Professions, Olivia's comment suggests, resemble clothes in that they actively assist in the construction of attractive femininity by providing women with respectable social identities. While Olivia is thus preoccupied with thoughts about her future, the first part of Lehmann's novel presents her with an array of different but ultimately uninspiring female role models: Miss Robinson, the spinster dressmaker living with her ailing mother; Mrs Wells-Straker, widow extraordinaire, who has elevated mourning for her husband to the rank of a proper profession; Mrs Wainwright, the sweep's fertile and impoverished wife with her horde of children and the pram of 'unique design' (56); Mrs Skinner, former femme fatale whose 'flame of beauty' is 'almost swallowed up now in billowing fat' (51); Miss Mirvart, James's reluctant botany tutor, whose 'fantastic garb' proclaims 'her status of gentlewoman in reduced circumstances' (59); and the lace-girl, who swindles Olivia out of money and who is a repulsive counterpart to Miss Robinson. The list is completed by Olivia and Kate's mother, Mrs Curtis, the prototypical 'Angel in the House' and by the formidable matron Lady Spencer, of whom the reader is told that 'every action she performed was so fitting and so right' (153). This impressive line-up of female role models is contemplated, evaluated and analysed by the perceptive Olivia, and although all these femininity designs turn out to be unsuitable for Lehmann's academically minded protagonist, her extensive meditations on women's social opportunities mobilise political readings of the novel. Different femininity constructions are on display in its first part, and Olivia is invited to contemplate all these as potential future careers.[15]

In this manner, Lehmann's novel assesses 1920s gender constructions and points to the complicity of the fashion industry in the creation and commercialisation of prototypical femininities. However, *Invitation to the Waltz*, reminiscent of some of Wharton's texts, also, and somewhat inconsistently, uses sartorial tropes to represent writing and authorship. In Lehmann's literary imagination, terminology referring to text or textiles, to writing or clothes, that is, continually overlaps: 'Don't try to understand him', advises the young, moody Oxford aesthete, Peter Jenkins, when talking to Olivia about the poet Brian Carruthers's literary achievements at the Spencers' ball: 'Let his pattern sink in' (146). Lehmann's correspondence during her Girton years shows the very same preoccupation with sartorial concerns and artistic aspirations. Some of her letters sent home from Cambridge in 1920 and 1921 thus interlace comments on her writing progress with obsessive accounts of new clothes and garments. 'Mummie darling', she writes on 4 February 1920, 'that cloak!! . . . I just stood & gasped & clutched Helen & said "Oh! Oh! Oh!" It's what I've always wanted, but the material and colour are beyond my wildest dreams.' In the same letter, Lehmann, who is anxiously hoping for her parents' approval, also provides a detailed overview of her recent literary achievements:

> I enclose the latest [poem] & do so hope you & Dad will like it. Tell him I've tried to make sound express sense, that the changing metre is intentional, &, I hope, all right; & will he – or you – mark what you disapprove of, & let me have it back soon as I must 'get busy,' for I want to earn some money. I've two others ready, & shall try 'The Nation.' I hope this one is good enough to send? (RNL2/341/16/1)

Similarly, a letter dated 19 November 1921, which contains specific requests for modish garments – 'Love to Helen and Peg. Tell the former that much as I should love scent, I think stockings, – nigger-brown. – would be more the ideas, & many many thanks' – ends on the fervent exclamation: 'Oh, *how* I want to publish a book!' (RNL2/341/16/2). If writerly ambitions and nice clothes were the two, seemingly contradictory, forces that determined Lehmann's youthful sense of self, it should not surprise that *Invitation to the Waltz* similarly shows that for Lehmann dressmaking and the work of the imagination had a lot of common purchase. The lace-girl, however repulsive she might be, is – in an analogy to a prominent trope already used by Emily Dickinson and Woolf – compared to a spider.[16] She is the producer of pathetic textile designs and the weaver of intriguingly sad stories about bedridden mothers – stories convincing enough to stimulate

Olivia's vivid imagination and induce her to forfeit a ten-shilling note for an unwanted collar. Also important is this use of the spider trope in the novel's first chapter where it is employed to draw out the analogies between the creative imagination and the production of (textile) webs. Here, the narrator suggests, when describing the Curtises' home and family history, that 'at once the imagination is engaged' (4) in a scenario in which 'continuity is spinning a web from room to room, from year to year' (5).

But if Lehmann's novel so deliberately aligned dressmaking with artistry and the creative imagination, how does Kate fit into the picture here – Kate, who is the producer of the most striking sartorial compositions and who uses perfume that has been chosen to match, like the dress, her personality, features and colours? There can be no doubt that this young woman knows about the importance of setting oneself apart from the crowd since she strongly rebukes Olivia for failing to choose 'scents and colours' that 'suit [her] personality' and for the attempt at 'copy-catting' her sister (93). But is she – because of this unmistakable insistence on individuality – also the character most immediately representing Lehmann's notion of artistic creativity? In the novel, Kate obviously functions as a narrative construct introduced to articulate Lehmann's awareness that imitation and originality, conformity and differentiation, are the 'two antagonistic principles' that according to Georg Simmel determine the 'vital conditions of fashion as a universal phenomenon' (1971: 295–6). In describing Kate's resolve to emphasise her distinction, Lehmann certainly showed awareness of the fashion industry's production of easily identifiable feminine types.

But Kate is, as we have seen, also an enthusiastic follower of sartorial patterns. Her dress design has been taken 'straight from Vogue', without any alterations worth mentioning in the text. And, as *Vogue's Book of Practical Dressmaking* reminds its readers, 'the success of a frock' depends on 'an accurate pattern' that 'keeps the spirit of the original design and scrupulously reproduces every last detail of its construction'. It is important, the manual states, 'not to deviate a hair's-breadth from the pattern' and to *'follow the rules'* (Anon. 1926b: 2, 4; italics in original). According to the *Vogue* guide, perfection in dressmaking requires copying, faithful imitation and the confirmation of a specific pattern. A similar awareness of the importance of following rules is apparent in Lehmann's Girton letter, in which she identifies and justifies metrical irregularities in her poetry as deliberate composition strategies. Written at a time when she was aiming to follow the latest sartorial fashions, Lehmann's epistolary note to her parents indicates that she was, in some cases, more than willing to bend a few rules and change inflexible or preconceived patterns. In *Invitation to the Waltz*, we see that Kate, the model of feminine elegance and sophistication, is also well aware that in textile compositions faithful reproduction that incorporates the suggestion of personal and sartorial distinction generates success and social approval. Lehmann's novel therefore exposes her as a skilful copyist. Conversely, Olivia is, due to her uneven hems and the ill-fitting dress, established as a sartorial rebel. Needless to say, the unhappy Miss Robinson has violated practically every golden rule of successful dressmaking when creating and fitting Olivia's gown. Although she takes the design from the fashion journal, *Fashions for All*, she has meddled with the original pattern, producing a lopsided frock that has 'a draiping [sic] one side only' and 'a graiceful [sic] bow' on 'Olivia's left hip' (Lehmann 1981: 37). Approximating the 'crimson ribbon slotted through an early white party frock' in Olivia's childhood wardrobe, which is 'exiting, evoking again the drop of blood of the fairy story piercing the cold, blank, startled snow, piercing her smooth mind indelibly, as she read, with sudden stain' (Lehmann 1981: 35), Olivia is clearly aligned, in these early scenes in the novel, with nonconformity and disobedience.

Even further accentuated is Olivia's potential as sartorial and social rebel during the Spencers' dance. Left alone and drifting into sleep, she visualises her red dress as 'blood on snow' – as a striking foil to Nicola's white dress: 'She went on thinking drowsily of white velvet, of its whiteness, its sheen and texture, thinking of the colour of her dress against it . . . red on white, blood on snow' (223). The end of *Invitation to the Waltz*, through these sartorial images, already foreshadows the relationship between Olivia and Nicola in Lehmann's next novel *The Weather in the Streets*: female counterparts marked by their roles as Rollo's wife and mistress. In the sequel, Nicola will be emblematic of the feminine role model rejected but at the same time desired by the adult Olivia. But as *Invitation to the Waltz* insists, in her adolescence Olivia has a much stronger inclination to like the unconventional, the uncommon. She does not seem to fit into a pre-planned domestic paradise of dressmaking and clothes manufacturing, and she consequently emerges as the more imaginative and inventive of the two Curtis sisters. It is Olivia, then, who has the potential to be intellectually original, creative and independent. She might see herself as something of a social misfit, but *Invitation to the Waltz* welcomes her opposition to the cultural machinery that regulates gender roles in post-war Britain, that immerses women in the fabrication, production and consumption of clothes and that is complicit in producing a world dominated by patterned femininities.[17]

But while Lehmann's novel noticeably favours this sartorial and social nonconformist, it subscribes, paradoxically perhaps, through its own appearance to the ideology of perfect designs and patterns that is promoted by the fashion industry as emblematic of modern, desirable femininity. Foregoing remarks have already indicated Lehmann's employment of colours and of particular imagery that everywhere suggests an overlap between sartorial, social and textual composition vocabulary in *Invitation to the Waltz*. To advance this discussion of female clothes and authorship as mutually responsive concepts in Lehmann's fiction, the next section of this chapter extends this analysis of the novel's design – a design that was described by contemporary critics (and many other Lehmann scholars since) as a 'perfect vignette' as well as 'a small but significant thing, done perfectly' (Pollard 2004: 78, 79). As I will suggest, it is through its reverential imitation of a particular precursor that its debate with modern fashion unexpectedly resurfaces. It is also in *Invitation to the Waltz*'s textual interactions with another novel that Lehmann's affiliation with modernism becomes extremely apparent.

'She has a clear hard mind, beating up now & again to poetry': Lehmann's well-knitted prose

Originally, Lehmann had planned to incorporate material later used in *The Weather in the Streets* – her first book to be released by the mainstream publisher Collins – into her earlier novel. But this plan was abandoned to develop the final well-ordered, tripartite structure of *Invitation to the Waltz* – a structure that already makes apparent Lehmann's aim to create a balanced textual composition (Pollard 2004: 76). Enclosed by two longer parts, depicting Olivia's birthday and the Spencers' dance, is the short core section, which covers the Curtis sisters' fervent preparations for their first appearance as debutantes. This middle part of the novel contains Olivia and

Kate's most extensive discussions of colours, frocks, underwear, perfumes and manicures – of their sartorial and cosmetic make-up for the evening. They recall incidents from the novel's first section such as Olivia's fatal collaboration with the dressmaker, Miss Robinson, and they envision impending ballroom scenarios. Kate, in particular, worries about Reggie Kershaw and their escort's unsuitability for the important occasion, gloomily anticipating that he will 'go falling over everybody's feet' (Lehmann 1981: 90) should he decide to take off his unbecoming spectacles for the dance. Equally retrospective and proleptic, the second section is, without a doubt, the novel's thematic centre. It connects the discrete temporal scenes of Part One and Part Three and – in detailing the ordinariness of the sisters' dressing-up routine – carefully keeps the balance between the singular events described in the other two sections (birthday and ball). However, not only is Lehmann's *Invitation to the Waltz* carefully constructed, it is also, as I will suggest in a moment, closely modelled on another text: *To the Lighthouse* – of Woolf's works the novel admired most by Lehmann (Hastings 2003: 121). This intertextual correspondence between the two texts, it might be argued, is not particularly significant in itself: Lehmann had obviously read Woolf's work, was deeply impressed by the older writer's aptitude as a novelist and therefore aimed to re-use themes already addressed by Woolf. But in the context of the current discussion of fashion as a key concern in Lehmann's work, this reverential imitation of another woman's work throws into sharp relief how much the younger novelist's mode of writing was conditioned by fashion's social causalities. To note these intertextual resonances between the two novels is to realise how much imitation and differentiation, reproduction and originality – desires that, if Simmel is to be believed, determine every single sartorial choice – effected the development of Lehmann's text. Their existence also offers a welcome opportunity for a discussion of Lehmann's position in the literary field of the interwar years. They can tell us a lot, in fact, about the self-conception of a novelist, who hoped that her work would appeal not only to a general audience but also to Woolf's Bloomsbury circle as the artistic elite of her time.

Needless to say, by the time of *Invitation to the Waltz*'s publication Woolf and Lehmann were by no means strangers. Together with her second husband, Wogan Philipps, Lehmann orbited, from 1930 onward, around the notorious 'Bloomsberries' (Hastings 2003: 121). But by the time Lehmann had published her first novel in 1927,

Woolf was already a well-established novelist, and the apparent age gap together with Woolf's towering reputation, clearly intimidated the younger writer. Woolf herself seemed to have responded to Lehmann, initially at least, with a mixture of condescension and friendly aloofness. A letter dated 2 July 1928 shows her mild arrogance in claiming comprehension of Lehmann's intellectual efforts and modes of thinking: 'Are you able to go on with your book?' Woolf asks before stating:

> I like walking about in your mind, & telling myself this is what is going to happen next, and so on. No doubt I'm all wrong. Are you writing about the same people, or have you come out in an entirely new world, from which you see all the old world, minute, miles & miles away? (RNL2/699)

Here, competitiveness might well masquerade as friendly inquiry. Although the relationship between the two women would become decidedly more cordial throughout the 1930s, Woolf reassured herself, at the beginning of their acquaintance, that Lehmann's achievements to date – although she has a 'clear hard mind, beating up now & again to poetry' and 'all the gifts (I suppose) that I lack; can give story & development & character & so on' – were nothing but fashionable literary ephemera: 'these books dont matter', she accordingly noted in her diary in 1930, 'they flash a clear light here & there; but I suppose no more' (Woolf 1980b: 314–15).[18]

Lehmann herself was a very perceptive critic of Woolf's work. A typescript in the Rosamond Nina Lehmann Papers at King's College, Cambridge – in all likelihood a memorial address for Woolf – evidences Lehmann's appreciation of the much-admired acquaintance and role model. It also illustrates the part that writers such as Lehmann played in popularising modernist artwork during the interwar period and thereafter. '[A]s regards her technique', Lehmann wrote here, '[Woolf] had two styles, one clear, logical, and concise, an admirable instrument for her admirable critical prose; the other for her imaginative work, a poetic style, full of light flexible expanded rhythms' (RNL1/1/5/2). Especially commendable in Lehmann's opinion is *To the Lighthouse*, in which Woolf 'grasped and expressed with the greatest sweep and lyrical ecstasy, the most moving imagery. There is not one paragraph that flags or falters; and it contains more human love, grief and happiness than do any other of her books'

(RNL1/1/5/2).[19] *To the Lighthouse*, Lehmann argued, was clearly setting new paradigms for novel writing. For the development of this aspirational writer's own modish modernism, which hoped to balance plot elements of the conventional romance with such modernist concerns as interiority and representation of subjective consciousness, it was beyond doubt a very desirable model to follow.

The suggestion that *Invitation to the Waltz* in some ways redresses Woolf's earlier novel by appropriating some of its easily recognisable imagery can therefore hardly be surprising. Although I hesitate to suggest a relationship of direct literary influence that approaches copying or – worse even – plagiarism, some textual components shared by Woolf and Lehmann's novels indicate that *To the Lighthouse* must have been at the fore of Lehmann's mind at the time when she was conceptualising *Invitation to the Waltz* and when the relationship between the two novelists intensified. On closer scrutiny, the texts' compatibility is, of course, apparent enough. In the first place, they resemble each other in their formal appearance. In both cases, a short second part is enveloped by two correspondingly longer sections: '[t]wo blocks joined by a corridor', Woolf explained when describing *To the Lighthouse*'s H-shaped structure in her notebook (Woolf 1982: 48). Both texts also share a thematic interest in examining the design of Britain's post-war society, especially in regard to the changed nature of women's social and professional roles. Two different generations and their respective social views collide in both texts. In *Invitation to the Waltz*, the stability and respectability of pre-war times is represented in the figure of Mrs Curtis and that of the awe-inspiring Lady Spencer. Likewise, the Ramsays in Woolf's text embody a similar image of Victorian respectability – a picture implying outmoded marital conventions against which Lily Briscoe, one of the novel's many daughter figures, openly rebels. Additionally, *To the Lighthouse* resembles Lehmann's *Invitation to the Waltz* in being a text that is extremely self-conscious about patterns, shapes and forms. 'Then beneath the colour there was the shape', notes Lily (Woolf 1992a: 23), whose painting also becomes the site for metatextual remarks about artistic composition – in a manner reminiscent of the role that clothes and garments play in *Invitation to the Waltz*. Frustrated with the 'disproportion' that 'seemed to upset some harmony in her own mind' and with her inability to 'achieve that razor edge of balance between two opposites forces; Mr. Ramsay and the picture; which was necessary' (209), Lily expresses exasperation not only with a particular social perspective captured in the Ramsays as 'symbols of marriage, husband and wife' (80), but also with her own artistic vision.

Most importantly, however, both texts make strategic use of an image that evokes the domestic ideology of the Victorian period: the matriarch occupied in the production of useful, functional garments. In Lehmann's *Invitation to the Waltz*, Mrs Curtis, readers are told, 'knitted. To-night it was stockings for James [Olivia's brother]. To-morrow night another kind of wool would be wound, another work embarked on' (Lehmann 1981: 83). *To the Lighthouse* opens with a similar scene: Mrs Ramsay, who sits next to her son, James, is knitting a 'reddish-brown stocking' while sitting for Lily's painting (Woolf 1992a: 8). The strewn references to a 'stocking', 'James', and above all, 'wool' in *Invitation to the Waltz*, which unmistakably cast Olivia's mother in the role of Mrs Ramsay, therefore consolidate the intertextual relationship between the two novels. Additionally, they also remind readers that both women, Lehmann and Woolf, repeatedly relied on dressmaking vocabulary to convey their views on artistic composition. Woolf, for instance, would use such an image in her 1939 essay 'Reviewing', in which the figures of seamstresses sitting in 'certain shop windows' in London, represent modern-day 'poets, playwrights and novelists', whose literary achievements are publicly scrutinised by critics who 'comment aloud ... upon the skill of the workers, and advise the public which of the goods in the shop window is the best worth buying' (Woolf 2011: 195).[20] But it is clearly Lehmann, even more so than Woolf, who self-consciously identified herself as the intellectual progeny of nineteenth-century authors who had explored the interdependent, at times conflict-ridden, relationship between writing and needlework as the expression of female creativity. As Patricia Zakreski argues, the 'opposition between the needle and the pen was a familiar device used by women authors throughout the eighteenth and nineteenth centuries' to consolidate an 'image of female authorship in which woman's conventional roles and responsibilities were represented as constraints to creativity' (2006: 19). Writers such as Elizabeth Barrett Browning and Elizabeth Gaskell acknowledged the act of sewing as a feminine-coded activity that sometimes hindered but sometimes also assisted women in the fulfilment of their poetic aspirations. Analysing the often intricate 'relationship between women's literacy in print and their literacy in textiles', Christine Bayles Kortsch therefore argues that 'literacy in dress culture was specifically gendered as a type of feminine knowledge in Victorian social practice' (2009: 4). As such, women's 'dual literacy' (Kortsch 2009: 4) and their conscious exploitation of sewing metaphors to represent female artistic labour offered them a powerful counterpoint to the exclusive rhetoric of Victorian patriarchy that discounted women as the producers of serious art. Resourcefully, a particularly expressive image of Victorian women's domestic responsibilities was re-appropriated by women writers and artists to describe creative pursuits.

Woolf's well-documented impatience with the domestic ideology of the Victorian period might make her an unlikely candidate for an author who would deliberately draw on nineteenth-century debates about women's 'dual literacy'. Even so, the knitting imagery placed so prominently into the opening sections of *To the Lighthouse* suggestively evokes intertextuality and references the novel's awareness of its textual borrowings – George Eliot's *Middlemarch* (1871–2) and Alfred Tennyson's 'The Charge of the Light Brigade' (1854) are only two of the texts that are woven into Woolf's literary design. It also offers the opportunity for more complex readings of Woolf's acknowledgement of Victorian women's creative achievements. Mrs Ramsay might not be an obvious artist figure in *To the Lighthouse*, but Woolf nonetheless introduces such thematic concerns as creative productivity through the image of her knitting. *To the Lighthouse* thus follows in the tradition of novels that use sartorial imagery to represent women's artistic practices.[21] It is also Woolf's indebtedness, in composing *To the Lighthouse*, to this particular canon of female writing that employed the image of garment production as a shorthand for thinking about women's creative practices that further accentuates the intertextual correspondences between her own and Lehmann's novel. Both texts, I argue, use dressmaking terminology to emphasise moments of self-conscious reflection about artistic composition strategies. In Lehmann's case, the use of this particular image also foregrounds the younger writer's intellectual reliance on Woolf's textual model and with such an indicative array of correspondences between the two texts, it is clearly very tempting to define *Invitation to the Waltz*'s relationship to its textual precursor as one of evocative imitation. Percipient to her literary role model's achievements, Lehmann seems to have recycled, when writing *Invitation to the Waltz* in the early 1930s, aspects of Woolf's novel. This would mean, of course, that Lehmann's text not only illustrates the conflict between adaptation and differentiation that determines women's fashion choices in 1920s Britain, but that it also interrogates, through its resemblance to Woolf's novel, the relationship between originality and imitation as common practices in novel writing. As a young, ambitious novelist well aware of Woolf's monopolistic claim to novelty and innovation in female authorship in the 1920s and 1930s, Lehmann based her attempt at writerly creativity, at least in part, on resourceful adaptation and skilful reproduction.

Lehmann's *Invitation to the Waltz*, especially through its fidelity to textual patterns found in and taken from another woman's novel, therefore seems to belie its own rebelliousness – its critical interrogation of fashion's responsibility in standardising women's sartorial appearances. But in choosing a particular well-fitted narrative design that is to a certain degree modelled on Woolf's text, Lehmann obviously accentuated, once again, the interdependent relationship between costumes and customs that shaped women's social and professional experiences in the 1920s and 1930s. As the example of *Invitation to the Waltz* illustrates, authorship was considered a vocation by Lehmann that was dependent, like many other careers open to women of her generation, on difference and adaptation as incompatible forces. Creative independence, the desire to update novelistic conventions, as well as the concurrent need to obey the dictates of the literary marketplace determined Lehmann's literary productivity in those early years of her career. Her case shows that in the interwar period, female authorship and not only feminine image construction through clothes had to negotiate the provisions of contemporary fashion practices.

It might appear, therefore, as if Lehmann's early work is stuck in an ontological double bind, that her attempt to create an independent literary persona is made impossible by the overbearing presence of another writer whose work she felt she had to imitate. However, such a pessimistic interpretation of *Invitation to the Waltz* can be sidestepped by underlining the one apparent difference between Lehmann's novel and Woolf's *To the Lighthouse*. Both self-consciously engage visual imagery as tropes for novel writing. But Lehmann departs from Woolf in her choice of symbolic infrastructure. Although Woolf certainly drew on the prominent nineteenth-century concept of women's 'dual literacy' in her representation of Mrs Ramsay, her actual artist character in *To the Lighthouse* is a fabricator of abstract (modernist) art. Lehmann conversely relies on modern consumer culture in the development of her thoughts on authorship. Not high art but fashion provides the vocabulary essential for a representation of Lehmann's own mode of textual composition. And it is precisely through its choice of this conceptual imagery that Lehmann's novel offers an alternative understanding of literary composition, one that is more intentionally inclusive in making an aspect of mainstream culture, fashion, an obvious rather than disclaimed inspiration. Lehmann wanted to signpost her work's awareness of contemporary women's experiences. *Invitation to the Waltz*'s focus on fashion gave her the opportunity to speak about feminine identity formation and the conflicting demands made on women to define their social roles in response to significant demographic changes brought about by the First World War – concerns that would have preoccupied many of her female readers in the 1920s and 1930s. It is no wonder, then, that she reached out to fashion's conceptual vocabulary when self-consciously thinking about her work as a woman writer.

This is, of course, not to say that Woolf's writing was not socially aware or that the older novelist was unresponsive to the needs or the political interests of her readers. In fact, the concluding chapter of *Modernism, Fashion and Interwar Women Writers* will demonstrate that Woolf had begun to think extensively about her audience during the late 1920s and that she hereafter agreed to make certain compromises with mainstream publishing and its operational procedures to reach a wider readership for her books.[22] But Woolf certainly had a more complex relationship than Lehmann with the emerging creative industries of the interwar period. Not only did she associate mainstream publishing firms, journalists and popular literary periodicals with the commercialisation of artistic tastes. For Woolf, these commissaries of mainstream culture were also similar to such institutions as universities and libraries in being strongholds of a patriarchal culture that marginalised and silenced women such as Woolf who, determinedly but often unsuccessfully, aimed to trespass on male territory and thereby challenge social and cultural hegemonies (Woolf 1992b: 6–7). Lehmann, in contrast, seemed to have been relatively unperturbed by her professional affiliation with the interwar culture industry. Nowhere in her letters or in her published work did she suggest that her highbrow ambitions were in any way compromised by her commercial and popular success. On the contrary, she was happy, from the beginning of her career as a writer, to raise her public profile by promoting and capitalising on the image of the beautiful lady-novelist with high-society connections.[23] But as I have argued, Lehmann willingly accepted and sought commercial success because it allowed her to raise awareness of women's (often passionately emotional) experiences in a culture that continued to be dominated by patriarchal imperatives. In the final part of this chapter I will also suggest that Lehmann's emulation of other women authors' writing practices was consistent with, if not essential to, the development of her modish modernism – a mode of writing that satisfied her artistic aspirations but that also aimed to reach the largest possible audience for novels in which an emancipatory agenda is clearly emerging among numerous and detailed descriptions of those patterned femininities to which women of Lehmann's time were still expected to aspire and conform.

'One imagines a sympathy': female solidarity and Lehmann's design of a modish modernism

When she published her first, bestselling novel *Dusty Answer* in 1927, Lehmann later claimed, she 'knew no other female writers, young or old' and was 'with the exception of May Sinclair . . . singularly ill read in fiction published in the twentieth century'. It was 'the nineteenth-century literary giants' whom she 'revered, loved' and who were regarded as her 'great ancestresses' (Lehmann 1998: 68–9). In the course of the next decade, however, Lehmann would become decidedly committed to reaching out and getting to know other authors – and women writers in particular. In fact, the relationship with Woolf was only one of the literary friendships with other women that Lehmann sought to develop in the 1930s. There were others, and it is important to review a couple of those she regarded as significant to understand Lehmann's self-conception as a novelist who showed immense responsiveness to the literary fashions of her time. Doing so will illustrate that her mode of textual composition, imitative and extremely conscious of other women novelists' thematic interests, was in keeping with the hope to create, in her novelistic scripts, room for the type of collaborative practices she aspired to in real life. Inside and outside of her texts, that is to say, Lehmann cultivated her relationships with other women writers. She did this to learn from them and to advance her own career as a novelist – but, more importantly, she did all this to acknowledge the importance of female solidarity in attempts to explore, talk about and critique women's real-life experiences.

Among these literary friendships, the one with Elizabeth Bowen was most certainly of immense importance to Lehmann and surviving correspondence shows how consistently they provided feedback on each other's work. For example, on 12 October 1935 Lehmann admiringly wrote:

> Well – I've read the 'House in Paris' twice now – and as it's the only novel – practically the only book – I've read for I don't know how long – I got its full flavour. You don't need me to tell you at this late date how successful it is. I think it's a triumph, & I do congratulate you. (EBC2/11/6)

The publication of *The Heat of the Day* was received with similar praise in a letter from 4 March 1949:

> Darling Elizabeth, I have finished The Heat of the Day again – and again in a state of almost unbearable emotion – exaltation & scorching tears. It is now embedded deep deep in my consciousness: an over-pouring experience for which I am eternally grateful. (EBC2/11/6)

The full extent of Lehmann's admiration for the older novelist, however, is apparent in her obituary of Bowen printed in *The Times* in February 1973:

> Elizabeth was a woman of the most compelling charm, which, unlike many magnetic personalities and spellbinding talkers, she exercised with total self-disregard. People of all ages and in all walks of life expanded in her presence. More than anyone I have ever known she was a life-enhancer. (RNL2/64)

Almost forty years earlier, in 1936, Bowen, in turn, had written one of the most perceptive and encouraging reviews of Lehmann's novel *The Weather in the Streets*.[24]

More notorious among Lehmann's literary acquaintances was certainly Jean Rhys, with whom Lehmann tried to establish a personal association based on dialogue and intellectual exchange. And even if Lehmann's attempts to befriend a drunk and depressed Rhys would ultimately be thwarted, their correspondence of the time indicates the persistency with which Lehmann tried to establish rapport: after their first meeting, Lehmann reassuringly wrote on 21 January 1935, that she has 'been meaning to write for days and tell you how much I enjoyed meeting you the other day' adding that she has 'guessed, and now [is] sure' 'that you are frightened of people'. In the same letter, the sender details her plans for travelling up to London before anxiously asking: 'Might we meet?' As they continue, the tone of Lehmann's epistles becomes increasingly concerned but also encouraging. Rhys is sent asparagus from Lehmann's garden, is told that she has 'a lot of admirers that you don't know about', and that 'you don't seem to realize you are a writer' (JRA2/7/4). The news of a car crash, fabricated by Leslie Tilden Smith to cover up Rhys's involvement in a drunken brawl, is answered, in the last letter from Lehmann, with a gush of sympathetic inquiries.

Hidden among these caring notes is Lehmann's firm commitment to talk about writing. While she hopes that Rhys's 'new book goes well', she confesses that her own work 'goes like trying to haul a great piano out of a bog single-handed'. Elsewhere, Lehmann describes her attempt to work 'in a strangulated though quite excited way'. Rhys is told that Lehmann 'cannot see the end of this novel' and that 'the children rather swallow me up' (JRA2/7/4). However, due to Rhys's inability to live up to Lehmann's expectations, the wished-for intimacy and friendship between the two women writers did not materialise. When she was finally confronted with Rhys's alcoholism, Lehmann realised that the pursuit of this acquaintance would have to be aborted. But if she was disappointed in her efforts to reach out to the other writer who shared her concern with representing women's lives in the radically changed and changing interwar world, Lehmann, who wrote to Rhys 'that sometimes one imagines a sympathy that turns out not to exist', nonetheless found other ways to acknowledge the other writer's influence on her own work (JRA2/7/4): in *The Weather in the Streets*, the bohemian, now 27-year-old Olivia faces an unexpected pregnancy. And although she ostensibly rebels against the middle-class decorum dictating marriage and legitimate biological reproduction, Lehmann's protagonist ultimately decides to abort her pregnancy. This decision is driven, as Andrea Lewis has demonstrated, by the fear that it will jeopardise her middle-class status through its 'potential associations with lower-class indiscretion' (2002: 84). With the veneer and the progressive vista of the New Women gone, Olivia is unmasked to act in accordance with 'hegemonic social and political modes of thinking' (Lewis 2002: 84). Patriarchal structures continue to be overriding principles in the world inhabited by Lehmann's protagonist, who remains, at the end of the novel, suspended between the conflicting desires to conform and rebel. *The Weather in the Streets*, like other Lehmann novels, therefore offers a sustained assessment of patriarchy's ongoing monopoly over women's psychological experiences in the interwar period.

By thus combining the abortion motif with a well-thought-out critique of patriarchy, Lehmann situated herself very clearly in Rhys's thematic territory. Only two years before the publication of *The Weather in the Streets*, Rhys's *Voyage in the Dark* had dealt openly and scandalously with the same themes. To be sure, the textual parallelism between the two novels does not go beyond the description of a visit to the abortionist and of the ensuing recovery of the protagonist. Other than that, middle-class Olivia and Rhys's chorus girl, Anna Morgan, have as little in common as the authors who created them. But as Elaine Showalter noted as early as 1977, both texts stand out from the stack of female-authored novels of the 1930s because of 'a new frankness about the body and about such topics as adultery, abortion, lesbianism, and prostitution' (299). There were few women novelists who took up the challenge to represent such and other physical details with the frankness found in Lehmann and Rhys. It should also be noted at this point that Lehmann's correspondence with Rhys dates from the year immediately following *Voyage in the Dark*'s publication. The encounter with Rhys's novel, that is, inspired Lehmann to contact its author and it also gave her the confidence to comment, in the most daring and explicit manner to date, on the realities and consequences of extra-marital sexuality. This means that Lehmann, once again chose to develop an intertextual dialogue with another women writer of her generation, a mode of writing reminiscent of her intellectual engagement with Woolf in *Invitation to the Waltz*. Spurred by the desire to mark her intellectual affinity with a contemporary female novelist, Lehmann created a textual scenario that makes her protagonist re-enact situations found in the pages of a Rhys novel. If Lehmann herself was unable to reach out to the author of *Voyage in the Dark*, the novel she was writing at the time of their correspondence succeeded in embedding, in its developing plotlines, a passing greeting to her fellow writer. *The Weather in the Streets* (like the earlier *Invitation to the Waltz*) was therefore the result of intellectual collaboration with other women writers that Lehmann considered a central feature of her mode of creative thinking. Writing about feminine experiences required sensitivity to other women's lives, fictional and otherwise. For this reason, conversations with other women novelists and the engagement with their fictional worlds were practices that were more than desirable. For Lehmann, they were essential.

Inclusivity and interest in dialogue therefore emerge as central aspects of Lehmann's writerly concerns. If the thematic focus of novels such as *Invitation to the Waltz* is the experience of women (and sorority in particular),[25] the novel replicates this longing for mutuality and social connectivity – indicated also by its title – by absorbing textual details found in another woman's writing. Lehmann, that is, was committed to a mode of writing that assessed the world of women from the perspective of a shared, communal point of view. Even if *Invitation to the Waltz* spotlights Olivia's personal experiences, this analytical concentration on individual consciousness was part of Lehmann's ongoing attempt to explore the complexities of modern femininity, of social constellations and of situations recognisable to many women of her generation. 'Novelists must be able to love men and women', she noted in an article on the future of the novel published in 1946. In her view, this '[a]ppreciation' and this 'compassion for humanity' felt by 'the great nineteenth century novelists' was one important reason why these particular writers remained relevant for and popular among modern readers (Lehmann 1946: 10). Lehmann herself also aspired to this mode of writing that made energetic sociability its main ingredient.

Fashion, this chapter has shown, offers an expedient critical lens through which to read Lehmann's self-conception as a writer. It has been identified as a discursive organiser of female experience, regulating the behaviour of young middle-class women such as Olivia (and Kate), who have to negotiate the mutually exclusive desires for assimilation and differentiation with the help of their clothes. But it was also my aim in this chapter to complicate readings of Lehmann's position in the literary field of the interwar period. While the attention paid to fashion by her writing would assume a straightforward association with mainstream culture and commodity aesthetics, I have conversely suggested that her obvious interest in contemporary style guides (sartorial and literary) can serve as a useful starting point to assess the complex, and perhaps conflicting, influences that made their presence felt in novels such *Invitation to the Waltz* (and *The Weather in the Streets*). The hallmark of Lehmann's fiction was a two-pronged allegiance. On the one hand, she sought affiliation with avant-garde writers such as Woolf and Rhys whose work she admired and referenced in her novels. This aspect of Lehmann's writing signalled her intellectual aspirations, her interest in formal experimentation and her dedication to political commentary. On the other hand, it can be argued that literary productions such as *Invitation to the Waltz* and *The Weather in the Streets* followed and relied on aspects of the conventional romance plot – that they hoped to attract a wide readership and that they aspired to modes of consumption more in line with the expectations of commercial publishing. Unlike Wharton, Lehmann obviously did not associate commercial success with the surrender of intellectual standards. If this had been the case, she would have hardly agreed to publish *Invitation to the Waltz*'s sequel, *The Weather in the Streets*, with Collins – the commercial publisher who represented, among other things, titles of the famous 'Crime Club' series and who promised to launch 'the first novel to be published by them from their prestigious new recruit' with 'a major advertising campaign' (Pollard 2004: 89–90).[26] Although she confessed in a 1928 letter to her Chatto & Windus editor that 'the very words "publicity," "advertisement," – and "commercial value" make me shudder' (quoted in Pollard 2004: 45), Lehmann was, in the mid-1930s, by no means averse to the idea of moving to a mainstream publishing firm that promised exactly the kind of marketing strategies that would raise the 'commercial value' of her work. Even before she turned to Collins to increase her sales figures, however, Lehmann had created, in *Invitation to the Waltz*, a textual scenario that tried to reconcile aspects of modernism's innovations – an interest in spotlighting the subject's psychological realities and a self-reflexive composition technique – with a mode of writing that appealed to many readers because it dealt with recognisable aspects of everyday life: the cut and colour of a dress or the choice of the right perfume. The result of Lehmann's complexly structured artistic loyalties is the production of her modish modernism – a writing style that paid tribute to the demands of a market interested in disseminating literary hits for profit but one that also heeded the intellectual mandates of Britain's literary avant-garde.

Beyond revealing Lehmann's self-conception as a literary artist, however, the hybrid textual structure found in *Invitation to the Waltz* is noteworthy because it shows how much its author was involved in a cultural transaction that made modernism's revolutionary composition techniques and some of its political propositions available and accessible to readers who were not the recipient of little magazines or of coterie publishers' catalogues. By developing her modish modernism, Lehmann became an important populariser of modernism's artistic practices, a writer who assisted in transforming modernism from countercultural impulse into an artistic movement that would eventually become a particularly dominant, if not mainstream, feature of twentieth-century intellectual life. Elizabeth Bowen, as the next chapter will demonstrate, engaged in similarly complex intellectual negotiations with literary modernism. But unlike Lehmann, whose imitations of modernist models were entirely affirmative, Bowen managed her artistic association with Woolf and other modernist precursors and contemporaries differently. If Lehmann reverentially imitated modernist textual practices, Bowen hoped to update some of its programmatic accents by developing alternative modes of writing that replaced modernism's focus on interiority with a more complex depiction of subject-object relations. But in stressing her critical departure from modernism in this manner, Bowen obviously confirmed her ongoing involvement with modernist concerns. The next chapter will provide more details of Bowen's personal and textual affiliations with modernism, showing how some of its conceptual features were complexly refracted in the interwar work of this particular woman writer.

Notes

1. The artistic aspirations and talents of Lehmann's family are well known. Rosamond's father R. C. Lehmann was an author, publisher and regular contributor to *Punch*. Her sister Beatrix became an actress, theatre director and producer, and John Lehmann, Rosamond's brother, a poet

and editor himself, was managing director of the Woolfs' Hogarth Press in the 1930s before he set up his own publishing company in 1946. Born into this upper-class English family distinguished by strong literary connections, Lehmann attended Girton College, Cambridge before marrying Leslie Runciman in 1923. Unquestionably, everything in her sheltered and socially privileged upbringing should have prepared her for a contented life at the side of this Newcastle industrialist. But, for Lehmann, intellectual and, above all, literary ambitions jarred with the image of matrimonial bliss built on feminine subservience. While her marriage to Runciman disintegrated, Lehmann ascended to literary stardom: the publication of her first novel *Dusty Answer* in 1927, a *succès de scandale*, instantly turned her into a celebrated writer at the age of twenty-six. From then on, her writing career unfolded alongside tumultuous emotional and romantic encounters that illustrate, as the critic Judy Simons puts it, 'that blend of the radical and traditional' in Lehmann's intellectual and emotional composition (1992: 13). A second marriage to the artist Wogan Philipps lasted from 1928 to 1944 and overlapped with a nine-year-long, emotionally exhausting affair with the poet Cecil Day-Lewis. The same period also marked Lehmann's greatest literary productivity. The successful *Dusty Answer* was followed by a string of novels: *A Note in Music* (1930), *Invitation to the Waltz* (1932), *The Weather in the Streets* (1936), *No More Music* (1939), *The Ballad and the Source* (1944) and *The Gypsy's Baby and Other Stories* (1946).

2. A record in a Girton College newsletter from 1921 illustrates how much Lehmann's early years were marked by fashion's influence. In the relevant issue, the *Girton Review* reports that the college's Debating Society, of which Lehmann became Vice-President during Lent term in 1921, chose to discuss if 'an interest in dress should be encouraged'. The article then explains that '[w]ith the exception of one speaker, who gave the House the result of her calculations as to the amount of time spent in a term in the business of dressing and undressing, members were agreed that it was a good thing to have an interest in dress; but those who opposed the motion thought that such an interest was spontaneous, and needed no encouragement'. The final vote – '[f]or the motion, 64; against, 16. The motion was therefore carried by 48 votes' – indicates that dressing well was an essential concern for women coming from Lehmann's socio-economic and academic background (Anon. 1921: 3). Whether they were in favour of or against the final motion that dressing *à la mode* was to be approved, women such as Lehmann – the article indicates – had to position themselves in relation to the discourse of fashion that determined lifestyle choices in the 1920s.

3. This statement was made in a short piece published in 1953 in *The Listener*. In Cambridge, Lehmann continued, she 'wished to excel as a scholar and as a literary figure' – once more indicating that recognition mattered very much to her at the beginning of her career as a writer (513).
4. Chatto & Windus, whose 1927 list already included such 'distinguished current authors' as Aldous Huxley, Roger Fry, Clive Bell, Sylvia Townsend Warner and Wyndham Lewis 'would certainly have been categorized', Wendy Pollard explains, 'as literary, rather than commercial, publisher' (2004: 25).
5. Indeed, as Judy Simons argues, Lehmann's fiction has been sidelined for a long time as conforming exclusively to 'literary models that have traditionally provided the staple diet of middlebrow "women's fiction"' (1998: 95). In 2001, Nicola Humble tried to revise this established reading of Lehmann by emphasising the thematic and stylistic complexity of her first novel *Dusty Answer* (202–3). This chapter aims to develop these already existing revisionist readings of Lehmann's work by offering a new interpretation of *Invitation to the Waltz*.
6. Lehmann clearly shared some biographical coordinates with many of her protagonists. The writer 'V. Glendinning might well describe my life as an emotional soap opera', she inferred in a letter to Selina Hastings on 22 September 1983 (RNL2/341/10).
7. The magazine's routine interventions into 1920s social practices are illustrated by its etiquette columns. *Vogue*'s early July 1924 edition, for instance, contained a feature entitled 'A Guide to Chic for the Debutante'. In this article, girls are advised to '[u]se no rouge and only a faint touch of that lipstick'; '[w]ear positively no jewellery except your string of real pearls at throat and wrist at night'; '[b]uy few and simple morning and afternoon dresses'; and to '[b]uy lots of simple evening gowns rather than a few grand ones, for dance frocks soil more easily than any others and you will always be meeting the same set of people at dances' (Anon. 1924a: 86).
8. The various intersections between this journal and members of the Bloomsbury group have been the subject of some critical explorations (Garrity 1999: 29–58). Throughout the 1920s and particularly under the editorship of Dorothy Todd (1922–6), *Vogue*, as Jane Garrity has shown, promoted itself as a magazine with distinctive highbrow ambitions and commissioned work by such modernist writers and artists as Virginia Woolf, Clive and Vanessa Bell, Vita Sackville-West, Roger Fry and Duncan Grant. Both Britain's artistic avant-garde represented by the Woolfs' circle and the fashion magazine thereby entered into a mutually beneficial relationship of self-promotion (Garrity 2000: 187, 191).

9. That is, in other words, the kind of sentimental romance novel that is parodied, according to Suzette Henke and Kimberly Devlin, in James Joyce's *Ulysses* through Gerty MacDowell's reading habits (Henke 1982: 132–49; Devlin 1985: 383–96).
10. The designation 'little book' was used twice in a review published on 30 October 1932 in *The New York Times* (quoted in Pollard 2004: 78).
11. Wendy Pollard has already commented in more detail on the novel's interest in socio-political commentary (80).
12. Celia Marshik uses Lacan's 'mirror stage' theory to discuss such moments, in which garments 'participate in a process of self-recognition and self-consolidation' for a child or young person that is, according to Marshik, 'always, already fraught' (2017: 16).
13. Readers today might be uncomfortably aware of the racial connotations implicit in Lehmann's expression 'nigger-brown', a term that also appears in her Girton correspondence with her mother. It is beyond the scope of this chapter to analyse Lehmann or modernism's problematic association with contemporary racial politics but readers might want to consult Jane Garrity's *Step-Daughters of England: British Women Modernists and the National Imaginary* (2003) or Andrew Gibson's *Joyce's Revenge: History, Politics, and Aesthetics in Ulysses* (2002: 127–49) for scholarly discussions of this topic.
14. Throughout the novel, Olivia is repeatedly associated with the colour red. She blushes 'darkly' when embarrassed (Lehmann 1981: 104, 125, 160) and fantasises about 'break[ing] in flame upon the Spencers' ballroom' (19) in her red silk dress. Interestingly, J. C. Flügel associates the 'supported type' with a certain auto-erotic tendency that demands the choice of striking clothes. The psychological conflict that torments the 'supported type' is thus the negotiation between two opposing desires: to cover up one's body and to expose it proudly (Flügel 1966: 100). Olivia falls neatly into this category. She imagines her appearance at the ball in an eye-catching frock but when the occasion arises thinks it too conspicuous and feels overdressed and uncomfortable: 'She glanced in the long mirror . . . so red, so definitely the reverse of well cut' (Lehmann 1981: 197).
15. In analogy to its first part, the novel's final section introduces Olivia to a correspondingly wide selection of suits and suitors. Different dance (and matrimonial) partners are encountered at the Spencers' ball: the future curate Reggie Kershaw; Maurice (the navy soldier); Peter Jenkins, the moody Oxford aesthete, who tells Olivia that it 'takes a man to teach a woman how to dress' (Lehmann 1981: 149); George (the aristocratic friend of the Spencers); Etty's devoted suitor ('old Podge' (128)); the lecherous 'old fogey' (175); Timmy Douglas (the blind war

veteran); and finally Rollo Spencer, who mesmerises Olivia and who will monopolise her romantic feelings in *The Weather in the Streets*. Indeed, Lehmann's line-up of suitable and unsuitable dance partners reads a little like 'Wild Bachelors I Have Met: Some Agonised Entries in the Notebook of a Débutante', a comical feature from *Vogue*, which lists the following types: 'the seasoned blade'; 'the bored young man'; 'the human siphon'; 'the silly ass'; 'the handsome Argentine'; 'the expert' and 'the goat' (Anon. 1925: 70). *Invitation to the Waltz* therefore records that women are by no means alone in being assessed and typecast according to specific, preconceived standards of class, sex, upbringing and education. In fact, how conscious Olivia remains of the pressure of 'fitting in' is illustrated everywhere at the Spencers' dance. It is probably due to Lady Spencer's awe-inspiring presence that Olivia, once she finds herself immersed in the alluring world of the coming-of-age ball, obsesses about matching pairs and appropriate or correct fits. When dancing with George, she aims to 'fit [her]self to his simple but correct style' (Lehmann 1981: 155). Later, when observing Rollo and Nicola, Rollo's wife-to-be, Olivia notes their compatibility: 'She watched him and Nicola meet at the foot of the stairs and start to talk earnestly, their heads close together. They do suit . . . She went away' (217).

16. Emily Dickinson used this image to represent female creativity and authorship. In the 1873 poem 'The Spider as an Artist' (1275), this 'Neglected Son of Genius' is taken 'by the Hand', whereas the spider's 'unsubstantial Trade' creates 'Tapestries' destroyed in due course by 'the Housewife's Broom' in the 1862 'The Spider holds a Silver Ball' (Dickinson 1975: 297, 557). Woolf used the image of the 'spider's web' in *A Room of One's Own* as a trope for 'imaginative work' that is 'attached to life at all four corners' (Woolf 1992b: 53).

17. Lehmann was the most explicit, perhaps, in expressing her sceptical attitude towards clothes' auxiliary function in determining women's social well-being in a review of C. Willett Cunnington's *English Women's Clothing in the Nineteenth Century* (1937). Here, she wrote: 'To swallow this book at a draught is to be visited by a morbid melancholy; the sadness after the voluptuary orgy. There are too many women. All is vanity. And one is haunted by the obverse side of the spectacle; by the limitations implied by these extravagances, by the rigid compulsions and enslavements expressed in these decorated shackles. One thinks of governess and companion, of the half-dozen spinster lady daughters, disappointed, fading bitterly all together, to whom all this proved of no avail, and who were forbidden other uses' (1937: 4). Cunnington's book on women's clothing was also reviewed, as we will see in the next chapter, by Elizabeth Bowen.

18. At this point, it might be worth considering Clare Hanson's suggestion (2000: 26) that Lehmann's *Dusty Answer* anticipated some of the political concerns about women's lack of educational and professional opportunities that Woolf would articulate a couple of years later in *A Room of One's Own* (1929). If Hanson is correct, there is ample evidence that Woolf might have felt a little threatened by the younger woman's ability and by the success of her debut novel.
19. At a certain point, exchanging artistic opinions in letters was an important component of Lehmann and Wogan Philipps's courtship. Indeed, it looks as if Lehmann carefully directed the reading activities of her husband-to-be and most certainly Woolf's 1927 novel was on her select list of books. Philipps, in any case, dutifully noted in August 1927 that he 'sat up most night reading "To the Lighthouse." It is too beautiful for words' (RNL2/478/2/4).
20. More dressmaking vocabulary appears in Woolf's diary when she discusses the composition process of *The Years* (1937). Here, she acknowledges that she has 'no idea of the whole'. On another day she asks herself: 'Does it hang together? does one part support another? Can I flatter myself that it composes; & is a whole?' (Woolf 1983: 245, 360).
21. Through the creation of the Mrs Ramsay character, Woolf also seems to offer an image of literary composition that is private and domestic – 'a nostalgic vision of writing', Patrick Collier argues, that is 'independent of the mediations and complications of modern commerce' (2006: 75). I will return to Woolf's views on creative labour and the literary marketplace in Chapter 5.
22. In his reading of *Orlando* (1928) Patrick Collier finds that even here, in this earlier Woolf novel, 'the tension between the urge to decry the institutions of the literary marketplace and the need to master and manipulate those institutions, for prestige and cultural capital if not for popularity per se – between the writer's desire to be heard and her desire to remain true to her artistic ambitions' becomes apparent (2002: 363).
23. As I show in a forthcoming essay (Plock 2017), Lehmann made a lot of use of her high-society connections when promoting her first novel: in 1927, she made repeated appearances in such British women's magazines as *Eve: The Lady's Pictorial* where she was being introduced to readers as 'Mrs Leslie Runciman: Mr. Walter Runciman's daughter-in-law, who has just published, under her maiden name of Rosamond Lehmann, an exceedingly clever first novel "Dusty Answer"' (Anon. 1927b: 133).
24. In this review, Lehmann is praised for her 'power to give emotion its full value and play' and 'to transcribe into prose emotion that is grown up and spontaneous, fatalistic but not abject, sublime without being high-pitched'. Lehmann's style has, according to Bowen, 'a sensuous,

vital simplicity, to which her brain gives edge'. Bowen ends the review on a note of high praise claiming that the novel 'has lovely qualities that are inimitably its writer's' and is 'outstanding as a sheer piece of good work' (Bowen 1936: 54).
25. Even if such later novels as *The Echoing Grove* (1953) deal with such darker and distressing themes as sexual rivalry and competition between women, they still return Lehmann to a topic that should be listed alongside romantic love as an important and recurring feature in her work since the beginning of her career: the emotional transactions between women in general and sisters in particular.
26. Lehmann's biographer puts the differences between her two publishers in no uncertain terms when she writes that Harold Raymond, Lehmann's Chatto & Windus publisher, was 'privately convinced that Rosamond would come to regret leaving the publisher of Lytton Strachey and Proust for a firm which owed its huge commercial success to the Bible, school textbooks, thrillers, *Little Grey Rabbit* and the British rights to Walt Disney' (Hastings 2003: 162).

Chapter 4

Ties: Elizabeth Bowen

> In theory, dress is an art. The architecture of textiles ought to rank only less high than the architecture of stone in so far as textiles are less durable . . . (Bowen 1950: 112)

This chapter concentrates on Elizabeth Bowen and continues the investigation into the organisation of the interwar literary field by showing how a woman novelist, who assisted in shaping modernism's critical afterlife from the very beginning, coordinated her engagement with the sartorial and the literary fashions of her time. Like Lehmann, it needs to be remembered, Bowen was inspired by modernist writers such as Woolf, who is commonly regarded as her 'friend, mentor and, in some ways, her model as modern, professional female author' (Bennett 2009: 29). But Bowen was, unlike Lehmann, also very keen to develop her literary reputation as a serious novelist in response to a market that favoured the mass production of fiction that 'is written to formula' and 'created', as Bowen explained in 1950 in one of her reflections on contemporary publishing practices, to accommodate 'the wish of the public to be told, yet once again, what it knows already, or to have the same tune played, with slight variation, on a range of feelings of which it is already aware' (Bowen 1952b: 152).

Here I suggest that Bowen tried to safeguard her reputation as a highbrow writer precisely at the time when her work was beginning to become 'a prestige commodity' on the early 1930s literary marketplace (Glendinning 1978: 98). In doing this, I shall further suggest, she indirectly engaged with two programmatic concerns commonly associated with modernist experimentation. In the first place, she developed epistemological considerations of intersubjectivity and of subject-object relations that challenged modernism's conceptual focus on interiority. For Bowen, I will argue in the following pages, fashion proved to be such a rewarding topic because her critical engagement with its social causalities advanced her thinking about the construction of interpersonal relations in twentieth-century mass market economies. As we shall see, Bowen's writing consistently associates objects such as dresses with the quick pace of modern fashion and its insistence on seasonal renewal. These sartorial items obtain more agency than the characters who wear them.[1] They work as connective devices and they function, as I shall show, as dynamic agents of intersubjectivity in Bowen's fiction.

This animation of the world of everyday objects is, as recent criticism has established, a well-known aspect of Bowen's idiosyncratic mode of writing. Later on in this chapter, I will review these critical comments on Bowen's use of objects and explain how my chapter develops these, but here I also want to propose that the development of this peculiar object-ontology was very much in keeping with Bowen's aim to individualise her writing style and thereby ensure her standing as a literary rather than commercially minded novelist. In fact, her business correspondence with her publishers and editors, to which I will turn in the final part of this chapter, makes this determination to accentuate and protect the eccentricity of her novelistic prose extremely apparent. These letters clearly expose Bowen's dislike for editorial interventions that tried to polish her prose by removing some of its peculiarities. They also reveal, in no uncertain terms, her insistence on accuracy in the portrayal of her characters and their interpersonal relations on book covers and jackets. In both cases, I will conclude, Bowen's protectionist stance can be explained by her resolution to guard the idiosyncrasy of her mode of writing that had made the focus on intersubjective relations an important trademark. In this manner – in insisting so firmly on the distinctiveness of her authorial signature – Bowen therefore resembled the high modernists of the previous period who had similarly championed the idea of the 'imprimatur' that marked, according to Aaron Jaffe, the 'modernist literary object' with 'the stylistic stamp of its producer' (2005: 20).

'Ties' emerge, as will become apparent, as extremely important accessories that organise the sartorial connections that Bowen's characters develop in one of her most cosmopolitan novels *To the*

North (1932) – a text that is of twofold interest for the analysis that follows. First, I will show that this Bowen novel relies heavily on textiles (especially the image of the tie) in a development of literary character that evidences this writer's dissatisfaction with modernism's insistence on interiority.[2] Novelistic immediacy, a trademark of Woolf's modernist style, is here replaced by a more cautious approach to character development. Although readers certainly become familiar with Bowen's protagonists – and their innermost concerns – this readerly connection to Bowen's characters is established by examining exterior markers such as clothes.[3] By the same token, *To the North* associates, as I have already suggested, conductive energies not with individuals but with clothes as objects of daily use. If the belief in the individual's ability to imaginatively transcend and reconstruct reality distinguished the work of many writers associated with the modernist tradition, Bowen therefore challenged such affirmative constructions of the creative subject whose imagination had transformative potential. In her fiction, individuals themselves often lack the resourcefulness to creatively think alternatives into existence. It is no longer people but consumer articles that make things move and happen in the modern world of commerce and commodities.[4]

But *To the North* also matters to my analysis because its publication occurred at a point in Bowen's career that marked her transition from emerging to established writer. Indeed, this was the first of her novels that was released by the more commercially focused publisher Victor Gollancz. While the previous decade had been one of immense professional struggle – editors in the 1920s, Bowen explained in one of her essays, 'still cared, it seemed, for nothing but the establishment' – the 1930s witnessed the growing success of this 'new-comer' who 'hope[d] to break through those ranks' (Bowen 1952b: 90–1).[5] In this particular decade, Bowen became a well-known and much-acclaimed novelist, and her reputation as a successful writer of fiction made her an attractive addition to Gollancz's list. It also allowed Bowen to embark on a second career as a journalist that provided necessary income, especially during and after the Second World War, but that also became the source of immense anxiety because Bowen was convinced that these shorter, commissioned pieces lacked the quality of her novelistic prose. As a result of much extensive thinking about her self-conception as a writer, Bowen therefore began to distinguish – in her critical writing on artistic standards, authorial productivity and the literary marketplace – between authors who are 'imaginative' and those who are merely 'inventive', a distinction that can also be applied to her own work that she firmly segregated into prose writing and journalism (Bowen 1952b: 152). At the very same moment when commercial success was secured, in other words, Bowen became exceptionally worried about being turned into a literary commodity herself. Extremely fashion-conscious throughout her life, she was clearly very guarded when fashion's assumed tendency to synchronise, standardise and assimilate was directed at her own work.

In these multifarious negotiations with the market, Bowen emerges, like her friend and contemporary Lehmann, as an important disseminator of modernist concerns. This was because she developed her own would-be object-orientated ontology in response to modernist preoccupations with subjectivity and interiority.[6] But in presenting herself as an 'imaginatively creative' writer in the modernist tradition – someone whose fiction 'carries', as Bowen explained, 'the stamp of inherent originality' (1952b: 206, 207) – she also situated herself very clearly in the vicinity of such modernist writers as Joyce or Pound, who similarly promoted, according to Aaron Jaffe, the singularity of their writerly signatures. Even if her alternative portrayal of literary character had rejected a significant aspect of high modernist experimentation, in other words, her concern about the commercialisation of literature nonetheless led her to affirm another item from modernism's broad catalogue of innovations. By comparison, Bowen's engagement with modernism is therefore more complexly organised than Lehmann's. Whereas the latter was extremely inclined to emulate aspects of Woolf's work – for reasons examined in the previous chapter – Bowen, in the 1930s, tried to countermand modernism's influence in the same way in which she rejected too strong an allegiance with a literary market that threatened to incorporate her into an expanding list of 'literary hits' (Kracauer 1995: 90). In this manner, Bowen's fiction clearly announced its complex ties with modernist aesthetics – it indirectly rather than directly affirmed the literary practices of this artistic movement as significant benchmarks for her own work. Bowen's writing, that is, is critical and revisionist, disseminating the artistic propositions of her modernist contemporaries through complex refractions.

'That subtle blend of individuality and fashion': sartorial objects in Bowen's fiction

At the outset, it must be noted that Bowen's encounters with the world of fashion were far from opportune. Apparently, her 'dress sense' was 'atrocious' at the time of her marriage to Alan Cameron, who took on the daunting task of organising her wardrobe (Ellmann 2004: 33). Victoria Glendinning, Bowen's biographer, notes that 'large earrings, necklaces of false pearls or great glass bobbles, and flashy fake jewellery' were classic accessories of a writer who was, throughout her life, extremely uncomfortable about being photographed and who approved the use of only a small number of 'permitted' images for publicity purposes (Glendinning 1978: 47, 280–1).[7] One glance at those existing photographs of Bowen makes clear that she was hardly ever following sartorial protocols. That said, one can still discern an apparent affinity with the vagaries of the modern fashion industry in Bowen's writing as this was a topic she often addressed in her journalism. In a 1956 essay, for instance, she justified stylish idiosyncrasy by stressing the need to avoid conformity and a slavish devotion to the norm:

> Fashion, today, no longer is a dictator, rather a would-be ally of the identity; it deals no longer in 'musts' but in possibilities. There are [sic] an infinity of ways of avoiding the mass-produced look. Even what may seem to be universals, the grey suit or the black dress, subtly are invitations to personality; everything depends on the way of wearing them, the unique touches, the language of the accessories. (Bowen 2008: 415)

Clothes and other fashion ornaments, in other words, can be effectively manipulated in order to create what Bowen called a 'subtle blend of individuality and fashion' (Bowen 2008: 189). Indeed, in her essays, Bowen repeatedly stated that fashion and subjectivity are intimately linked. 'Clothes', she suggested accordingly in a review of the design historian Willett Cunnington's *English Women's Clothing in the Nineteenth Century*, 'never remain a question of pure æsthetics; far too much personal feeling is involved in them' (Bowen 1950: 112). Were it not for this intriguing connection between dress and psychology, garments, robes and other sartorial objects would not be such complex and intricate texts waiting to be deciphered.

Although sartorial references pervade all of Bowen's writing, I will here consider the centrality of fashion and garments in *To the North* – her 1932 novel that investigates the auxiliary function played by fashion accessories in forming personal attachments in a modern, ephemeral world driven by excessive consumption and by the velocity of modern travel in trains, planes and automobiles.[8] Needless to say, the composition of social networks (and their volatility) is a classic Bowen topos and by focusing on this particular theme in *To the North*, Bowen returned to a subject that had been of ongoing interest to her. After all, her first novel, *The Hotel* (1927), had already examined the fleeting nature of personal attachments formed among guests convening coincidentally in an Italian Riviera boarding house, whereas a later novel is more explicitly entitled *Friends and Relations* (1931). A 1950 lecture on 'The Poetic Element in Fiction' similarly illustrates the extent to which prose writing was, for Bowen, connected to the exploration of interpersonal relations:

> Is it to be allowed that the only spokesman for our time, the only remaining voice for our time, and a voice which may not always be easily heard, should be the voice of the poet, and of the lyrical and self-contemplative poet, at that? . . . There must be the outward action, however placed and however staged. There must be the conflict between consciousness of the one and of the other person. There must be the movement and the impact of the passion upon the passion, the project on the project. We cannot really accept, even in our most introverted individualism, the idea of a one-man world, of the solitary consciousness reflecting everything else. And that really, that fact that it concerns itself with two people, with three, with an unnumbered cast of persons, placed in a pattern relating to one another and acting upon one another, does constitute the hold and the future promise of the story, whether it be in . . . the novel of sensation, whether it be in the novel of allegory, the Kafka novel, or whether it be in the short story with its simplified invisible view, the fact of reaction and opposition, the consequence of one person upon another and one action as following another, will always be desired and will always be needed to be made plain. (Bowen 2010: 159–60)

As this passage suggests, Bowen regarded the novel as a predestined literary medium for addressing the question of how individuals relate to one another in social networks and configurations.[9] However, if the topic of human interactions figures prominently in all of Bowen's texts, I want to suggest that *To the North* occupies a special place in her literary universe because it spotlights, like few of her other works, the instability of interpersonal relations in modern, metropolitan London. In this text, the urban environment provides the backdrop for a story about two young women, sisters-in-law Cecilia and Emmeline Summers, who set up house together in 1920s London after the death of Cecilia's husband and Emmeline's brother. While the glamorous and unpredictable Cecilia contemplates a second marriage to the eligible bachelor, Julian Tower, Emmeline, co-owner of a small Bloomsbury travel agency, forms an ill-fated emotional attachment with the predatory Markie Linkwater. Their affair ends catastrophically and the novel concludes on a cataclysmic note: after a constrained and awkward dinner with Julian and Cecilia, Emmeline, in an emblematic death-drive scene, provokes a car accident that will, in all likelihood, kill herself and Markie.[10]

The contextual setting for this novelistic description of the characters' complex emotional and personal transactions is a world in which consumption and personal relations have threatened to become interchangeable, and the novel's apparent interest in metropolitan consumer culture might well be responsible for the abundance of sartorial references in the description of Emmeline's personal tragedy and Cecilia's blossoming romance: meteorological conditions are referenced indirectly through allusions to '[w]et lace' and 'sopping chiffon' (Bowen 2006: 219); Cecilia, we are told, is 'charmingly dressed' (4) in 'pink folds' (307) or an expensive 'fur coat' (1); Lady Waters, Emmeline and Cecilia's exasperating and exasperated relative, exhibits, in 'her black moiré skirt' (15), an 'expensive disregard of the fashions' (14). And elsewhere in the novel, Bowen draws attention to a 'white tie' (24), a 'black tie' (60), Emmeline's 'green dress' (138), her 'long yellow dress' (81) and her 'red leather slippers' (125). More unconventionally (and disturbingly perhaps), a schoolgirl's 'blue knickers' are on display in a 'dignified but dégagé somersault' (94), while the novel, in its final scene, zooms in on 'Markie's white scarf that he had forgotten' and 'Emmeline's gloves that she would not wear' (307).

Even to a reader who does not ransack Bowen's novel for references to clothes, fabrics and textiles, this sartorial colour chart must seem over-determined. While Bowen herself admitted that '[t]en minutes talk about clothes (except between perfect friends) tends to make everyone present either overbearing, guarded or touchy' (1950: 111), her novel, like its author, seems guilty of over-accessorising. What can be the point of this slightly inelegant and ungainly accumulation of sartorial references in Bowen's narrative? A possible answer can be found, I want to propose, by briefly reviewing existing criticism on Bowen's representation of objects. Maud Ellmann, for one, has compellingly argued that Bowen's fiction anthropomorphises inanimate objects, especially furniture, and provides them with mnemonic abilities (2004: 142). Things become guardians of the past – a past that characters no longer want to assimilate or confront. Ellmann, it could be said, registers a certain psychological emancipation of Bowen's artefacts. They are no longer figuratively tied to the human mind. Instead of simply representing characters, objects take on a more active and autonomous role in Bowen's fiction. Maintaining that the 'idea that places and things could have sentience and cognition', 'regardless of whether or not a human mediator is present to act as the source of or inspiration for such acts of personification', Elizabeth C. Inglesby has further advanced the study of Bowen's 'literary animism' (2007: 306–7). In Bowen's fiction, Inglesby argues, artefacts form connections with each other. Not only does Bowen's writing insist on the spiritual independence of the material world, but it also reveals objects' potential and desire for independent agency.

My own reading of garments in *To the North* is influenced by the critical consensus that things matter in Bowen's fiction. But clothes, I want to argue, can be distinguished from many of the objects that have been given specific attention by Bowen's critics. Whereas houses, furniture and other domestic items represent tradition, customs and history (nostalgia made material), clothes are consumer products, temporary of nature, transient and short-lived. Unsurprisingly, in 1902 Werner Sombart had already identified the instability and vicissitude of human nature as one of the inevitable consequences of an emergent capitalist economy. While he had noted that '[c]hange has been transformed from an individual into a social fact', he had also suggested that 'the relationship between human beings and articles of daily use has been stripped of [its] sentimental and romantic attraction' (1902: 10).[11] Clothes and other disposable consumer articles as they are presented in Bowen are certainly no memorabilia and they lack precisely the kind of 'sentimental and romantic attraction' identified by Sombart as the legacy of traditional social organisations built on close kinships between people and their things. Conversely, they represent – in a way that houses, tables or chairs do not – the energy and the mobility associated with modern capitalism. At this point, it is therefore tempting to suggest that Bowen, in *To the North*, is endorsing a specific ideological perspective: Karl Marx's well-known theory of commodity fetishism. And as we shall see later on, traces of capitalism's alienating influence on human relations are certainly apparent in her novel, while Bowen, in another place, overtly acknowledged modernity's sedating and paralysing influences. As she argued in 'The Poetic Element in Fiction', '[w]e could be very easily numbed and very easily made anonymous, unaware of ourselves, by this heavy looming up of invention, of buildings, of process of speed, of similarity, of mass production' (Bowen 2010: 159). However, in *To the North*, garments and fashion ornaments are also infused with a particular energy, and it is their vitality that is responsible for mobilising interpersonal dynamics among characters. While the ontological distinction between subject and object becomes increasingly blurred in *To the North* – her protagonists often appear like passive chessboard pieces – it is, paradoxically, through their reliance on sartorial objects that characters in Bowen's fiction seem to be able to bond at all with other individuals. In *To the North*, in other words, clothes determinedly generate interpersonal energies.

The 'tie question': sartorial connections in *To the North*

That Bowen consistently associated clothes with connective sociability is suggested early on in the novel when Emmeline and Cecilia's social behaviour is assessed with the help of a sartorial image: 'Mutability seemed to Emmeline natural; if her own friends, like her evening dresses, outlasted Cecilia's, it was simply because she did not wear them so hard or – to pursue the sartorial image – cut so close to the figure' (Bowen 2006: 24). Cecilia, it seems, is a consumer, Emmeline a collector. But while the two women obviously differ in their feelings towards clothes and friends, this passage already shows that *To the North* synchronises its apparent interest in sartorial matters with an equally decisive analysis of its characters' social networks and connections. Unsure whether or not to accept Julian's offer of marriage, to form a new attachment, Cecilia, we are told, displaces her indecision onto the equally problematic task of selecting new items for her wardrobe:

> Besides the agonies of decision – green, white or flame-colour? – she could never order a new evening dress without a sense of fatality: how much would have happened before it was worn out? . . . On Saturday there had been that disturbing passage with Julian. (105)

Cecilia's thoughts about the purchase, consumption and the wear and tear of garments parallel her attitude towards her social engagements. Does she, who 'loved strangers, strangeness' and who 'could enjoy in a first glance all the deceptions of intimacy' (6), really want to form an attachment that is to outlast her new evening dress? Does one want to find stability and permanence in a swirling world that pays lip service to the 'slick mundanity of *Vogue*' (7)? As excessive consumption is not a problem unique to the flighty Cecilia, this is a question many of Bowen's characters have to face. Accused by his siblings of going 'through life too easily, forming too few ties and buying too many pictures' (40), Julian, Cecilia's suitor, is equally accountable for a too fashion-conscious attitude to life. In Bowen's novel consumption and intimacy, like mismatched ornaments, do not seem to go together.

But if some of Bowen's characters seem reluctant to form lasting attachments, her own fiction is nonetheless loyally focusing on one particular sartorial object: the tie. Cravats, neckties and their close sartorial relatives, scarves, are everywhere in *To the North*. While the school tie of Julian's adolescent niece, Pauline, becomes the subject of an aesthetic debate (195–6), readers are also told that Emmeline, during her first meeting with Julian at a party, glances 'once or twice at his white tie' (24). Likewise, Cecilia reports that her first conversation with Markie on the train came to pass because she 'looked at his tie' (18) – 'at his Old Harrovian tie: the only tie, for some reason, she ever recognised' (3).[12] In this last case, a sartorial accessory motivates a fleeting encounter on the train, which has, nevertheless, more long-term and ultimately unfortunate repercussions because it brings together Markie and Emmeline, Cecilia's sister-in-law. Once again, it might be argued that this unconcealed concern with a particular sartorial accessory is nothing but another example of Bowen's tendency to 'over-furnish' her novel.[13] However, if *To the North* repeatedly references this particular garment, it is, of course, for the explicit purpose of exploiting the semantics of the homonym 'tie' and to stress the associative connection between sartorial objects and social attachments. In an early scene in the novel, Bowen's socio-sartorial concerns already become apparent when Emmeline's business partner maintains 'an air of slightly disdainful discretion' during her telephone conversation with a parlour-maid, 'as though', the text reveals, 'he were thankful he had no ties' (36–7). Such playful conceptual fusion on Bowen's part more than confirms Neil Corcoran's proposition that her fiction is extremely alert to the 'semantic, acoustic, and etymological interconnections between words' and that she consistently aimed to merge discursive fields associated with particular linguistic referents (Corcoran 2004: 4). Extremely apparent (and comical) is this overlap between the sartorial and the socio-psychological when Lady Waters hopes that Cecilia, after her marriage, will 'travel with Julian, or have more ties' (Bowen 2006: 274). In Bowen's *To the North* – a text that develops bizarre grids of ties – sartorial ornaments and personal relationships, in a deft (or daft) play with linguistic signifiers, have clearly become interchangeable.

Bowen, it should be added, was extremely fond of this particular image and used it again in *The Heat of the Day* (1948), another of her novels exploring the ephemerality of human connections – this time in London at the height of the Blitz. Forced to reconsider the 'ambiguities of her tie' with her lover Robert Kelway (Bowen 1998: 114), who may or may not be a Nazi spy, the protagonist Stella Rodney, in one of the novel's key scenes, is asked to provide an opinion on Robert's necktie: '"Don't you agree," he asked, "it's about time I scrapped this tie?"' (Bowen 1998: 101–2). This conversation about Robert's tie, odd as it must appear in the first place, is awkwardly pinned to a chapter reviewing emotional rapport between individuals – personal ties – in the time of war. Death and the dangers faced daily and nightly during the Blitz function, according to Bowen's narrator, like an aphrodisiac:

> So, among the crowds still eating, drinking, working, travelling, halting, there began to be an instinctive movement to break down indifference while there was still time. The wall between the living and the living became less solid as the wall between the living and the

dead thinned. In that September transparency people became transparent, only to be located by the just darker flicker of their hearts. . . . There was a diffused gallantry in the atmosphere, an unmarriedness: it came to be rumoured about the country, among the self-banished, the uneasy, the put-upon and the safe, that everybody in London was in love . . . (92, 94–5)

Intruding on this atmosphere of romance and passion is a man called Harrison, who forces himself (and certain unwanted information about Robert's intelligence work) on Stella. With her suspicion awakened, Stella, who is unable to confront her lover directly, nonetheless decides to investigate Robert's case: what follows is an intricate dialogue about Harrison, Stella's 'friends' (102) and about Robert's relatives – a conversation that produces uneasiness, the crucial 'tie question' (102) and an emotional outburst:

'The thing is,' [Stella] cried, kneeling by him with the tie in her hands, 'that really I cannot judge any tie you wear. Just as I cannot judge . . . How should I feel, for instance, if somebody tried to tell me something preposterous about you?' (102)

In the emotionally charged atmosphere of wartime London where human associations form rapidly and intimacy becomes discountable, all sorts of ties, it seems, might easily become oppressive or burdensome and finally will have 'to go' (102).[14]

In *To the North*, Bowen's interest in exploring clothes' potential to function as agents of connective sociability resurfaces in a scene involving Emmeline and her secretary, the neglected (but appropriately named) Miss Tripp, 'recently down from Lady Margaret Hall' (Bowen 2006: 35). Oblivious to the stenographer's display of increasingly striking clothing, put on for 'Emmeline's eye alone' (149), and to Miss Tripp's bottled-up emotions, Emmeline suddenly finds herself in a tight spot one day when walking into the office in an arresting green silk dress. Arriving late, 'agitated and bright-eyed' (143) from a lunch date with Markie, she must realise that her unpunctuality and her unusual choice of dress provoke an emotional crisis in the office. Unfortunately for both women, Miss Tripp has misread the significance of the green frock. In principle, Emmeline is a version of J. C. Flügel's 'duty type' – a person for whom 'certain kinds of clothes have indeed become outward and visible signs of a strict and strongly developed "Super-Ego" or moral principle' and who would 'draw a sharp distinction between clothes worn for work and the less severe and more ornamental garments worn for rest or recreation' (1966: 97–8). Emmeline, we should not be surprised to hear, 'never came to work in anything but a coat and skirt, or a linen dress as severe', so Miss Tripp is partly vindicated in thinking that there is really 'no reason why this departure from precedent should be allowed to pass without comment' (Bowen 2006: 143).

Evident in the tense exchange between employer and employee now ensuing in Emmeline's travel agency is the alienating aspect of modern office work that threatens to mechanise and standardise human life and labour. It is precisely this 'impersonality' (Bowen 2006: 148) that Doris Tripp criticises in Emmeline's behaviour – especially in a place that prides itself on taking 'personal care of clients' (26). Although Doris knows better than to allow 'personal feeling to impinge on business relations' (148), she refuses to be regarded as 'an automaton' or, worse even, 'a platinum blonde' (151). 'But where was the confidence', wonders Emmeline's employee, '[w]here were the smiles, the gleams of satirical understanding, the dear sense of impositions endured together, of jokes shared grimly enough, that should cement an association between females?' (150). Tripp, who takes up Emmeline's request for dictation, 'smiling, as though at an invitation to dance' (146), wants intimacy while her employer expects nothing but 'punctuality, bridling diligence' (153) and 'the seductive efficiency' 'implicit in [the] use of "stenographer"' (154). It is partly due to these conflicting expectations that Bowen's characters become entrenched in their respective positions in the ensuing argument. But in writing this specific scene from *To the North*, Bowen also registered that fashion dictates, to a certain extent, the problematic office politics depicted in such detail. By associating the image of modern and stylish femininity with the attractive picture of women's competence and efficiency, the 1920s fashion industry had started to set standards for female dress and demeanour in the workplace. 'Uniform working relations and collective contracts condition [the salaried masses'] lifestyle, which is also subject . . . to the standardizing influence of powerful ideological forces', noted Siegfried Kracauer in *The Salaried Masses* (1930). 'All these compulsions have unquestionably led to the emergence of certain standard types of salesgirl, draper's assistant, shorthand typist and so on', he continued, 'which are portrayed and at the same time cultivated in magazines and cinemas. They have entered the general consciousness, which from them forms its overall image of the new salaried stratum' (1998: 68).[15]

Kracauer's comments are echoed in *To the North*, where a particular 'type' of employee seems to be required by the business partners – one who is 'cheap', 'wrote the King's English, absented herself at tea-time, and did not sniff' (Bowen 2006: 153). Not individuality, represented by Tripp's 'striped, checked or polka-dotted' dresses (149), but compliance with the ready-made image of female professionalism is in high demand on the 1920s job market. For this competition Tripp is, of course, extremely ill-fitted. But if she is not the kind of employee desired by Emmeline and her business partner, Bowen nonetheless shows compassion for this sartorial and social outsider. The scene from *To the North*, in spite of an underlying strand of satire, is sympathetic towards the young woman, who 'worked for ten shillings a week and the experience' (35). Indeed, given her well-documented taste for sartorial idiosyncrasy, Bowen – who argued elsewhere that 'beauty, once its early dazzle is past, is very very much a matter of identity' and 'the gentle brilliance of individuality' – could only have been concerned by fashion's regulation of female appearances and social roles through the alluring imagery of prêt-à-porter models (Bowen 2008: 356). In all likelihood, she would have classified herself as a 'non-combatant' in this battle for modish uniformity – someone who would have been responsive to the cry of 'the elderly and the old' who argue 'that everyone, nowadays, looks exactly the same as every one else' (Bowen 1950: 113), someone who would also pessimistically conclude in one of her essays:

> The truth, probably, is, that everybody would like to look like one preconceived person, a figure suggested to them by the propaganda of fashion: they believe the figure to be their private ideal and do not realise how general the figure is. Stenographers with good figures, quick eyes and uncomplex natures approximate to this ideal most neatly. (Bowen 1950: 113)

Bowen, in other words, sensed that fashion's authoritative prescriptions created expectations about feminine appearance and behaviour that threatened to erase personal differences and idiosyncrasies.[16]

However, Bowen's apparent critique of fashion's democratising influence aside, it must be said that Emmeline's dress, whose sleeves are 'rubbing against the desk' and whose 'silk was still warm from the sun' (Bowen 2006: 145), is certainly unsuitable for office work. In fact, the inappropriateness of the green frock is colourfully illustrated by a 1924 feature in British *Vogue* that offers 'A Guide to Chic for the Business Woman': '[A]ny woman who is working in the City among men may be said to be best dressed in the very plainest of smart ways', the writer asserts, before denouncing 'the sleeveless street gown' and very 'short, tight, bright dresses' as 'unsuitable' for the work place. Emmeline has committed the modern office woman's worst sartorial faux pas: adorning herself, as the *Vogue* fashion arbiter calls it, with 'an eye to the social side of life, and for the sake of mid-day or evening engagements'. She is therefore very 'ill turned out for [her] employment' (Anon. 1924b: 71). And Bowen herself is even more severe in her criticism of unbefitting clothing than the *Vogue* columnist, suggesting that '[a]n unsuccessful appearance is more than a pity; it is a pathological document' (Bowen 1950: 112). It is clear, then, that this author would have been extremely aware that Emmeline is 'ill turned out for her employment' in her green frock. But even if this is the case and Emmeline's dress is very unsuitable for work, Tripp's advancement is equally misplaced. Although the frock carries the distracting memory of her lunch with Markie and of their plans for a short trip to Paris, it is not an invitation to an intimate and friendly tête-à-tête between 'girls' (Bowen 2006: 143). Back in the office, Emmeline is once more detached and impersonal, as surprised by Miss Tripp's emotional outbreak 'as though the very furniture had complained' (148). Yet the green frock does motivate Tripp to speak and to seek Emmeline's confidence. However improvident, misguided or undesirable Doris's effort might have been, Emmeline's clothes become the reason for this attempt to establish intimacy. '"If I hadn't come in in this wretched dress"', Emmeline correctly concludes, '"she would not have spoken"' (155). Once more, we can see that clothes are responsible for producing emotional energies between Bowen's characters.[17]

Needless to say, the fact that *To the North* consistently interrogates the relationship between material goods and human relationships in this manner might also suggest that Bowen's text contributes to an ongoing debate about consumer culture's alienating effect on social relations. It is well known that Karl Marx – in his remarks on the fetishism of commodities – expressed a deep mistrust of consumer objects and their tendency to commodify human labour. In Marx's words, 'whenever, by any exchange, we equate as values our different products, by that very act, we also equate, as human labour, the different kinds of labour expended upon them' (Marx 1983: 78). But in contrast to Marx's assumptions, Bowen shows in *To the North* that sartorial items can also obtain assembling powers. In her fiction, material items such as clothes and other fashion accessories have significance because they encourage the development of personal relationships. Bowen's use of dress accessories thus moves beyond critical paradigms that pessimistically envision, *pace* Marx, estrangement and personal isolation as the logical consequence of capitalist modernity. Although she elsewhere frowningly recorded the evanescence of intimacy and personal connections in a modern world of mass production and consumption, Bowen's novel also shows that it is, paradoxically, through consumer objects that emotional rapport can occasionally be established.

While Bowen's characters are thus directed by the energy of their clothes and form what I propose to call sartorial connections, the novel's readers are also encouraged to develop strong links with Bowen's fictional personalities by familiarising themselves with their fashion accessories. We become intimate with her characters, in other words, by getting to know their clothes. When the emotionally tormented Emmeline, in one of the novel's last scenes, turns to her wardrobe for inspiration on what to wear for Cecilia's dinner party, she has the choice between 'the yellow in which she had dined with Markie, the silver in which she had first met Julian' (Bowen 2006: 284). Both dresses are associated, in the reader's (and Emmeline's) mind, with the men, who, in one form or another, have contributed to terminating her tenancy at Oudenarde Road and to interrupting her comfortable intimacy with Cecilia. And while the experience of spotting Emmeline in 'a long silver dress that he did not know' (286) rekindles Markie's sexual desire (289), the reader is aware, unlike Emmeline's former lover, that the silver dress does not represent a clean slate. Intimacy with Emmeline has intensified since we first saw her in the shiny silver dress. By associating the sartorial references strewn across *To the North* we are therefore able to follow Emmeline in recalling decisive moments in her past – like her first encounter with Julian during which she wore this particular dress and which triggered further meetings between Bowen's protagonists. By the end of the novel, when we re-encounter this particular dress, it has become apparent to the reader that the casual personal attachment desired by Markie is clearly incompatible with Emmeline's emotional intensity. And it is the fabrics in Emmeline's wardrobe that assist in connecting different elements in Bowen's textual design, thereby encouraging the reader's familiarity with the protagonists. In Bowen's fiction, in other words, exterior markers such as clothes generate ties between the characters and the reader as much as they develop interpersonal energies among the characters themselves. Not the protagonists but the consumer objects that surround them are, in many cases, the agents of the narrative. In *To the North*, it is the inanimate world of frocks and ties that provides characters with stimulating impulses, energetically determining their choices. Clothes, not literary characters, are responsible for directing the course of Bowen's plot.

This insistence on focusing on exteriors to allow readers access to her characters' emotional worlds becomes extremely apparent in an earlier scene in the novel – a scene that also shows how determinedly Bowen hoped to challenge a central tenet of modernism's conceptual apparatus: an insistence on abandoning realism's focus on exteriority, observation and the world of material objects. *To the North*'s fascination with ties, we can observe in this scene, is particularly seductive for the emotionally consistent Emmeline, whose strong attachment to Markie has such drastic consequences for everyone involved. Unexpectedly finding her lover in her garden one morning, she cannot help but notice his 'dishevelled white tie' (126), an ostentatious marker of an eventful night. And although Bowen's novel does not record Emmeline's discomposure and agitation directly, the sartorial image provides clues about Markie's nocturnal activities and Emmeline's emotional response. 'To get his tie like this', we are told, 'someone must have been holding him tight round the neck' (127). For Emmeline, we can deduce, Markie's 'crumpled tie' (127) advertises the possibility of sexual betrayal. But instead of giving the reader direct access to the internal, psychological organisation of the character, *To the North* externalises Emmeline's perceptions and emotional responses by recording her reading of a sartorial ornament. Throughout Bowen's novel, that is to say, garments can indirectly reveal characters' emotional states to the reader who turns, like the elusive Emmeline herself, into a vigilant examiner of clothes when examining what characters might feel or how they emotionally relate to each other. In this manner, Bowen developed a strategy for representing character in *To the North* that effectively communicates to the reader the intensity of Emmeline's emotions without taking recourse to the literary techniques employed by such modernist writers as Woolf, who had made the focus on interiority a central aspect of their writing. Woolf, it should be remembered at this point, had insisted in her 1924 essay 'Character in Fiction' that the writers of the previous period – Edwardians such as Arnold Bennett, H. G. Wells and John Galsworthy – had failed in representing human nature in fiction by laying 'enormous stress upon the fabric of things' (Woolf 1988: 432). 'What appalled her', Bowen wrote in a 1954 review of Woolf's recently published diaries, 'were the non-moments, the bridge passages, the "narrative business of the realist". . .' (Bowen 1999: 179). Opting instead for a representation of character that prioritises 'an intense inner existence' (Bowen 1946: 48), Woolf's modernism, Bowen proposed, radically challenged the conventions of twentieth-century novel writing.

Obviously, Bowen did not share Woolf's dislike for representing 'the fabric of things' in fiction. On the contrary, her writing relies, as we have just seen, on energetically interrogating the intricate relationship between subjective consciousness and material existence. As Maud Ellmann convincingly claims:

> The difference between Bowen and Woolf is that Bowen relishes the narrative business of the realist, insofar as it releases her from the stifling rose-house of inner life into the world of cars and cocktail-shakers, typewriters and telephones – in short into the modern world, which claims her attention just as much as the archaic phantoms of the mind. (2004: 5)

In *To the North*, Bowen, instead of affirming the modernist concern with interiority advocated by writers such as Woolf, therefore allows us to read her protagonists externally through their sartorial accessories. This means that Bowen's fiction evinces – in an all but realist fashion – a determined devotion to description and surfaces. For Bowen, the kaleidoscopic organisation of the modern social landscape marked by fast-paced consumption, commercial exchanges and the ephemeral nature of human connections, proved to be too exhilarating and fascinating to be neglected. Individuals, in her fiction, are shown to be thrown into a modern force field of competing social energies that can be anesthetising but also galvanising at the same time.

Nonetheless, since Bowen pays significant attention to sartorial markers but refuses to fall neatly into line with an unwavering materialist outlook, her aesthetic commitment to realist conventions, set up by critics as modernism's outdated but contending literary practice, must be further investigated. Whereas the realist writers criticised in Woolf's essay would insist on the solidity of the material world – the concreteness, the substance and the conceptual dependability of objects surrounding characters in fiction – Bowen foregrounded, like many modernist writers before her, the ephemerality of the world. Nothing is static. Human relations like subjective impressions are constantly in flux, subject to change and revision. Moreover, in her novel psychological interiors and external appearances form complex alliances. On the one hand, characters' clothes invite the reader to speculate about their emotional make-up. On the other hand, *To the North* everywhere illustrates the instability of these sartorial connections. Like Miss Tripp and Markie, readers might misjudge characters' garments and by extension their states of mind, both of which become attributes that are provisional and temporary of nature. In a modern world, in which experiences are short-lived and nothing is of permanent duration, personal characteristics seem to have become as volatile as fashion objects. And it is precisely this inability of Bowen's objects to create stable meaning that unhinges scholarly interpretations focusing exclusively on her writing's realist facets. Although she remained, throughout her career, attracted to the literary practices of the realist tradition by engaging with 'the fabric of things' as Woolf called it, Bowen nonetheless offered a different way of representing the interdependence of human subjects and the world of objects surrounding them, one that noted the variable nature of personal associations and one that brought into play the suggestion of consumer objects' energetic intervention in the world of human connections.

Testing her artistic ties with Woolf and the latter's dislike of the so-called 'narrative business of the realist' in this manner obviously assisted Bowen in refining her own writerly technique in response to modernism's propositions for experimentation and innovation.

But even if she opted for an alternative version of character representation – one that reinstated the significance of exteriors in the development of her protagonists – Bowen's fiction still confirmed her mentor's work as an important artistic standard, as a composition practice that might have been unsuitable but that was nonetheless influential for her conceptual thinking about writing. As such, Bowen acknowledged the radical artistic innovations devised and encouraged by the modernists as a programmatic reference point for authors working in their wake. As a novelist who gained critical acclaim in the 1930s, Bowen was clearly part of a generation of authors who knew that their work would be measured according to the artistic criteria introduced and practised by the high modernists of the previous decade whose claims to novelty and originality had nonetheless begun to wear thin at the time she was writing her major novels. It is, in fact, fair to say that at the precise historical moment when Bowen's role as a novelist was consolidated in the 1930s, modernism was already considered by many contemporary writers as an artistic practice in need of updates and revisions.[18] This was the decade, then, during which the 'specific law of change in the field of production' that Bourdieu has called 'the dialectic of distinction' ensured that one school or group of artists (modernism) that is 'inevitably associated with a moment in the history of art', is 'condemned to fall into the past and to become *classic* or *outdated*'. No longer the artistic avant-garde that pronounces the kind of 'discontinuity, rupture, difference, revolution' that Bourdieu associates with every newcomer on the artistic scene, modernism, in the 1930s was already in the process of being 'canonized, academicized and neutralized' (Bourdieu 1993: 105–6).[19] This meant that the work of Woolf or Joyce became more widely available and familiar to readers in this decade.[20] But it also meant that their work, in the very process of becoming canonised, lost some of its revolutionary energy and invited revisionist attempts by the next generation of writers, Bourdieu's 'newcomers' whose aim it was to 'push back into the past the consecrated producers with whom they are compared, "dating" their products and the taste of those who remain attached to them' (Bourdieu 1993: 107).

Bowen, it is my contention in this chapter, played an important role in this emerging debate about modernism's critical acceptance which would lead to the institutionalisation of the work of its main exponents but which also redefined this movement as an artistic formation that had now lost some of its claim to novelty. As the above remarks about *To the North* have shown, Bowen's work aimed to revise, update and thereby 'push back into the past' some of Woolf's artistic imperatives. At the same time, however, her fiction but even more so her critical writing acknowledged modernism's ongoing relevance for writers and readers of her own generation. She simultaneously reacted against, but also disseminated and helped to popularise the work and the intellectual interests of modernist writers by making the discussion of their work, biographies and critical significance recurrent themes in the essays and reviews she was writing from the 1930s onwards.[21] And while this work as a modernist critic was in all likelihood motivated by the selfless desire to promote the writing of a group of artists who had had a significant impact on her artistic formation and her self-conception as a writer, it is important to note that Bowen, through her novelistic engagement with modernism, also managed to affirm her own credentials as a serious, highbrow artist – someone who was capable of comfortably inhabiting the role of intellectual descendant of an artistic formation that had made the importance of cultured refinement one of its most significant trademarks.

This issue – emphasising her intellectual affiliation with modernism's highbrow ambitions – became especially important to Bowen at the time when she began to occupy a more central place in the literary field of the interwar period and when her writing became more commercially successful. *To the North*, as I have already noted, was the first of her novels to be published under the imprint of Victor Gollancz Ltd, a relatively young publishing firm, whose innovative, eye-catching advertising campaigns expressed a more commercially orientated publishing philosophy than the one that had distinguished Bowen's former, more conservative publisher, Constable.[22] The publication of this particular novel therefore represents a clear shift in Bowen's reputation as a writer. No longer in her formative years as a novelist, Bowen, it can be said, was now an established writer who was courted by a publisher such as Gollancz who wanted to include her in his expanding list. Also beginning to emerge at about the time of *To the North*'s publication are Bowen's self-conscious reflections on art and commerce as contrasting yet often intersecting concerns for contemporary writers. As the final section of this chapter will show, Bowen continued to be preoccupied with her reputation as a highbrow writer working in the modernist tradition when she began publishing her novels with a more commercially orientated press. This reputation she hoped to guard throughout her writing life – especially at times when personal circumstances made it imperative to turn to writing for much-needed income.

'Job' writing: Bowen, commercial obligations and artistic commitments

Bowen's growing reputation as a novelist and a short story writer coincided with, and made possible, a parallel career in journalism, and Allan Hepburn, in noting that Bowen made the strategic choice to boost her income by writing reviews, essays and short stories, paints a vivid picture of the economic conditions that forced her to write for profit:

> By the late 1930s, Bowen had earned an international reputation. Throughout the 1940s, her reputation grew further because of unstinting hard work: she wrote essays for money; she wrote in aid of charities. She wrote to pay for repairs to the house on Clarence Terrace, which was twice damaged by bombs during the war. Her output of short stories and non-fiction was prodigious, but she scarcely had time for novels. (Bowen 2008: 4)[23]

It was exactly during this time that Bowen, forced by 'the necessity of paying household bills', started her busy career as a journalist for *Vogue, Mademoiselle* and numerous other journals and magazines (Bowen 2008: 5).[24] But in spite of, or rather because of, this diligence and apparent productivity as a critic, essayist and reviewer, Bowen felt uneasy about the quality of her non-fiction. 'Despite evidence to the contrary', Hepburn notes, 'Bowen persisted in believing that her essays and prefaces were inferior to her fiction. In her view, criticism remained subordinate to creativity.'[25] No doubt, what explained Bowen's pejorative opinion of her journalism – '"job" writing' as she called it somewhere – was its commercial nature (Bowen 1999: 227). Written under immense time-constraints with a view to meeting a particular deadline, these essays and reviews were artistically compromised and, in Bowen's opinion, by no means the qualitative equals of their novelistic siblings. This means that for Bowen the tension between artistic distinction and commercial success remained in some ways irresolvable and could be negotiated only by conceptually separating writing that was meant to satisfy the need for the one or the other. Because she considered her non-fiction pieces predominantly as money-spinners, these outputs had to be segregated from her novelistic works whose literary value she elevated and relentlessly promoted.

How much and how intensely Bowen thought about qualitative differences in her own and in other people's published work is evidenced by the frequency with which she returned to the topic in her critical writing from the mid-1930s onwards. In an essay from 1936, for instance, she accused the contemporary novel of 'mawkishness'. 'Middle-class repugnance to an essential subject', she stated in this essay, limits the scope of and 'must exercise the strongest possible censorship over the artist' who 'remains the pensioner of middle-class taste' (Bowen 2008: 308). The main problem with contemporary writing for Bowen, that is, is a novelist's desire to respond too explicitly to the demands of a (middlebrow) reading public with limited interests.[26] The outcome, Bowen proposed, is 'timidness' and a 're-translation of *clichés*' in modern fiction. 'It is not that subjects do not exist', she claimed, 'but that writers are not empowered to tackle them' (Bowen 2008: 309). And according to Bowen, the reason for this responsiveness to readers' questionable tastes that creatively restricts many contemporary writers is the hope for commercial success. As she stated in a letter to Graham Greene in 1948, writers who have published two or three books and who have thus moved beyond the formative years of their career, 'divide off into those who, honestly planning to make money, have reason to think themselves, now, on to something good, and those who, now, find themselves ridden by an impersonal obsession on the subject of writing for its own sake' (Bowen 1999: 227). Although she acknowledged that both authorial types 'have to make money . . . to pay their own and their families' way through life' (Bowen 1999: 227), Bowen clearly assigned them different motivations for artistic production. Whereas the first considers writing as 'honest work' undertaken 'because one must have money', the other regards it as a 'creative' pursuit that generates 'a pleasure elsewhere equalled only in love' (Bowen 1999: 227, 228). Given the persistence with which she was thinking about such topics as creativity and artistic labour, it is hardly surprising that Bowen would, two years later, write an essay that categorically distinguished between an 'inventive writer', whose ideas 'have been taken from stock', and an 'imaginative writer', whose work 'causes a long, reflective halt in the reader's faculties' – an essay, in other words, that identified creative interests and economic needs once more as contemporary authors' conflicting motivations (Bowen 1952b: 152).[27]

No doubt, Bowen would have insisted on being described as an imaginative, creative novelist whose work, she proposed, 'demands to be reread, to be brooded over, to be ingested, to be lived with and *in*' (Bowen 1952b: 153). 'Writing', she explained in an interview from 1959, 'appealed to me as a way of doing something that hadn't ever been done before, because nobody but me could write the particular thing that I would write' (Bowen 2010: 329). According to its author, this singularity of vision and purpose permeated her novelistic work, and it was for this reason that Bowen never failed to emphasise the artistic considerations that went into the production of her carefully crafted fiction. 'I am a great rewriter', she stated in a biographical sketch from 1956, 'each page represents from two to ten discarded drafts'. In the same piece, she also confirmed that it was some of her 'longer short stories, such as 'Summer Night, The Disinherited, The Happy Autumn Fields' that have 'nearly completely satisfied' her artistically while *The House in Paris* and *The Heat of the Day* were singled out as those of her novels that have given her 'the most pleasure' or are considered her 'best . . . so far' (JC106/8). Importantly, only in the case of her prose fiction (novels or 'longer short stories') is the question of literary merit given any consideration. Only these creative and imaginative works, we can assume, are deemed fit to stand the test of Bowen's very high standards for writerly perfection.

It is no wonder, therefore, that her correspondence with her editors and publishers is replete with comments that confirm the exactitude with which Bowen considered every aspect in the production process of her novels. Although she worried, as she stated in a letter to her editor from 18 June 1968, about appearing 'fussy' (JC106/8), she nonetheless took immense care that all her wishes were respected. In particular, she was adamant that cover images adequately reflected the complex interpersonal dynamics she depicted so comprehensively in her novels. In the case of *Eva Trout* (1969), for instance, she rejected a jacket that was designed by the French illustrator Philippe Jullian because it showed two characters 'sitting side-by-side' in a boat. This image, she explained in a letter from 23 September 1968, 'requires correction as to one vital matter' because the characters Eva and Henry '(in the story) were not seated side-by-side in the boat (as P. J. depicts), but at opposite ends of it; psychologically, typical of their weird relationship!' (JC106/8). Interestingly, Bowen had already made the very same point in an earlier letter to her publisher where she noted:

> <u>They were sitting at opposite ends of the boat, facing each other. This is, for various reasons, very important</u>. They always <u>did</u> sit at opposite ends of things – e.g. the long sofa in the vicarage drawingroom. That characterises their whole (peculiar) relationship. (JC106/8)

The repetitive appeal for correction together with the underlined passages in the earlier letter thereby convey Bowen's determination to resolve what she considered a very obvious misrepresentation of her intentions. As she saw it, an accurate depiction of her characters on the book cover was essential because 'a jacket portrait', she explained in another letter dated 19 May 1968, 'pins the physical personality of a character down, indelibly, where the reader is concerned' (JC106/8). If nothing else, previous remarks about *To the North* have shown that the focus on interpersonal relationships was an essential aspect of Bowen's writerly agenda. It is far from surprising, therefore, that this author conscientiously monitored the design of those jackets that aimed to pictorially represent the nature of those intersubjective relations.[28] As a novelist who wanted to be seen as an 'imaginative writer' of distinctive novels that did not seek, like the literary materials produced by 'inventive' authors, the economic rewards synonymous with commercial publishing, Bowen understandably demanded from publishers and editorial production teams the same attention to detail she herself devoted to her novelistic work. Her authorial interventions into the production process of her books therefore express more than fastidiousness. Rather, they show that in the years after the Second World War when she 'was widely recognised as an established and major author' (Glendinning

1978: 214), Bowen's self-image as a novelist continued to hinge on a writing philosophy that saw her own work in essential opposition to a market that relied on the quick and above all cheap production of literary ephemera.

In fact, nowhere does Bowen's self-conception as an artist dedicated to creative pursuits in novel writing come to the fore more prominently than in her resistance to tolerate editorial interventions. Many critics before me have commented on the idiosyncrasy of her novelistic style that openly disregarded syntactical, lexical and semantic conventions.[29] But what her business correspondence also reveals is the obvious apprehension with which Bowen guarded the formal eccentricity of her prose. Daniel Bunting George, a reader at Jonathan Cape was only one person who had to deal with and respond to her protectionist approach once this firm began publishing Bowen's work after the Second World War. A letter from 2 June 1948 about the editing of *The Heat of the Day*, written at a time when Bowen was busy churning out texts for commercial profit, shows in no uncertain terms that this novel had become an opportunity for the author to present herself as the producer of exclusive, high-quality prose that 'demands to be reread, to be brooded over, to be ingested, to be lived with and *in*':

> What I am, in the main, sticking to my guns about, are various word orders which you query. I cannot, myself, bear <u>fanciful</u> arrangements of words in sentences. But, in this novel, many sentences in which the order is queer are deliberate, because the sentences won't (as I see it) carry the exact meaning, or – still more important – make the exact psychological impact that I desire in any other way. E.g., 'This tarnished open air theatre in which no plays had been acted for some time . . .'. You suggest 'in which for some time no plays had been acted . . .'. But <u>I</u> want the psychological stress to fall on 'time', not on 'acted'; so therefore I like to give 'time' the more <u>sounding</u> position of the two. . . . The same applies to 'Nothing more now than suffering the music he sat on tensely . . .'. If I reversed this to 'He sat on tensely, nothing more now than suffering the music', something I wish from the effect (impact) of the sentence would be lost. . . . I'd rather keep the jars, 'jingles' and awkwardnesses – e.g. 'seemed unseemly', 'felt to falter'. They do to my mind express something. In some cases I <u>want</u> the rhythm to jerk or jar – to an extent, even, which may displease

the reader. . . . So, all these things I'm sticking to, I'm sticking to very much <u>at</u> my own risk. If I'm either jumped on or ridiculed by the critics because of them, I shall remember (as you and William will be too nice to remind me) that I <u>was</u> warned. (EB2/10/4)

At a time when economic necessities demanded the production and publication of short, journalistic pieces that did not live up to her high artistic standards, Bowen remained committed to presenting the novel she was currently writing as a work of art that was untainted by financial concerns – even at the price of having to accept responsibility for its potential 'failure'. In this, as in similar cases, it seems as if Bowen could not be prevailed upon to make any compromises with the public taste that editors were asking her to consider when suggesting stylistic changes. Even if Bowen had become a 'celebrity writer' by the 1940s who 'fashioned herself', as Hepburn has suggested, 'according to the dictates of commercial publishing' (DiBattista and Wittman 2014: 98), letters such as the one above illustrate how carefully she tried to safeguard her reputation as highbrow novelist whose work demanded minute attention and repeated perusal – that these were texts that hoped to challenge rather than entertain, texts, in fact, that were written for a readership with a similarly well-developed sense for taste as that of the author. She might have actively assisted publishers in advancing her career, in other words, but Bowen had nonetheless found an extremely successful strategy to make it clear to her editors (and to herself) that literary stardom and her professional commitments as a journalist were not to compromise her artistic integrity.

In practice, it is of course most unlikely that Bowen's writing can be neatly divided into commercially lucrative and artistically valuable prose. If her reputation as an accomplished prose writer allowed her to work as a remunerated journalist and critic, this type of writing also cemented her public profile as a novelist and helped to advertise, and sell, the fiction she was writing thereafter. In terms of professional image generation, these two modes of writing, fiction and non-fiction, were obviously interdependent and mutually responsive. However, my intention in the previous paragraphs was not to argue for or against Bowen's construction of her authorial persona and her self-conception as a writer of highbrow fiction. Rather, I wanted to illustrate this author's unease about the growing market value of her work. While she shared with other women novelists of her generation a fascinated interest in fashion and commodity culture, Bowen also felt apprehensive about becoming a commodity herself. Writing for profit might have become a necessity with the onset of the Second World War. It had to be done to meet various financial commitments, and Bowen approached this task with diligence and professionalism. At the same time, however, she became a determined guardian of the Bowenesque style and resisted attempts made by publishers and editors to make her novels more formally and stylistically conventional. Insisting in this manner on the 'awkwardnesses' of her novelistic prose was therefore, like the demand for accuracy in pictorial representations of her novelistic character sketches, an important strategy adopted by Bowen to artistically upgrade her fiction and prevent its absorption into a canon of mass-produced work that was 'written to formula'. Only in this manner, by pursuing these strategies, could she overlook her complex alliances with a literary marketplace that favoured the production of prose texts that were recognisable, consumable and extremely disposable.

Fashion, this chapter has shown, was a central and ongoing concern for Bowen in that it influenced the way in which she depicted her literary characters' complexly structured sartorial connections. But fashion also mattered to Bowen because it affected her self-image as a novelist who aimed to preserve a semblance of artistic autonomy at a time when publishers fashioned celebrity authorship and when many critics and writers such as Wharton deplored the standardisation of writing practices as well as the deterioration of artistic standards. Bowen, as her literary criticism suggests, was extremely responsive to such pessimistic debates about deteriorating values in writing and refused to consider those composition modes considered safe and acceptable by her editors at Jonathan Cape – mainly because she feared that such concessions might turn her into one of those 'pensioner[s] of middle-class taste' already crowding the literary marketplace. She nonetheless worked with the very same editors and publishers and complied with publicity campaigns designed to raise her public profile as a novelist of international renown.[30] Her case thus illustrates the complex situation of a woman writer who came to maturity in the 1930s and who tried very hard to consolidate commercial success with intellectual ambitions. A type of literary criticism distrustful of the ideological underpinnings of the mid-century culture industry was thereby the most apparent result of Bowen's extensive considerations of the contemporary literary field and of her own position within it. This critique of commodity literature, however, was generated but also compromised by Bowen's occasional compliance with modern-day publishing practices, and the directness with which she sometimes censored the mass production of literary commodities might confirm rather than obscure her collaborations with a literary market that threatened to erode the artistic autonomy she so fervently defended.

In all of these deliberations of the contemporary literary field, modernism remained, as previous remarks have shown, an important provider of artistic imperatives for Bowen. Although she might have assisted in condemning modernism, to use Bourdieu's phrase once again, 'to fall into the past and to become *classic* or *outdated*' by challenging its focus on interiority with a considerate return to realist conventions, she nonetheless confirmed the ongoing relevance of some of its paradigmatic suggestions in the process of updating and revising them. By the same token, the modernist insistence on clearly identifiable authorial signatures provided her with an artistic model to emulate when commercial success threatened to affect her self-understanding as the writer of highbrow prose. In this manner, Bowen emerges as an important disseminator of modernist concerns who publicised its intellectual suggestions and who assisted in turning into cultural commodities works of art whose radical impetus for novelty and innovation had initially, but perhaps somewhat misleadingly, signalled incompatibility with the economic demands of the market. As modernism aged and its main proponents were in the process of being replaced by younger writers such as Bowen, the economic purchase of their work very significantly increased. Perceived as less radical but also as more culturally influential, some modernists of the later interwar years were beginning to form complex alliances with an emerging culture industry that hoped to capitalise on their status as cultural icons. Woolf, as the next chapter will show, was one of these modernist authors who began to reconsider her relationship with commercial publishing practices in the second half of her career when she realised that the historical realities of the 1930s urgently required the widespread dissemination of her feminist and anti-fascist propositions.

Notes

1. As noted already in this study's introduction, Celia Marshik's *At the Mercy of their Clothes: Modernism, the Middlebrow, and British Garment Culture* has made a very similar point about the representation of sartorial ensembles in interwar British fiction. But as I have already explained, my reading of Bowen parts company with her interpretation of garments in interwar fiction by showing that Bowen believed in the conjunctive capacities of sartorial items.
2. As scholars such as Maud Ellmann and Neil Corcoran have noted, Bowen's writing style, which shows influences of both realist and modernist literary techniques, is difficult to place on existing critical maps (Ellmann 2004: 5; Corcoran 2004: 4). Generically fluid, her novels and short stories include aspects of the Gothic romance, the ghost story, the spy thriller, the comedy of manners, classic realism and the Anglo-Irish Big House novel. As its author vehemently claimed in her unfinished autobiographical sketch 'Pictures and Conversations', 'Bowen terrain cannot be demarcated on any existing map; it is unspecific' (Bowen 1975: 35). This conceptual elasticity of Bowen's writing is one reason why scholars continue to claim her fiction for incorporation in different critical fields. Even though she chose Ireland as a setting only for a marginal part of her fiction, the surfacing of Irish Studies as an academic subject was nonetheless instrumental in putting Bowen onto the critical map in the 1980s and 1990s. Critics such as Vera Kreilkamp have rightly claimed that the 'tensions and discordances of her Anglo-Irish experience' are central to understanding Bowen's art (Kreilkamp 1998: 143).
3. In fact, *To the North* marks the beginning of Bowen's experimentation with literary character – one that she fully accomplished, according to Spencer Curtis Brown, with the writing of *The Little Girls* in 1964: 'In *The Little Girls*, she for the first time deliberately tried, as she said when discussing with me the writing of it to present characters entirely from the outside. She determined never to tell the reader what her characters were thinking or feeling' (Bowen 1975: xxxviii). Even if this challenge to write a book externally was only mastered as late as 1964, I want to suggest that traces of this new form of character development were apparent as early as 1932 when she published *To the North*.
4. It needs to be acknowledged at this point that critics such as Douglas Mao have recently questioned the problematic theory that modernism maintained a strained relationship with materiality and with material culture. When stating that modernist writers aimed to 'show how the discrete object . . . could exert a powerful hold on the imagination at a

time when questions about the meaning of existence seemed unusually pressing' (1998: 17), Mao illustrates modernism's evident fascination with the material organisation of the modern world.
5. In this essay, originally published as a new preface for her short story collection, *Ann Lee's*, Bowen speaks candidly about her 'assault on magazine editors' (1952b: 90) – an activity that produced (in spite of two already published short story collections to her name) by and large only unsatisfactory results.
6. In an essay from 1949, Bowen spoke about inanimate objects in a manner that anticipates aspects of Bill Brown's 'thing theory': 'Don't just use a chair, for instance, as a "property" for the action of a story, *or* as a four-legged thing seen through subjective distortions', Bowen argues here, 'no, every time you write the word "chair" force yourself to break off and contemplate the chair-ness of a chair' (Bowen 2017: 4).
7. Bowen's lover, Charles Ritchie, also felt that her unorthodox taste in jewellery demanded commentary: 'E was wearing a necklace and bracelet of gold and red of the kind of glass that Christmas tree decorations are made of . . .'. (Glendinning 2008: 28). Bowen herself addressed the constant pressure of dressing adequately in the 1956 broadcast 'On Not Rising to the Occasion': 'When I was fourteen, fifteen, the dress-problem raised its ugly head. It was necessary to look nice, as well as be nice. Still more, it was necessary to look "suitable." But, my heavens, suitable to what? . . . Fashion, now so kind to that age-group, took no account of us. So trial-and-error it was, for me. Outcome: error' (Bowen 2010: 110).
8. Not for nothing is '[m]ove dangerously' the slogan of the protagonist's travel agency, which aims to distinguish itself from its competitor Cook's (Bowen 2006: 25).
9. As Allan Hepburn suggests, for this author novels 'cannot but take up the dilemmas of human interaction in all their diversity. Novels reveal the complexity of human relations, not as a transcription of contemporary life but as an artistic pattern.' Bowen, he continues, 'therefore insists on the value of the novel as a social force: the interaction among characters brings them into being' (Bowen 2017: xxiv–xxv).
10. Needless to say, clothes also feature prominently in other Bowen novels. However, in many cases – such as *The Last September*, where 'crisp white skirts and transparent blouses clotted with white flowers' denote girlish innocence and sexual inexperience – sartorial objects often obtain a more straightforward symbolic function to represent characters' states of mind (Bowen 1952a: 3). In its deployment of sartorial markers, *To the North*, due to its explicit urban setting, differs significantly from, for instance, Bowen's 'Big House' fiction.

11. 'Es ist härter geworden und damit sind auch die Beziehungen des Menschen zu den Gegenständen seines täglichen Gebrauchs jenes oft so gemüthvollen und romantischen Zaubers entkleidet, der in die Zimmer unserer Eltern trotz aller ästhetischen Versündigungen doch jene Wärme hineintrug, die heute den glänzenden Salons der Enkel ... fehlt' [my translation]. Bowen practically parrots Sombart's comments on the temporary nature of human associations in a 1952 *Vogue* essay, 'The Art of Respecting Boundaries': 'Our parents and grandparents, possibly, were either less eager than we are or less impulsive. They gave more time, all time, to getting to know their friends; they were reticent or more adroitly guarded; and intimacies, such as there used to be, were rarer, more temperate – were they perhaps more lasting?' (Bowen 2008: 398).

12. In a memoir of her friend, the American publisher Alfred A. Knopf, Bowen recorded that she was, during their first encounter, similarly arrested by his tie: 'Circling the room, I succeeded in getting my back to the windows, put on my spectacles (I am near-sighted) and again looked round, more worried if less blinded. There seemed to be several women in their thirties (my then age) any one of whom might well have been I. It struck me that Alfred might be in the same quandary as myself: possibly he might have become bored by the puzzle and gone home? Or, had something gone wrong, had he not come? He could not possibly be anyone I had looked at so far. Then my eye lit on a tie, some distance away. The sun glinted on it. The tie was not so much magenta as the dark-bright purple-crimson of a petunia, and it was worn with a shirt of a light green, just too blue to be almond, just not blue enough to be verdigris. Tie and shirt were at some height from the ground; their wearer stood leaning in a doorway or archway, a vantage-point some way away from the throng. He looked almost sleepy. With an onlooker's great calmness, one might say indolence, he was considering everybody, including me. "I wondered how we should find each other," I said, as we shook hands' (Bowen 2010: 222).

13. This expression is Willa Cather's. In her essay 'The Novel Démeublé' (1922), she accused contemporary novelists of overcrowding their fiction with descriptive details rather than focusing on the development of their literary characters (Cather 1988: 43).

14. A typescript marked 'alternative version' in the Elizabeth Bowen Collection in the Harry Ransom Center illustrates that Bowen, at some point, wanted to make more explicit this link between the sartorial and the social. First of all, the optional ending of the chapter emphasises sexual jealousy on Robert's part when he asks Stella overtly not to '"two-time with Harrison, will you?"' Moreover, the two lovers

discuss their relatives and relations in more detail. Accordingly, Stella provides a reason for her request to meet Robert's family: '"After all, you've met Roderick [Stella's son] not only once but often – in fact, I should be miserable if you hadn't."' Likewise, Robert volunteers more personal information: '"Oh, so should I; but we both know perfectly well that my mother and Ernestine aren't to me anything like what Roderick is to you. He is part of you; they're my origin – if you like".' Finally, the 'khaki tie' features more prominently as a focal point in the scene. Stella, in an exchange that references a famous case of mistaken affection, even wonders if it could function as keepsake: '"Yes," she said, looking straight at the tie, "this will have to go. To feel I should like to keep it is idiotic." "Like Harriet Smith and Mr Elton's toe-nails?" "No, dear; it was sticking-plaster she kept"' (EB1/5/2).

15. The German original reads: 'Gleichförmige Berufsverhältnisse und Kollektivverträge bedingen den Zuschnitt der Existenz, die überdies, wie sich zeigen wird, dem uniformierenden Einfluß gewaltiger ideologischer Mächte untersteht. Alle diese Zwangsläufigkeiten haben unstreitig zur Heraufkunft gewisser Normaltypen von Verkäuferinnen, Konfektionären, Stenotypistinnen usw. geführt, die in den Magazinen und den Kinos dargestellt und zugleich gezüchtet werden. Sie sind ins Allgemeinbewußtsein eingetreten, das sich nach ihnen sein Gesamtbild von der neuen Angestelltenschicht formt' (Kracauer 1971: 65).

16. It should be noted again that Bowen was, in spite of her critical inspection of fashion's tendency to standardise appearance, extremely entranced by clothes and other fashionable items. Indeed, her correspondence with Blanche W. Knopf and Charles Ritchie after the Second World War shows how delighted she was whenever they sent her clothes or cosmetics (Glendinning 2008: 69, 74–5). In an unpublished letter to Blanche from 26 October 1947, Bowen's pleasure about the arrival of new shoes becomes particularly apparent: 'Dear Blanche, I was in the middle of a more than belated letter to you when I got your cable – I'm now beginning again, as I feel so <u>awfully</u> bad you didn't know the shoes had arrived. Alan said he had sent off a line to you saying they'd come – <u>I</u> was then here, in Ireland. He was nearly as thrilled as I was: you know how he loves shoes! (short, I think, of being a fêtichist [sic]). I got back to London for a few days early this month, fitted them on and they are <u>perfect</u> – as easy to wear as they are on the eye. I can't tell you what they will do for my morale, this coming depressing London weather, or how angelically thoughtful I think it was of you to send them – not least to <u>find</u> them, for I know that elegant shoes in my outsize are far and few' (AK/3/685/14).

17. Even the capricious Cecilia is not immune to the seductive allure of the personal – as long as it speaks to her and lets her speak through sartorial referents. Having finally decided to tie the knot with Julian, she faces the task of befriending Pauline, Julian's teenage niece. Confronted with the girl one evening during one of Lady Waters's tedious country outings, Cecilia, after a number of awkward attempts to build rapport, finally offers to assist Pauline in getting dressed: '"Does your dress do up at the back?"' she wants to know before suggesting: '"Perhaps I could hook it"' (Bowen 2006: 201). Although Pauline rejects the well-meant offer, Cecilia's concern for Pauline's dress and hair produces a 'burst of confidence' (201) in the young girl. Bowen's novel leaves no one in doubt that Pauline and Cecilia have formed a bond, especially since Pauline recalls the scene for the benefit of her uncle Julian: '"A girl of my age might easily feel *de trop*"', she says, '"but they are all determined to make me feel quite at home. Mrs. Summers came in last night and offered to hook my dress, but it hooks at the side"' (210). Clothes consolidate, once more, a personal connection.
18. This is a point forcefully made by Tyrus Miller who argues that 'late modernist writing appears a distinctly self-conscious manifestation of the aging and decline of modernism, in both institutional and ideological dimensions' while it also 'anticipates future developments, so that without forcing, it might easily fit into a narrative of emergent post-modernism' (1999: 7).
19. It is, of course, difficult to establish the exact moment when a particular writer can be said to have become canonised. For the present purpose, I shall use the example of the publication of the Uniform Edition of Woolf and Bowen's work as a starting point for the difficult business of putting a date on an author's inclusion into the literary establishment. While the Hogarth Press began publishing the first titles of a Uniform Edition of Woolf's work in 1929 (HPA MS2750/A/28), it was roughly twenty years later, in 1948, that the first two titles in the Collected Edition of Bowen's work were published by Jonathan Cape (JC A6/2/1).
20. A key event in the consolidation of high modernism as accepted literary movement and practice was certainly Judge Woolsey's decision to remove the ban on *Ulysses* in 1933 (Potter 2013: 133–5).
21. As already noted in this study's introduction, Bowen wrote numerous book reviews and articles on modernist authors and their work (Bowen 2008: 239–47, 272–83, 284–7; Bowen 1952b: 53–74, 155–8; Bowen 1950: 78–82).
22. Victor Gollancz, who set up his publishing firm in 1927, was, Beverly Schneller acknowledges, 'widely recognized as an advertiser nonpareil, whose book jackets and advertising displays employed subtle claims about

the books he was selling. Words such as "Best Ever," "Sensational," or "Spellbinding" were intertwined with excerpted comments from reviewers printed in different typefaces to attract the browsers. . . . The Gollancz jacket', she continues, 'was recognized by book designers as a typographical masterwork, its drama enhanced by the use of grey or yellow as the background colour.' All this and Gollancz's equally well-known demand for 'huge pressruns, often for unknown authors' first books', made him a quintessentially modern, adventurous entrepreneur who was able to capitalise on new developments in book publishing (Rose and Anderson 1991: 126–32). Constable, Sondra Miley Cooney states, was a firm distinguished by 'a basically conservative and traditional publishing philosophy' (Rose and Anderson 1991: 66–70). Bowen stayed with Gollancz until 1945 when her collection of short stories, *The Demon Lover*, was published by Jonathan Cape.

23. Even if I am in danger of pointing out the obvious, I want to elaborate on Hepburn's point about the trajectory of Bowen's novelistic career. Looking at the publication dates of her novels, it becomes apparent that her productivity in the 1930s far exceeded that of later years. Her first novel, *The Hotel* (1927), was followed by *The Last September* (1929), *Friends and Relations* (1931), *To the North* (1932), *The House in Paris* (1934) and *The Death of the Heart* (1938). Only four more Bowen novels would be published after the Second World War: *The Heat of the Day* (1948), *A World of Love* (1955), *The Little Girls* (1964) and *Eva Trout* (1969). If Bowen was able to devote her energy to writing novels in the interwar period, her changed economic conditions during and after the Second World War forced her to turn to more profitable forms of writing.

24. Bowen's contributions to *Vogue* in the 1940s and 1950s included such diverse articles as a 1948 evaluation of 'Prague and the Crisis', a reflection of post-war Christmas rituals in the 1950 'The Light in the Dark' or the 1946 essay 'Ireland Makes Irish' on Irish castles and country houses (Bowen 2008: 37–40, 81–5, 155–61).

25. To illustrate this point further, Hepburn quotes the following passage from one of Bowen's unpublished autobiographical notes: 'I do not really consider myself a critic – I do not think, really, that a novelist *should* be a critic; but, by some sort of irresistible force, criticism seems to come almost every novelist's way. I write, at intervals, for the *New Statesman*, the *Listener*, *Vogue*, *Harper's Bazaar*; and do request articles, from time to time, for papers too diverse to enumerate' (Bowen 2008: 5).

26. 'There are startling few things that the public cares to hear about', Bowen noted in her essay 'What We Need in Writing'. 'Sex, or love, is a popular

subject', she continued, 'because self-love and the private imagination luxuriate around it. Adventure, being fantasy, is safe ground', she went on to assert before concluding that '[c]hildren, animals and the upper classes appeal to tenderness and to curiosity' (Bowen 2008: 307).

27. Another essay in the same collection, written and published in 1953, similarly distinguished between the 'imaginatively creative' and the 'merely cerebrally inventive' writer (Bowen 1952b: 206).

28. The case of *Eva Trout*'s jacket is thereby by no means an isolated one. In a letter from 11 September 1948, Bowen complimented George Wren Howard at Jonathan Cape on the chosen design for the cover of *The House of Paris*. Here, she noted that 'the whole effect is just as envisaged by me' before adding 'but I feel that the knickerbockers should be shorter, as I am almost sure I speak somewhere of Leopold as "examining his bare knees"' (JC A6/2/1). In 1963, shortly before publishing *The Little Girls*, Wren Howard is once more provided with 'some afterthoughts on the jacket drawing', that indicated Bowen's concern 'about the artist being so widely "out" where the period is concerned. Sartorially', Bowen explained in a letter dated 24 July 1963, 'these 3 little girls' on the proposed cover image, 'might be 3 of the young Miss Marches of Little Women'. This, Bowen continued, 'is so misleading as to the nature of my book that it could well set The Little Girls off on the wrong foot. "Ah another book about a Victorian childhood," anyone might pardonably think' (JC21/1 836485-1001).

29. Susan Osborn provides a vivid description of Bowen's eccentric style that is representative of this particular type of criticism: 'With willful disregard for the reader, she often inserts ugly sounding words into otherwise mellifluous sentences when more euphonious ones would do just as well if not better; her syntax is often anfractuous and strained; her images are frequently bizarre, unexpectedly macabre in places, even nonsensical; and her punctuation is so often ungoverned that one wonders, at times, if the errors were intended or the result of negligent proofreading' (2009: 38).

30. Jonathan Cape's decision to begin publishing a Collected Edition of her works was one such marketing campaign designed to capitalise on but also further raise Bowen's profile as an internationally renowned writer. Another one was Blanche W. Knopf's attempt to get her nominated for the Nobel Prize in Literature in 1963. Blanche's attempts are documented in various letters now held at the Harry Ransom Center at Austin (AK3/686/1).

Chapter 5

Uniforms and Uniformity: Virginia Woolf

On Monday, 9 October 1936 Sir Oswald Mosley, founder of the British Union of Fascists (BUF), attended a luncheon organised by a group of local businessmen at the Grand Hotel in Birmingham. According to the Report of the Birmingham City Police Investigation Department, Sir Oswald rose to his feet after the meal to address the assembled crowd. This time, he said, it was 'not his intention to give a generalised speech on such subjects as foreign affairs or the broad policy of the British Union of Fascists'. Instead, the BUF leader used the occasion to discuss new government legislation passed earlier in the same year: the Public Order Act that aimed to curb the spread of extremist political parties and movements by banning the public wearing of uniforms during rallies and meetings. 'As usual', Sir Oswald contended confidently in response to this governmental attempt to dissolve his party, 'our opponents were two years too late with their legislation.' In his view, 'the banning of the blackshirts at this stage would not make the slightest difference to the organisation' because a 'flame had been lit which would not be quenched by such legislation. . . . The time to have attacked the blackshirt uniform', he concluded, 'was two years ago, but now the uniform had achieved its object' (KV2/884). If Mosley was to be believed, the rise of the fascist world order could, in 1936, no longer be prevented. The black uniform had played its part in organising the movement in its infancy but had become obsolete precisely at the time when the BUF had turned into a recognisable feature of Britain's political landscape.

Although its expendability was publicly announced by the BUF leader in 1936, it must be said that the blackshirt uniform had, during its short history as the party's official garb, obtained a significant reputation. While the party's official publications aped Mosley in stressing the uniform's significance in attempts to unite a disparate party base,[1] it had also become synonymous – in the public imagination – with scenes of organised violence and brutal brawls, finding the most extreme expression in the aftermath of the notorious Olympia rally in 1934.[2] The ban of the black uniform, it was hoped by many, would put an end to such politically motivated mass scuffles and riots. More than that, it might assist in dispersing an extremist movement that relied to no small extent on the group spirit generated by a set of sartorial signifiers with decidedly militaristic features. If nothing else, it might be argued, the Public Order Act of 1936 responded to a widespread fear about the misuse to which uniforms and other items of clothing could be put. Appropriated to this effect by political extremists, clothes could be utilised to control, dominate and manipulate individuals for the explicit purpose of overthrowing democratic institutions. As the visual manifestation of the fascist threat in Britain, the blackshirt uniform became, in the mid-1930s, the site of a protracted public debate about political stability. For the time being, its prohibition in 1936 was the logical conclusion to this debate.

The controversy surrounding the BUF and its radical mobilisation of sartorial markers in the 1930s is the historical background relevant for the concluding chapter of *Modernism, Fashion and Interwar Women Writers* that deals with Virginia Woolf and her views not just on uniforms but also on uniformity as a cultural phenomenon propelled by modern fashion. If Wharton had previously worried about too much standardisation in texts and textiles, Woolf's later works show her concerns about the misuse to which clothes could be put by political extremists who organised mass spectacles that threatened to eradicate the individuality of conglomerated subjects. In the years during which Mosley's party members paraded the streets of Britain in their blackshirts, Woolf, who was in the process of writing *The Years* (1937) and *Three Guineas* (1938), increasingly turned her attention, I argue in this chapter, to the question of how clothes and other sartorial objects constructed identity and coordinated individuals in social settings and configurations. In particular, she investigated how a trend towards uniformity in dress affected the construction of female identity at a time when uniforms became increasingly prominent aspects of the visual landscape. What were the sartorial alternatives available to women who hoped to challenge this synchronisation of individuality that had become an essential feature of modern mass politics in general and of fascist dictatorships in particular? Were there any such alternatives? My chapter shows that Woolf was thinking extensively about these questions while she was clipping newspaper articles in preparation for writing *Three Guineas* and *The Years*.

Her obvious suspicion of a uniform dress culture was thereby matched by a corresponding rejection of sartorial conspicuousness as uniformity's conceptual antithesis. As Woolf suggested in *Three Guineas*, too much insistence on sartorial conspicuousness could reinforce the hierarchical modes of thinking found in patriarchal institutions that, for her, provided fertile ground for the growth of fascist mentalities. In the desire to unsettle the contemporary drift towards a uniform dress culture – a desire that was tantamount to challenging an associated political extremism – this mode of dress would have to be carefully employed by women lest they were prepared to confirm the sartorial politics on which the organisation of much of patriarchal thought relied. To be clear, Woolf certainly saw political potential in extravagant dress – but only if adopted temporarily and in a self-conscious, critical way since a permanent appropriation of sartorial distinctiveness was too closely aligned for her with the highly decorated regalia that featured prominently in contemporary male-dominated institutional society. And for women, the wearing of conspicuous dress had one further disadvantage: as numerous passages from *The Years* suggest, Woolf believed that it unfavourably affected community building and that it prevented the formation of emotional attachments among women who desire mutually sustaining social relationships. What I propose in the following pages, therefore, is that the critical focus on uniformity reveals Woolf's awareness of the political use to which fashion can be put. For Woolf, in other words, clothes always had immense political significance – in such obvious contexts as fascist rallies but also in the more complexly structured lived experiences of women who became – through their compliance with, or resistance to, accepted sartorial practices of the 1930s – firmly enmeshed in the socio-political structures of this politically unstable decade.

However, even if Woolf was frequently critical of uniformity in a manner reminiscent of Wharton, it is interesting to note that she was also extremely aware of and willing to exploit her own complicity in a culture industry that produced and favoured easily recognisable forms and looks. In concentrating on the second phase of Woolf's professional life as a writer and publisher when her name began to be confirmed as an established brand, my chapter turns, in its final pages, to an analysis of her possible reasons and motivations for a surprising acceptance of a certain type of uniformity. As we shall see, the appearance of her work in the Hogarth Uniform Edition signalled Woolf's compromise with dominant market conditions whose potential exploitation by patriarchal and totalitarian impulses could only be addressed, Woolf would have realised, if she made strategic use of the position that this partial affiliation with uniformity afforded. It would be wrong, therefore, to associate Woolf's thinking with an absolute resistance to uniformity in the manner promoted by Wharton. Rather, I shall show, by discussing Woolf's position as a publisher and a bestselling author, that the political conditions of the 1930s made her receptive to embracing particular types of uniformity in the form of uniform-looking publications. While she ruminated on fashion's ability to both abolish and generate diversity, Woolf noted, I shall argue, that the best strategy for publicising her diagnostic statements about modern cultural politics was to capitalise on some of the opportunities that commercial publishing had to offer. As such, this chapter can function as an important corrective to critical views expressed, among others, by scholars such as Patrick Collier who have argued that Woolf saw 'the literary marketplace – which exists in the intertwined institutional context of the press and publishers and the social context of literary professionalism – as *potential* obstacles to healthy relations between artists and the public' (2006: 104). By the 1930s, both Woolf the novelist and the publisher had come to some kind of agreement with aspects of interwar mass culture and the standardised productions associated with modern fashion. Although she certainly remained suspicious of its potential misuses and although she continued to compose critical and at times caustic statements on literary productivity in the age of mass publishing, Woolf, I want to suggest, also knew that a tactical compromise with modern fashion as the initiator of uniform looks for bodies and books was essential in her attempt to reach her readers.

In what follows, I therefore read Woolf's support of the Uniform Edition of her works – a turn to more commercial publishing practices – not simply as a straightforward capitulation to the commercial pressures of an aggressive literary marketplace. Instead, I propose that her decision was strategic and that it was taken to further disseminate her critique of socio-political formations that threatened to erase difference and convert individuals to a mass standard through collectivising. As the 1930s drew to an ominous close, Woolf thought incessantly about the political alternatives to patriarchal democracies and its most radicalised extremity, fascism. Uniforms and uniformity, I shall argue in the following pages, are extremely useful focalisers for analysing her political vision that developed and matured in response to the rise of totalitarian politics in the interwar period. Even more so than in previous chapters, we will see how intimately clothes and fashion were related to the political thinking of an interwar woman writer. As Woolf noted in so many places in her writing, no choice of dress or outfit is ever simple. It always carried with it the immense weight of complex political meanings.

'The connection between dress and war': tailoring the fascist subject

In spite of her well-documented 'clothes fear' (Woolf 1983: 302), Woolf enjoyed spending money on new dresses and she warmly welcomed the advice of her dressmaker, Ronald Murray (Woolf 1983: 307) on all matters sartorial. It was also not beneath her to pass on 'smart gossip' about couturiers and their high society clients. In 1933, for instance, she imparts information about 'the man milliner' Charles James who had started dressing Mary Hutchinson in clothes that were 'symmetrical, diabolical and geometrically perfect. So geometrical is Charlie James', she told Vita Sackville-West in a letter, 'that if a stitch is crooked . . . the whole dress is torn to shreds' (Woolf 1979b: 157–8).[3] All this demonstrates Woolf's awareness and appreciation of fashion and clothes even before she began her determined analysis of sartorial markers in patriarchal and fascist configurations. However, her critical observations of uniforms and uniform modes of dressing began to make more regular appearances in her writing and she turned her critical attention to examining fashion's social causalities more systematically precisely at the point when she became aware that fascist identity politics had started to pose a new and so far unmatched threat to civil liberties.

Woolf, it must be remembered, directly encountered Continental fascism in 1935. In that year, the Woolfs toured Central and Southern Europe and their itinerary included a three-day drive through Germany, an experience that was apprehensively but also eagerly awaited by Virginia, who records in her diary scenes of mass gatherings – 'ranks of children with red flags' (Woolf 1983: 311) – observed in regions that were now controlled by Hitler's National Socialists.[4] No doubt, the Woolfs' decision to enter Nazi Germany was driven by an interest to see the kind of social and cultural changes put into effect by the new state authorities in charge since 1933. So far, they had only hearsay knowledge of Hitler's impressive oratorical skills and of obedient German crowds, 'the passive heavy slaves' or the 'brown jelly' that offered no 'resistance' to police or governmental orders (Woolf 1983: 304).[5] Once in Germany, the Woolfs encountered banners and signs predictably greeting them with messages such as 'The Jew is our enemy' and 'There is no place for Jews in – ' (Woolf 1983: 311) and they watched, with alarm and consternation, the 'docile hysterical crowd[s]' forming in Nazi Germany (Woolf 1983: 311). Nobody who visited this country could be in any doubt about the fact that the socio-political landscape in Central Europe had changed, and changed for the worse. Disquietingly hiding behind the facade of cheering crowds and friendly looking mass spectacles were the xenophobic, racist principles for which Nazi Germany's 'completely equipped & powerful machine' was beginning to become notorious (Woolf 1983: 304).

Shortly before embarking on this trip, Woolf had already noted in her diary a trend towards increasingly militaristic clothes styles at home. On Sunday, 28 April 1935, Alix Strachey came to dinner and while the conversation circled around war and men's enthusiastic response to military action – topics that would resurface later in *Three Guineas* – Virginia observed almost in passing: 'Alix like a blackshirt, all brown & tie & tailor made' (Woolf 1983: 307). The irony is apparent. While Britain's liberal pacifists (and Freudian devotees) organised themselves in active opposition to totalitarian regimes, they were oblivious, Woolf suggested here, to their own, very obvious, sartorial concessions to fascism's visual aesthetics. Although she might not be aware of it, Alix, with her sleek, austere and masculine attire that is reminiscent of the blackshirt uniform, represents, for Woolf, the standardised look adopted by many British intellectuals during the interwar period. This look of severe chic and sartorial asceticism, as Woolf's 'blackshirt' simile unmistakably shows, might have been 'tailor made' but it was also embraced and aggressively developed to suit the fascist insistence on uniformity that threatened to offset difference and distinctiveness in appearance and character. Given her perceptive observations about corporatist dress codes at home, Woolf could hardly have failed to notice, during her short visit to Nazi Germany, the role played by clothing in structurally organising and unifying individuals under the political banners of the NSDAP.

A few months after returning from Nazi Germany, Woolf once more recorded her growing alarm about the public visibility of fascist propaganda in Britain. In a diary entry from 4 September 1935, she observed: 'Writing chalked up all over the walls. "Don't fight for foreigners. Briton should mind her own business." Then a circle with a symbol in it. Fascist propaganda, L. said. Mosley again active' (Woolf 1983: 337). A very similar passage appears in the 'Present Day' section of *The Years*, which was written at the time during which Woolf had noted her awareness of Mosely's political slogans in her diary.[6] Here, however, the reference to British corporatist movements is brought into more explicit dialogue with propagandistic exploitations of sartorial markers: North Pargiter, recently returned from Africa after long years of exile, accordingly notes a 'chalked' BUF sign 'on a wall' (Woolf 1992c: 270), and he deliberates how organisations such as Mosley's BUF manipulate uniform dress codes in the attempt to mobilise group energies. North, 'to whom ceremonies are suspect' (359), subsequently rejects the 'reverberating megaphones', the 'marching in step after leaders, in herds, groups, societies, caparisoned' while he correctly identifies the 'black shirts, green shirts, red shirts – always posing in the public eye' as effective devices for group identity formation (358). In view of imminent dangers posed by corporatist organisations that propagate 'a world . . . that was all one jelly, one mass' (358–9), North insists on 'begin[ning] inwardly', on emphasising the importance of the individual and so keep 'the emblems and tokens of North Pargiter' (359). Yet while he is thinking about the modulation and the structural organisation of personal identity in political configurations, *The Years* is quick to expose North as indecisive and hesitant. 'But what do I mean, he wonder[s]', unable to clearly formulate 'other sentences' because he cannot grasp 'what's solid, what's true; in my life, in other people's lives' (359). In spite of these obvious shortcomings,[7] however, this character who values individuality and resists uniformity productively illustrates Woolf's thoughts about the relationship between subjectivity and communal life in a time overshadowed by the rise of mass political movements.

The notes and newspaper clippings in the Monks House scrapbooks held at the University of Sussex further illustrate how systematically Woolf collected information on uniform dress codes and practices in preparation for writing *Three Guineas* – the text that is the product of her most sustained thinking about the organisation of patriarchal societies and of corporatist political movements. This material, which includes substantial references to clothes and sartorial protocols, can be divided into two sections and, as subsequent remarks will show, it is in these newspaper clippings that the focus on gender in Woolf's thinking about the political significance of clothes truly comes to the fore. In the first instance, Woolf seemed to have collected facts about 'ceremonial' clothes. Numerous articles discuss dress regulations for the coronation ceremony in 1937. '[P]eers and peeresses attending the Coronation, on May 12 next year', readers are informed in the article 'No Coronets for Peeresses', 'will wear full Coronation robes of their degrees' (MHP B16/2/32). Attendees at George V's funeral on 28 January 1936 at Windsor are similarly reminded in the note 'Dress for Guests at Funeral' that '[f]ull dress, that is full uniform or Court dress, cloaks or great coats [are] to be worn' by men. 'Those not in possession of uniform or Court dress will wear evening dress with white tie and black waistcoat – cloaked.' Women, the columnist continues, are supposed to wear '[m]ourning dress with small hats, veils 18 inches in front and 11/2 yards behind. No decorations will be worn by ladies' (MHP B16/2/1).[8] These and similar articles provide a sense of the regulations strictly organising official events and society congregations in the interwar period in Britain. In all of these cases, sartorial guidelines enforce the correct apparel of those in attendance. However, if uniformity in dress is encouraged (or demanded) for these high-profile occasions, a thematically related article from *The Times* of 9 March

1932 evocatively recalling 'The Chaperonage Age' notes the way in which ceremonial dress can function as a clear marker of distinction for men. 'The balls at Buckingham Palace', the article reminiscences, used to 'bring ... together the whole of Society'. And according to the writer, it was '[t]he uniforms and kilts and Court dresses of the men and their decorations' that 'added immensely to the brilliancy and interest of the scene ... making it easy to identify persons of distinction' (MHP B16/1/29). As Merry M. Pawlowski explains, '[w]hile consciously clipping articles which take up the issue of women's place (and lack thereof) in public space, Woolf was encountering evidence of masculine society as "spectacle"' that values the use of male uniforms as a means to represent distinction (Pawlowski 2003: 35).

In sum total, then, the collected notes on ceremonial dress are supportive of men's interest in sartorial conspicuousness. A second cluster of observations and articles, which relates specifically to women's professed desire for sartorial 'extravagances', conversely shows that Woolf's female contemporaries fared less well when attempting to demonstrate distinction through the strategic use of dress. Noting that women 'differ extravagantly and aboundingly one from the other', one of Woolf's typewritten notes entitled 'Womens [sic] Dress at Ascot' comes to the relatively obvious conclusion that 'women resent being cut to patterns' (MHP B16/3/1). More problematic is a preserved article 'Sex Allurement', which disconcertingly infers: '[i]n matters of dress women often remain children to the end' because a 'reasonable indulgence in dress is needed to counterbalance ... the inferiority complex of women'. Contemporary sartorial politics, Woolf seemed to have wanted to suggest by keeping this article, take for granted but simultaneously condemn women's desire for sartorial displays. In their case, sartorial overindulgences – censored as extravagant, frivolous and economically imprudent – are positively discouraged. 'The law has rightly laid down that the rule of prudence and proportion must be observed', the same article declares. 'A husband is not to be exposed to ruin by the extravagances of a wife, and the feminine instinct for variety and grace of decoration must be curbed to the needed extent' (MHP B16/1/12). Sartorial idiosyncrasies and overindulgences are frowned upon in cases in which women hope to mark their individuality through the use of distinctive clothing. To all these topics briefly referenced in the Monks House scrapbooks Woolf would return in her novel, *The Years*, but even more extensively and forcefully in its thematic companion, her 'war book' (Woolf 1983: 361) *Three Guineas*.⁹

Here, dress and uniforms repeatedly arrest Woof's critical attention. In fact, in establishing conceptual links between 'dress and war' and in devoting space to an analysis of the 'sartorial splendours of the educated man' (Woolf 1992b: 180), Woolf is consciously making clothes the focal point of some of her socio-political and socio-psychological observations. She suggests, for instance, that male dress or uniform 'in its immense elaboration ... not only covers nakedness, gratifies vanity, and creates pleasure for the eye, but ... serves to advertise the social, professional, or intellectual standing of the wearer' (Woolf 1992b: 179). Elsewhere, she notes, by addressing men directly in her text, that 'your finest clothes are those that you wear as soldiers'. For this reason, she argues, 'the connection between dress and war is not far to seek' (Woolf 1992b: 180). To put it simply, men thrive on the thought of war because it provides an opportunity to advertise their physical and social superiority through the wearing of uniforms, regalia and other military insignia. As signs of military rank and social status, uniforms, in this particular reading, are aestheticised and fetishised. As Brandon Truett argues, for Woolf 'male fashion's *raison d'être* is to reify and to perform a specific station; that is to say, male morality, as representative of patriarchy, is intrinsically tied to nationalism or an expression of Englishness, which is reflected in male sartorial fashion' (2014: 27). But, as Woolf discovers, 'in courts and universities, we find the same love of dress. There, too, are velvet and silk, fur and ermine' (Woolf 1992b: 180). 'Your clothes', she summarises, 'make us gape with astonishment. How many, how splendid, how extremely ornate they are – the clothes worn by the educated man in his public capacity' (Woolf 1992b: 177). Here, Woolf reads male ceremonial dress in a manner reminiscent of Herbert Spencer as insignia of authority, hegemonic power and control. Clothes, in other words, regulate professional and socio-psychological relations among men in a far from subtle manner. As Woolf suspects, these homosocial dynamics rely on clothes to develop hierarchies and authoritarian structures – exorbitantly magnified in fascist and in totalitarian political systems. In this manner, Woolf conceptually links patriarchy and fascist militarism in her thoughts about male dress.

But what about women's clothes? After J. C. Flügel's *The Psychology of Clothes* was published by the Hogarth Press in 1930,

Woolf must have been aware that clothes, thus fetishised by men in military and professional contexts, played a similarly significant role for identity formation in everyday contexts.[10] *The Years*, it must be remembered, is a novel focusing deliberately on descriptions of domestic, quotidian events to present Woolf's feminist views on women's educational and social opportunities in the late nineteenth and early twentieth centuries. Nonetheless, as my analysis will show, Woolf did not abandon her ambition to investigate how sartorial markers assisted in fashioning, sustaining or unmaking social relationships among individuals. In *The Years*, in fact, Woolf demonstrates that women's behaviour and thinking is as regulated and as determined by clothes as that of men. In particular, she investigates if making use of singular or extravagant dress could be a deliberate and useful strategy for women to mark personal distinctiveness. Can the resolute choice of peculiar or extraordinary dress assist in safeguarding individuality? Can it serve to empower women in the way men feel empowered when wearing their magnificent clothes? Is it at all desirable to divert from contemporary fashion protocols and its organisation of feminine beauty according to uniform types? Woolf, while occasionally experimenting with extravagant dress in real life,[11] deliberated these questions in the different but interconnected historical tableaux assembled in *The Years*.

Social configurations and the construction of the self: 'frock consciousness' in *The Years*

Dealing variously with nationalism, public life and the relationship between the sexes as its principal themes, *The Years* is a text that truly tries 'to take in everything' (Woolf 1983: 129). Characteristically for Woolf, however, it focuses on female experiences, and the novel's clear sequential organisation – it begins in 1880, moves, in Chapter 2, to 1891, includes chapters focusing variously on the years 1907, 1908, 1910, 1911, 1913, 1914, 1917, 1918 and finally jumps ahead to the present day (between 1931 and 1933) – enables her to examine how women's lives have changed during her own lifetime.[12] In the 'Present Day' section, for instance, *The Years* contrasts the young woman doctor, Peggy, with her aunt Eleanor Pargiter, who grew up without any formal schooling during the Victorian period.

In these final scenes, Peggy Pargiter is presented as a professionally successful woman doctor confidently holding her own in a male-dominated career.[13]

Clothes and sartorial practices consistently evoke the kind of historical particularity Woolf needed to convey in *The Years* to choreograph her thoughts on women's changed social status diachronically, across a comprehensive span of time. For example, the 'flounced dresses' (Woolf 1992c: 1) of the Victorian period, evoking faint images of sartorial divertissement and frivolity, have 'so many hooks and all at the back' (51) that the act of dressing and undressing becomes a time-consuming as well as challenging activity. In this particular case, it is easy to see how the (not so) simple act of putting on one's clothes becomes, in Woolf's extremely observant notation, a powerful expository illustration of women's social restrictions. Tight-laced and firmly ruled by contemporary dress practices, Woolf's middle-class women of 1880 really have very few opportunities to explore alternatives to their domestic responsibilities. By comparison, the 'Indian cloak' worn by Eleanor in the 'Present Day' section (324) is certainly expressive of the changed status of some (celibate) women in the 1930s, free to move, travel and wear the clothes that materially index some of their new-found freedoms.

But Woolf's comprehensive use of sartorial references is also integral to the composition of her penultimate novel because it establishes the text's significant interest in routines and customs and the ordinary events that structure human life. While significant historical events are indirectly acknowledged in *The Years*, these cannot compete for textual space with such everyday incidents as philanthropy, committee work or a shared meal. In this context, it is worth remembering that the descriptive, almost banal, meteorological summaries that contain many sartorial references and that introduce each chapter were last-minute additions to the text (Radin 1981: xxii). It seems as if Woolf tried to augment the novel's interest in the quotidian only a short while before the manuscript went to the printer. The jotted-down references to clothes and to sartorial practices in *The Years* therefore emphasise the historical particularity of each chapter and they make it clear that Woolf's focus would be the everyday, the quotidian and the lived experiences of women in both domestic and public settings in the time period chosen for analysis.

Most important for the present purpose, however, is Woolf's use of clothing imagery to examine women's 'frock consciousness' (Woolf 1980b: 12) – fashion's influence on women's self-perception and their subsequent engagement with their social surroundings. Throughout *The Years*, Woolf explored how clothes organise relationships and she critically assessed how uniformity and distinctiveness in dress determine social interactions among women. Often, she thereby shows that clothes problematically produce a crippling class-consciousness in her female characters. They have the power to dissolve but also to reinforce socio-economic hierarchies, and it is mostly for this reason that Woolf remained as critical of sartorial conspicuousness as of uniformity in clothing. Although we can see in *The Years* that she certainly noted fashion's complicity in obliterating individuality by standardising appearance, she was also aware that sartorial conspicuousness could prevent community building. Responsive to some of the conclusions reached in *Three Guineas*, *The Years* therefore articulates Woolf's suspicion that masculine strategies to mark status through the use of elaborate dress generate problematic psychological dynamics for women. By offering a very determined analysis of uniformity and distinction as fashion's conceptual opposites, *The Years* therefore develops Woolf's interest in sartorial themes that had already surfaced, more than a decade earlier, in such short, exploratory texts as 'The New Dress', in which the topic of sartorial conspicuousness had already been addressed.

In *The Years*, it is scenes involving Kitty, the Pargiters' Oxford cousin, that show how much the construction of autonomous individuality relies on sartorial practices. This young woman, as the novel's '1880' chapter reveals, is exceptionally aware that clothes are indispensable auxiliaries in establishing and reinforcing group identities that tend to eliminate individuality through uniform modes of dress. When she observes 'the old men in black gowns billowing; the young women in pink and blue dresses flowing; and the young men in straw hats carrying cushions under their arms' during an afternoon stroll through Oxford, she comes to the inevitable conclusion that everyone is 'dressed up' and is 'acting parts' (Woolf 1992c: 63). Clothes, Kitty recognises, have more than a practical role to play when going out for a walk. They locate the wearer in particular socio-economic configurations. The academics, the students and the young women who are out for a walk announce solidarity with social groups by donning appropriate costumes. As Woolf's frock-conscious young character is only too aware, not individuality but social affiliation is expressed by this conscious choice of uniform dress. But while she is thus musing on clothes' ability to strengthen group identities, Kitty is also extremely self-conscious about cutting too extravagant a figure. 'I'm too large' and 'I'm too well dressed' (57), she worries when visiting a friend's house, whose parents have made a conscious decision to invest in their daughter's education rather than her wardrobe.[14] Kitty, who desires the family's approval, asks herself anxiously if the Robsons will 'accept her in spite of her hat and gloves' (62). If ornate clothes were regarded, in *Three Guineas*, as a prop for masculine self-esteem, Woolf conversely shows in *The Years* that they frequently create uneasiness and embarrassment when functioning as symbols of women's socio-economic difference.

Already apparent in these early scenes, therefore, is Kitty's awareness that clothes are visibly indexing conflicting, but relational, desires: the need for social integration and for nonconformity. But it is the '1910' section, bringing together female members of the extended Pargiter family in the description of a lunch, a political meeting and a visit to the opera, which investigates, like no other passage in the novel, the role of dress as a marker of socio-economic difference. Class distinctions are reinforced, for instance, when Rose Pargiter, dressed in her 'tailor-made suit' (150), notes the sewing machine in her cousins' living room and interprets it as material evidence of poverty. Her relatives live in a shabby, 'noisy' (145) street, cook their own food, and make their own clothes (147) to save money. Yet, as on previous occasions, it is a scene involving Kitty (who is now Lady Lasswade) that brings to the fore the complexity underlying everyday experiences – and the role that clothes play in organising social encounters. Joining her cousins during a political meeting, dressed for the opera in 'ridiculous clothes' (153), as she calls them, Kitty feels, once more, ill at ease because of her showy appearance. Indeed, how much her shiny 'silver dress' ostracises her is emphasised by Woolf's text, which repeatedly, in this short passage, flags up how 'strange' and 'odd compared with the others' Kitty looked 'dressed in evening dress in the broad daylight' (154). Her cousin Eleanor certainly acknowledges that she 'felt suddenly shabby and dowdy compared to Kitty' (155).[15]

When reading these passages from *The Years*, we should recall for a moment the article in Woolf's *Three Guineas* scrapbook that advocated more sartorial abstinence for women. If the writer in question had denounced women's excessive interest in dress first and foremost for economic reasons, Woolf, who preserved this article, shows the strong cultural reverberations of its decrees in *The Years* when illustrating Kitty's frock consciousness. Although we can assume that it was not her aim to parrot this disapproving critic of women's dress culture by similarly accusing them of inappropriately donning extravagantly expensive clothing, she nonetheless shows that Kittly's elegant but unsuitable clothes isolate her and prevent the establishment of a harmonious relationship with her cousin Eleanor. If sartorial distinction had been identified in *Three Guineas* as a male strategy for confidently parading social superiority, this scene from *The Years* conversely shows that the wearing of extravagant dress does not similarly enable or psychologically empower women. Rather, it creates embarrassment, and it is responsible for the unease with which two women respond to each other who have clearly valued each other's company in the past.[16] Once more, Kitty feels too conspicuous and awkward because of her clothes. Unsurprisingly, she therefore reaches her final destination, the opera house, with a clear 'sense of relief'. As the narrator observes, now 'she no longer felt absurd. On the contrary she felt appropriate. The ladies and gentlemen who were mounting the stairs were dressed exactly as she was' (157). Suddenly, as *The Years* so knowingly protocols, Kitty experiences the pleasing sense of fitting in, of being adequately dressed. After the uncomfortable experience of attracting too much attention through her inappropriately elegant clothes, the sudden uniformity of dress in the opera house is a welcome respite. Now that she is surrounded by similarly clothed individuals, Kitty no longer attracts attention. Instead, she merges with the rest of the people who have dressed up for this daytime operatic event.

In all of these passages from the '1910' chapter, Woolf therefore investigates how clothes can make women feel ordinary or privileged, if not eccentric. But she also shows that the relationship between clothes and social context is mutually constitutive. Not only do clothes determine the social dynamics of any given moment but what turns clothes into conspicuous dress is, very often, their contextual inappropriateness. During the political meeting Kitty's remarkable dress makes her feel 'shy' (156) and it prevents intimacy with Eleanor. By the same token, Rose's desire for a friendship with her cousins Sara and Maggie is initially thwarted by material differences of which clothes are the most explicit expression. But if conspicuous clothes can thus become vehicles for social isolation, uniform dress can be similarly adverse for identity construction because it does not sufficiently distinguish the wearer from the environment. There is always the danger of looking ordinary when trying to dress suitably, appropriately or uniformly fashionable. In Woolf's text, Kitty practically disappears once she reaches the opera house. Although she remains, for a few more pages, the narrative's central consciousness, her singularity that was noted by everyone who attended the political meeting is suddenly far less pronounced when she is surrounded by individuals who 'were dressed exactly as she was'.

Reading these passages from *The Years* is to realise, therefore, that individuality and subjectivity are fragile compositions for Woolf, psychological entities that require careful and consistent maintenance. Clothes, in Woolf's novel, are the visual index of a particular tension. When they become extraordinary events as dress they tend to underline personal and economic differences among individuals even if their wearers seek to establish rapport and emotional connections. Throughout the novel, Woolf therefore remains sceptical about the merits of distinguishing oneself from the crowd with the help of one's clothes. For her, the desire for distinctiveness, expressed by specific sartorial markers, remained too closely associated with the 'splendour' of male uniforms – sartorial items that were complexly related to the production and the maintenance of social, professional and economic hierarchies and that prevent the formation of social attachments between women who long, like Eleanor and Kitty in *The Years*, for the extension of those shared experiences that enriched their childhood years. Fashionably suitable clothing, by contrast, frequently eliminates the peculiarities and individual characteristics that distinguish individuals. Indeed, Woolf notes in *The Years* that a turn towards uniform dress codes has the unfortunate tendency to eradicate individuality and abolish personal idiosyncrasies through collectivising.

As critics have often noted, with *The Years* Woolf created a novelistic scenario in which communal relations are constantly in the process of being threaded and unthreaded.[17] To this critical debate

I want to add the suggestion that she was particularly interested in discussing how clothes bring into play the mutually exclusive desires for social integration and personal distinctiveness that affect female subjects who form part of these communal relations. But – it must be noted next – throughout *The Years*, Woolf's observations remained interrogatory. A more authoritative contribution to the debate about contemporary sartorial codes would certainly have been anathema to a women novelist who aligned too much argumentative power with totalitarian viewpoints.[18] In fact, the novel's exploratory remarks on the auxiliary role that clothes may play in community building are best read in concert with those passages from *Three Guineas*, in which Woolf proposed the creation of an alternative social order for the 'daughters of educated men' – an organisation she suggests, that can temporarily undercut patriarchal authority and patriarchy's tendency to conserve its rule through the use of sartorial signifiers in public spectacles (Woolf 1992b: 315).

As Woolf accordingly suggested in *Three Guineas*, this 'Society of Outsiders' (Woolf 1992b: 320) 'will dispense with the dictated, regimented, official pageantry' and 'with personal distinctions – medals, ribbons, badges, hoods, gowns – not from any dislike of personal adornment, but because of the obvious effect of such distinction to constrict, to stereotype and to destroy' (321). Instead of supporting organised sartorial displays, Woolf's society was to 'increase private beauty; the beauty of spring, summer, autumn; the beauty of flowers, silks, clothes; the beauty which brims not only every field and wood but every barrow in Oxford Street' (321). It was to cultivate, in other words, the appreciation of aesthetic experiences that occur outside of public spectacles but that can nonetheless be experienced collaboratively, collectively. From now on, Woolf suggests, nothing organised, structured or easily reproducible can ever be the inspiration for aesthetic experiences. Beauty presents itself randomly, momentary but it is also ubiquitous. It cannot be found in any of Kitty's carefully made-up ensembles, for instance – in the appearance of a character who secretly wishes to 'fleece' other women 'of their clothes, of their jewels, of their intrigues, of their gossips' (Woolf 1992c: 227). No, in *The Years* it is Maggie's torn but exquisite 'silver dress with gold threads' (248) from Constantinople, looking extremely out of place in a dingy basement during an air raid, which provides an inspirational moment for appreciating 'scattered beauty' (Woolf 1992b: 321). This particular sartorial object momentarily disrupts expectations and marks difference. Even so, it does not ostracise its wearer from other individuals because it is worn in the company of an accepting group of friends. As such, it is representative of the kind of productive relationship among individual, garment and observer that Woolf associated with sudden manifestations of beauty – those aesthetic experiences that are noticed and appreciated by members of her Outsiders' Society and that can provide alternative sartorial experiences to the ones that dominate patriarchy and fascism's ritualistically staged performances. It is in short-lived moments such as these, Woolf believed, that clothes obtained significant political potential for unsettling established socio-sartorial hierarchies and for gesturing towards alternative modes of thinking not just about beauty but also about the formation of cooperative communities that are respectful of individual difference. Read in this manner – in tandem with *Three Guineas* – *The Years* therefore represents one of Woolf's most sustained attempts to investigate identity formation in the radically changed cultural climate of the 1930s when clothes, like never before in her lifetime, had obtained very obvious political significance. In this novel, Woolf made the intricacies of everyday sartorial rituals a thematic keynote, and she systematically debated the complex social tensions brought into play by fashion. Sartorial practices might well be part of everyday life. But as Woolf knew very well, as social performances they dominate individual and collective experiences – especially at a time when totalitarian extremists began to consciously manipulate clothes for political reasons.

In *The Years*, I have suggested, Woolf tried to address the topic of women's frock consciousness in all of its complexity. And as the novel's early critical reception shows, readers certainly responded well to this attempt to use sartorial imagery as a starting point for a debate about women's social obligations and opportunities. Although Woolf's diary indicates that its author was privately convinced that the book was a 'failure' (Woolf 1984: 65),[19] *The Years* turned out to be Woolf's most commercially successful book during her lifetime – a book with immense 'selling power' (Woolf 1984: 74). Released almost simultaneously in Britain and the US in the spring of 1937, its Hogarth edition sold over 13,000 copies in the first six months after publication, and over in the US, Harcourt, Brace's edition was published to even bigger public acclaim. It sold nearly 38,000 copies in the first six months.[20] As such, *The Years* easily eclipsed *Orlando* (1928) and *Flush* (1933) as Woolf's most popular publications to date and it confirmed that she had become a literary celebrity, someone whose novels commanded audiences on both sides of the Atlantic, whose public visibility had significantly increased and who had obviously established cooperative relationships with aspects of mass publishing.[21] Indeed, in the years leading up to the publication of *The Years*, the Hogarth Press had already adopted business practices more in keeping with commercial publishing, and particularly interesting for this chapter's debate of Woolf's engagement with contemporary mass culture and its standardised productions is the creation of the Uniform Edition of Virginia's works that began in 1929. She might have deplored the emergence of a uniform dress culture in many places in her writing. But as the example of the Hogarth's Uniform Edition will show, she nonetheless endorsed another form of uniform production, hoping that it would expand her readership and propagate her political views more widely. As Woolf would have realised, this partial compliance with uniformity provided her with a very effective means to voice her opinions about the political (ab)uses to which (uniform) dress codes could be put.

'The "fame" is becoming vulgar & a nuisance': Woolf's celebrity, the Hogarth Uniform Edition and the interwar literary marketplace

'How much difference does popularity make?' Woolf wondered in 1921 (Woolf 1980a: 106).[22] Strewn across her *oeuvre* are many such inquisitive remarks about her growing reputation and the pitfalls of careful authorial image management. Like Wharton and Bowen, Woolf, it can therefore be assumed, worried, at least occasionally, about being commodified, about becoming 'an established figure – as a writer' who is being taken 'for granted' (Woolf 1980b: 137). In 1928, for instance, her initial worry about not being awarded the Femina-Vie Heureuse Prize for *To the Lighthouse* was soon replaced by horror and consternation about the publicity surrounding the award ceremony. As she recorded in her diary, she feared that she had 'looked ugly in cheap black clothes', and she resented the attention she received from admirers and critics, eventually concluding that all 'the "fame" is becoming vulgar & a nuisance. It means nothing; & yet takes one's time' (Woolf 1980b: 183). Afflicted by her strongly developed 'clothes complex' (Woolf 1980b: 81), this writer was clearly ill-equipped to deal with the demands made of women authors by an interwar culture industry that awarded prizes, that sold books by trading on authors' names and that demanded that writers were visible or available at official functions, in published interviews or through mass-produced photographs. For Woolf, image marketing through advertising, media coverage and social performances remained a necessary but unpleasant strategy to make her voice as a writer of politically minded texts heard and understood.

Given Woolf's general unease about her own celebrity status, it is unsurprising that she repeatedly returned, in both fictional and non-fictional texts, to discussing the production or the guillotining of authorial careers by commercial publishing practices: *Orlando* and *A Room of One's Own* are certainly the principal locations for tracing, in Kathryn Simpson's words, some of 'Woolf's contradictory concerns about money, gift, fame, and the vicissitudes of the market' (2008: 110). The case of Shakespeare's imaginary and unfortunate sister in *A Room of One's Own* is thereby the most impressive example of a writing career cut short by the sexual and social expectations of a hostile patriarchal culture. For the present discussion, however, the years leading to the publication of *The Years* are particularly significant because they represent a moment in Woolf's career during which she and Leonard mapped out strategies for squaring artistic innovation more determinedly with commercial success. Woolf, whose novelistic career began with the attempt to remove her experimental scripts from the overbearing institutional governance of a patriarchal publishing industry embodied by such intimidating masculine figures as her half-brother Gerald Duckworth,[23] therefore learned to accept, in the late 1920s, that a partial and cautiously managed affiliation with commercial publishing practices was desirable because it allowed her to reach a broader audience for her feminist and anti-fascist writing. What follows here, then, is a discussion of Woolf's relationship with the interwar literary marketplace that takes her bestseller status of the late 1930s as the historical finale of a process of authorial image formation that began in the late 1920s. And as I will suggest, it was through the standardised appearance of her books in the Hogarth Uniform Edition that Woolf managed to reach an agreement with aspects of modern mass publishing and its associated cult of celebrity authorship: it is through these conveniently sized, uniform-looking volumes that she could speak to a wider readership without having to make her own person available for public inspection more than was absolutely necessary. It is true, she must have agreed to have her picture used in the promotional campaign of *Orlando* – a decision criticised severely by Wharton – but Woolf nonetheless continued to dislike the publicity associated with book promotion. Her professional access to a printing press, however, gave her the possibility of reaching a readership that exceeded the highbrow intellectuals of her own social and intellectual sphere without having to endure the kind of personal exposure required by authors on commercial publishers' lists. Not so much her own but the appearance of her books in the Hogarth Uniform Edition, in other words, became the visual manifestation of Woolf's partial cooperation with a culture industry that favoured the easily recognisable, standardised exteriors associated by many contemporaries with modern fashion's cultural ascendency.[24]

The Hogarth Press – it must be noted – obviously offered Woolf a very privileged position in Britain's interwar publishing world. As its co-owner, she was able to negotiate the creative and commercial sides of the marketplace in a manner most suitable to her. While others 'must be thinking of series & editors', she stated in 1925, she was lucky to be 'the only woman in England free to write what [she] like[d]' (Woolf 1980b: 43). But while the press released Woolf, the author, from the censoring views of editors and from interferences by profit-making publishers, Woolf, the editor and publisher, was of course directly contributing to the commodification of the written word – especially when the Hogarth Press began to develop from small, private publishing house to commercial press in the 1920s and 1930s and when it changed its business strategies and modes of production accordingly. Evidently, the histories of Woolf, the writer, and Woolf, the publisher, intersected in many interesting ways during the last years of her life. While Woolf herself developed into a brand name, the press expanded, assumed the outlook and operational procedures of a more conventional publishing enterprise and made good use of the growing marketability of its illustrious headliner. John K. Young therefore correctly surmises that only 'as author *and* publisher . . . could Woolf revise the aesthetic and commercial roles available to modernist women writers' (2010: 187).

The year 1929 is particularly relevant when considering Woolf's dual role as successful author and publisher. Encouraged by steadily mounting sales figures for her work – *Orlando* in particular – the Woolfs decided, at the end of 1928, to bring out a selection of Virginia's works in a Uniform Edition.[25] Although Leonard 'had taken quiet pleasure in the unconventional form and content of the early hand-printed press books' (Willis 1992: 155) and 'the Woolfs wanted to retain', as Helen Southworth explains, 'an element of amateurism' in their printing business (2010: 1), it seemed time to capitalise on Virginia's popular success and make available her work in cheaper reprints that conformed more directly to conventional printing standards. As Leonard explained to Gerald Duckworth in a letter from 10 December 1928, the Woolfs were now 'thinking of a cheap edition of Virginia's books' that was eventually supposed to be a 'complete edition', and they therefore required the rights of *The Voyage Out* (1915) and *Night and Day* (1919) from Duckworth (HPA MS2750/546). This 'inexpensive standard trade edition meant', J. H. Willis notes, 'to the press greater ease of production, lower reprinting costs, and certain marketing advantages' (1992: 155–6). It also cemented the ongoing transformation of the Hogarth Press from private publisher to commercial publishing house that was completed in 1932 when the Woolfs finally ceased to hand-print. In 1928, they had already decided to overhaul the publicity strategies of their press by asking the American designer E. McKnight Kauffer to create the iconic wolf's-head logo that would grace all subsequent Hogarth adverts and some of its publications. Henceforth, many Hogarth titles could be easily distinguished from those of competitors by their trademark appearance.[26]

The first four titles to be published on 26 September 1929 in the new Woolf Uniform Edition were *The Voyage Out*, *Jacob's Room* (1922), *Mrs Dalloway* (1925) and *The Common Reader* (1925), and these titles were followed in the next year by *Night and Day*, *To the Lighthouse* and *A Room of One's Own*.[27] And right from the beginning, these volumes were produced not with the art collector but with the general reader in mind. They were marked by the wolf's-head logo and they were standardised in size and appearance (Figure 3). As such, they represented a very noticeable visual departure from Woolf's earlier Hogarth publications that had been distinguished by Vanessa Bell's idiosyncratic jacket designs. What is more, adverts for this new Uniform Edition certainly included critical endorsements of Woolf's works, but they particularly focused on the affordability and the 'small and convenient size' of the publications – thereby emphasising the publisher's efforts to make her work available in standardised volumes that lent themselves to collecting as books rather than art objects (Figure 4). Interestingly, therefore, the same writer who had harshly censored *Vogue* editor Dorothy Todd in 1928 as a 'woman who is commercial' and who speaks 'of "getting my money back" as Gerald Duckworth might have spoken with the same look of rather hostile & cautious greed' (Woolf 1980b: 175–6), was a year later actively involved in

Figure 3   Cover of Uniform Edition of Virginia Woolf's *To the Lighthouse*, 1930. Mortimer Rare Book Room, Smith College

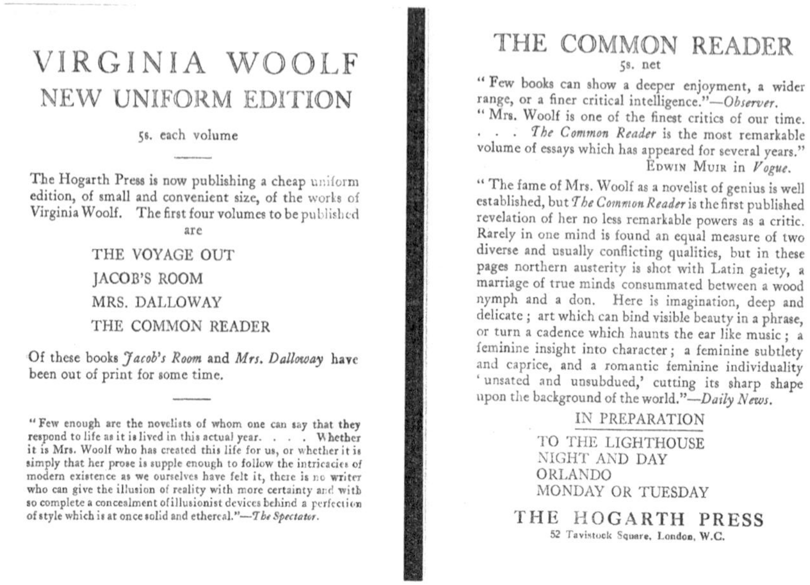

> **VIRGINIA WOOLF**
> **NEW UNIFORM EDITION**
>
> 5s. each volume
>
> The Hogarth Press is now publishing a cheap uniform edition, of small and convenient size, of the works of Virginia Woolf. The first four volumes to be published are
>
> THE VOYAGE OUT
> JACOB'S ROOM
> MRS. DALLOWAY
> THE COMMON READER
>
> Of these books *Jacob's Room* and *Mrs. Dalloway* have been out of print for some time.
>
> ---
>
> "Few enough are the novelists of whom one can say that they respond to life as it is lived in this actual year. . . . Whether it is Mrs. Woolf who has created this life for us, or whether it is simply that her prose is supple enough to follow the intricacies of modern existence as we ourselves have felt it, there is no writer who can give the illusion of reality with more certainty and with so complete a concealment of illusionist devices behind a perfection of style which is at once solid and ethereal."—*The Spectator*.
>
> **THE COMMON READER**
> 5s. net
>
> "Few books can show a deeper enjoyment, a wider range, or a finer critical intelligence."—*Observer*.
> "Mrs. Woolf is one of the finest critics of our time. . . . *The Common Reader* is the most remarkable volume of essays which has appeared for several years."
> EDWIN MUIR in *Vogue*.
>
> "The fame of Mrs. Woolf as a novelist of genius is well established, but *The Common Reader* is the first published revelation of her no less remarkable powers as a critic. Rarely in one mind is found an equal measure of two diverse and usually conflicting qualities, but in these pages northern austerity is shot with Latin gaiety, a marriage of true minds consummated between a wood nymph and a don. Here is imagination, deep and delicate; art which can bind visible beauty in a phrase, or turn a cadence which haunts the ear like music; a feminine insight into character; a feminine subtlety and caprice, and a romantic feminine individuality 'unsated and unsubdued,' cutting its sharp shape upon the background of the world."—*Daily News*.
>
> IN PREPARATION
> TO THE LIGHTHOUSE
> NIGHT AND DAY
> ORLANDO
> MONDAY OR TUESDAY
>
> **THE HOGARTH PRESS**
> 52 Tavistock Square, London, W.C.

Figure 4 Advert for the Hogarth Press's Virginia Woolf: New Uniform Edition, 1929. Mortimer Rare Book Room, Smith College

a commercial procedure that packaged her work in a standardised, 'inexpensive edition' of 'convenient size' and 'uniform binding'.[28] Suddenly, uniformity of appearance – often criticised elsewhere as a mechanism that can obliterate difference and diversity – became a convenient mechanism for increasing Woolf's public visibility and for consolidating her status as a leading woman novelist who could and who wanted to reach a larger audience.[29]

However, an exchange of letters between Leonard Woolf and Jonathan Cape from April 1929 also shows that the Woolfs' rapprochement with commercial publishing methods remained partial rather than wholesale. Leonard, who had meant to publish titles in the forthcoming Woolf Uniform Edition at 3s 6d, had obviously asked his more experienced colleague for advice on pricing. 'If you publish Mrs Woolf at three and six pence in the ordinary Crown Octavo format', Cape wrote in response, 'you then come in competition with the popular three and sixpenny fiction issued by Hodder, Cassell, Collins, and in fact almost every publisher' (HPA MS270/546). Cape was correct. Interwar publishing practices were relatively standardised and publishers conventionally released a new hardback title at 7s 6d before issuing a cheaper reprint at 3s 6d (Kingsford 1970: 119). If the Woolfs had published volumes from Virginia's Uniform Edition at 3s 6d as initially planned, these titles would have been indistinguishable from all those other cheap reprints that other interwar publishing houses offered to readers at the point when a title's initial popularity had waned. It was clear that this was not quite what the Woolfs had in mind. Although they aimed to make Virginia's titles available to new readers, they also hoped to carefully preserve her image as a writer of high-quality literary prose and distinguish Hogarth titles from that of other, commercially focused publishers of the interwar period. It is therefore no surprise that they accepted Cape's advice and brought 'out a five shilling edition instead of a three and sixpenny edition' (HPA MS270/546) as this slight irregularity in pricing gave them an opportunity to underline and market the particularity of Virginia's experimental prose.

But Cape also made another suggestion in his letter to the Hogarth editors. Indeed, after voicing his suggestions on effectively pricing 'Mrs Woolf', the publisher of H. G. Wells, Ernest Hemingway and Radclyffe Hall concluded his letter with the following proposition:

> If you and Mrs Woolf will consent to my publishing a Collected edition of her work at five shillings, under a joint imprint of The Hogarth Press and Jonathan Cape, I can offer you a royalty of twelve and a half per cent (12½ %), twelve copies as twelve, with an advance of five hundred pounds (£500) on account of royalties payable on signing the agreement. (HPA MS270/546)

Leonard's answer was posted five days later. After thanking Cape for his 'friendly and generous letter', he told him: 'I need hardly say that my wife and I have carefully considered your proposals. Your offer is very tempting', he stated politely and probably somewhat disingenuously, 'but', he concluded, 'we feel that as long as we continue to publish her books under the Hogarth imprint, we had better go the whole hog and also do the collection edition' (HPA MS270/546). Even if they were happy to consider, with the Uniform Edition, more conventional publishing practices, the owners of the Hogarth Press nonetheless insisted on their professional independence from Cape – for whom, Woolf had noted three years earlier, she 'should not much like writing' (Woolf 1980b: 116). They might have made inroads into the world of commercial publishing, in other words, but the Woolfs still remained attached to the idea of their 'commercial hippogriff', a printing press that retained, in spite of an obvious move towards commercialisation and professionalisation, aspects of the exclusivity that had characterised its early years as a coterie publisher.[30]

The example of the Uniform Edition therefore demonstrates how effectively the Woolfs negotiated the commercial and artistic purchase of Virginia's work, thereby challenging the notion that 'commodification became the sole available means of establishing textual authority' for women writers of the interwar period (Young 2000: 240). Although it accelerated the transformation of 'Virginia Woolf' into a recognisable brand after 1929, the Hogarth Uniform Edition still ensured that Woolf, the writer, maintained an element of her much fetishised 'freedom' (Woolf 1980b: 70) from the professional networks structuring the world of mainstream publishing. Had they taken up the offer to publish the Uniform Edition under a joint imprint with Jonathan Cape, Woolf would obviously have been only one among many other formally experimental writers already associated with Cape's illustrious list. And had they gone with contemporary publishing conventions and priced titles in her Uniform Edition at 3s 6d, the Woolfs would have lost the advantage to promote her work (and other Hogarth titles) as idiosyncratic and distinctive. That they had sought advice about this new publishing venture from a more commercially focused publisher was of course somewhat inconsistent with their attempts to distinguish their press and its titles very clearly from 'the *field of large-scale cultural production*' of the interwar period (Bourdieu 1993: 115). However, it seems as if this issue never bothered the Hogarth editors who were determined to accrue 'symbolic' rather than 'economic capital' for their publishing press (Thompson 2012: 8).[31]

Particularly privileged as a woman writer who owned a press, Woolf thus tried to preserve her intellectual autonomy while simultaneously finding a way to speak not only to specialised but also to general readers who would be attracted to the competitive price or the easily recognisable volumes of the Uniform Edition of her works. Indeed, it could be argued that in publishing her books at a reduced price in the Uniform Edition Woolf acted directly on a critical suggestion made during the radio broadcast 'Are Too Many Books Written and Published?' developed collaboratively with Leonard in 1927. Here, Woolf had argued that cheaper books would have the decided advantage of making reading more affordable to many, if not all, members of the British public. 'What is wanted', she had suggested, 'is some system by which private libraries could be thrown open to other people, so that readers living in the same neighbourhood could use each other's books' (Woolf and Woolf 2006: 242, 243). Although she did not quite throw open the doors of her private library to neighbourhood readers, the decision to reprint her works in a more affordable edition certainly shows an awareness that her readers' limited economic means did not necessarily amount to limited intellectual interests. In the same broadcast, she had also pronounced – five years before Q. D. Leavis would pessimistically declare the inevitable demise of literary culture through standardised tastes – that the mass production of printed material would lead to more rather than less cultural heterogeneity.[32] Claiming that the reader, whose 'appetite is insatiable', 'wants books written by all sorts of people; by tramps and duchesses; by plumbers and Prime Ministers' (Woolf and Woolf 2006: 241), Woolf refused to accept contemporary fears about levelled tastes and the diminished value of mass-produced cultural forms. Even if, she seems to want to reason, books were mass-produced in cheaper, standardised editions, a surprising variety in content could hide behind the uniform look of their covers.

As Woolf had determinedly stated in 1924 in 'The Patron and the Crocus', 'writing is a method of communication' and 'the fate of literature' depends upon the 'happy alliance' between an author and her readers (Woolf 1994: 215).[33] It is for these readers, Woolf suggested, that the author writes. They are 'in a very subtle and insidious way the instigator and inspirer of what is written' (Woolf 1994: 212). With the Hogarth publication of her Uniform Edition, she began to take note not only of 'the highbrow public' but also of 'the best-seller public' that had so far not been the particular target of her publications (Woolf 1994: 213). Although her relationship with her reading public and with the literary marketplace might not have been straightforward thereafter, as Patrick Collier rightly points out (2006: 76), Woolf's decision to embrace the possibility of making her work available to members of the 'unknown public' amounted to an awareness of her social responsibility as a political writer.[34] She might have continued to reflect critically on modern publishing practices in *Three Guineas* or the unpublished 'Anon', but it would be wrong to label these late evaluations of the literary marketplace, as

Collier does, as 'increasingly desperate and fanciful solutions' offered by an author who firmly resented writing for publication (2006: 105). Even if she suggested in *Three Guineas* that writers, especially the daughters of the educated men, should find non-commercial ways to address their readers by 'fling[ing] leaflets down basements; expos[ing] them on stalls; trundl[ing] them along streets on barrows to be sold for a penny or given away' (Woolf 1992b: 297), Woolf's willingness to engage, cautiously but determinedly, with the interwar literary marketplace and its publishing practices somewhat controverts these critical reflections. While she welcomed the widespread dissemination of her works in the Modern Library Series in the US, as Lise Jaillant has recently shown,[35] the Hogarth Uniform Edition of her works was similarly designed to introduce more readers at home to Woolf's feminist and anti-fascist pedagogies.

It could be said, therefore, that Woolf's more cooperative relationship with mass publishing was the result of a political activism that became increasingly vociferous. Indeed, it might be nothing more than an intriguing historical accident that the publication of *A Room of One's Own* – the first of her two critical assessments explicitly addressing patriarchal cultural politics – practically coincided with the Woolfs' decision to begin with the printing of her Uniform Edition, but I see these two as interconnected events that reveal this writer's desire to more forcefully express and popularise her views on contemporary social politics. While Woolf's subsequently published political prose and the factual realism of *The Years*, the 'Essay-Novel' begun on 20 January 1931,[36] allowed her to speak more directly and more concretely about the urgency for socio-political reform,[37] the Hogarth Uniform Edition is expressive of her concerted wish to broaden access to her politically minded writings. It is also indicative of her aspiration to refashion herself as a writer with a more pronounced appreciation of her heterogeneous and diversified readership – a readership that could gain access to her writing through the cheaper, standardised-looking volumes of the Hogarth Uniform Edition.

While some of her writings on contemporary sartorial practices might very well suggest otherwise, the foregoing analysis of Woolf's measured engagement with the interwar literary marketplace has shown, therefore, that she was by no means inclined to think that uniform covers inevitably amounted to nothing but standardised content or substance. Rather, Woolf firmly believed in the possibility of cultural pluralism, and if anything, her writings from 'The New Dress' to *Three Guineas* and *The Years* are inquisitive explorations into social dynamics that convey the desire for individual expression in a world in which standardised images and forms flourished because they rendered manageable the complexity of everyday life. By collectivising and grouping into clusters, clothes, as Woolf noted in numerous places in her writing, helped to organise the conceptual chaos of a world rendered unfamiliar to many by socio-political and technological change. In Britain during the last decade of Woolf's life, the blackshirt uniform was certainly the most drastic expression of this contemporary need to use sartorial markers for conceptually stabilising experiences. Its suggestion to categorically arrange individuals into units was no doubt appealing to many because it simulated straightforward approaches to analytically classifying the diverse and often confusing social experiences that made life in the interwar period unpredictable if not threatening.

Woolf, as analysed extracts from *Three Guineas* and *The Years* have shown, was critical of such reductive attempts to organise individuals with the help of sartorial emblems. She was clearly concerned about the use to which clothes, and uniforms in particular, had been put by patriarchal and non-democratic political movements. In these cases she worried about the place of the individual, whose rights and freedoms were, she believed, annulled by the all-consuming corporatist spirit of the collective. But her writing also shows us that she understood and often sympathised with this contemporary need for conceptual stability and that she regarded clothes as important props that mediated desires for affiliation. Time and again, her texts describe situations in which individuals long to efface distinction and adapt to their socio-sartorial environment. It is hardly surprising that Mabel Waring at the end of 'The New Dress' desires to wear the uniform of a nurse or a nun. The image of the respect-commanding uniform is comforting not only because it imparts authority on its wearer, but also because it promises the effacement of difference that had been the source of Mabel's suffering at Mrs Dalloway's party.

In concluding this chapter, it needs to be stressed once more that Woolf was, like Wharton, certainly concerned about too much uniformity in appearance. She thought that it compromised the expression of personal characteristics. But she also understood that a degree of uniformity in clothing could generate a pleasing sense of social belonging. Indeed, while she was pursuing her detailed research on contemporary sartorial practices for *Three Guineas*, she began to realise that a rigorous insistence on displaying personal distinction through clothes was socially harmful because it could isolate individuals rather than organise them into communities that acknowledge that expressing dissent and receiving support were equally important social mechanisms for the development of contented subjectivity. In *The Years*, Woolf developed, as we have seen in this chapter, very detailed investigations into the complexities of women's socio-sartorial desires, aspirations and commitments. Here, she confirmed what she had already suspected in 1919: that a 'woman's clothes are so sensitive that, far from seeking one influence to account for their change, we must seek a thousand' (Woolf 1986: 332). And all these socio-psychological and socio-sexual dynamics generated by women's clothes and sartorial practices were explicitly discussed by Woolf in publications that increasingly acknowledged and were willing to accept, in terms of their own appearance in the Hogarth Uniform Edition, that a measured degree of uniformity could be beneficial for the development of cooperative relationships between individuals in general and between a writer and her readership in particular – a readership that might have been vast and unknown but which was nonetheless diverse, intellectually curious and appreciative. As Woolf advised aspiring female writers in *Three Guineas*: when 'approaching "the public"; single it into separate people instead of massing it into one monster, gross in body, feeble in mind' (Woolf 1992b: 297). As this chapter has shown, her sartorial politics are expressive of Woolf's pronounced desire to find singularity in standardised products and collective social formations.

Notes

1. The 1933 'Special R.A.F. Pageant Number' of *The Blackshirt* contains an article entitled 'The Men who Sold You This', which explicitly addressed the uniform's power to bridge class divides among its members: 'You have been impressed by their smart appearance, their trim black and grey shirts and grey flannel trousers. You have noticed that one of these men will speak to you in the accents of Cambridge; and the next in the mannerism of Brixton. Yet, to you, they look equally smart.

The Cambridge man is as much at home selling papers in the streets as is his less educated brother. You notice no difference in the bearing of one to another. You are right: it is a wonderful spirit that governs these men' (Anon. 1933a: 4). Another feature appealed to the reader to '[t]hink of the uniform you wear – and of what it signifies. We are all Blackshirts together – bound in a common determination. Remember that – and the bugbear of "class" will disappear' (Anon. 1933b: 1).

2. Eyewitnesses unanimously noted the aggressive behaviour with which blackshirt stewards responded to attempts to interrupt speeches or the progress of the event. Storm Jameson, for instance, reported that it 'is certainly possible that the interrupters were "organised" but what actually happened was that a solitary man or woman stood up, made or began to make a remark inaudible to all but his close neighbours, and was instantly set on by a dozen or more Blackshirts, and kicked and pommelled unrestrainedly, before being ejected'. Vera Brittain similarly observed: 'I saw men and women knocked down and treated with violence for nothing more serious than a shout of "No!" or the very pertinent enquiry, "Does Hitler stand for free speech?"' (quoted in Montagu 1934: 12, 14–15).

3. Charles James was a Chicago-born couturier whose textile designs relied on geometrical shapes as principle construction elements. The term 'smart gossip' in the previous sentence is Woolf's.

4. On their way through Nazi Germany, Mitzi, the Woolfs' marmoset, diverted attention from the couple who were known for their anti-fascist stance. Woolf, however, was alarmed by her own response to these scenes of mass salutation. She noted that the crowds, actually waiting for a Nazi official, gladly 'cheered Mitzi' while she 'raised [her] hand' in salute. Not even the Woolfs as uncompromising critics of the fascist regime, her diary seems to suggest, were immune to the fact that they were having this kind of mass appeal (Woolf 1983: 311).

5. The Woolfs' most immediate link to fascism at home was Vita Sackville-West's husband Harold Nicolson, who was an early supporter of Mosley's New Party and who edited its journal *Action* in 1931. But he parted ways with Mosely when the BUF was created in the following year. For more information on Mosley, the New Party and Woolf's response to this new political movement see Jessica Berman (2001a: 105–21).

6. According to Woolf's diary, the writing of the 'Present Day' section was begun on 22 May 1934 (Woolf 1983: 221). The link between life and work is made even stronger by Woolf's marginal comment next to the diary entry about Mosley: 'And I think I will call the book "The Years"' (Woolf 1983: 337). It suggests that she was thinking about her novel while she was recording her anxiety about the BUF graffiti.

7. It should be remembered that this character is responsible, as David Bradshaw and Maren Linett point out, for an anti-Semitic outburst (Bradshaw 1999: 179–91; Linett 2002: 341–61).
8. Related articles discuss subjects such as 'New Uniforms for Army' (MHP B16/3/47) and new outfits for postal workers (MHP B16/3/4).
9. On the symbiotic relationship and parallel genesis of these two dissimilar texts, *Three Guineas* and *The Years*, see Grace Radin's *Virginia Woolf's The Years: The Evolution of a Novel* (1981: xvii) and Anna Snaith's introduction in the new *Cambridge Edition of the Works of Virginia Woolf* (Woolf 2012: xlv–lxxviii).
10. When acknowledging in *Three Guineas* that '[n]ot only are whole bodies of men dressed alike summer and winter – a strange characteristic to a sex which changes its clothes according to the season, and for reasons of private taste and comfort' (Woolf 1992b: 177–8), Woolf certainly shows awareness of Flügel's 'great masculine renunciation' theory (Flügel 1966: 111, 20). In further stating that 'every button, rosette and stripe seems to have some symbolical meaning' (Woolf 1992b: 178) in men's otherwise austere clothing, her argument also aligns itself very clearly with the psychoanalyst's suggestion that 'decoration' is one of the three reasons why human beings dress themselves (Flügel 1966: 25–52).
11. In a diary entry from 12 April 1935, for instance, Woolf applauded herself for her 'courage' to venture out in her 'silver corduroy'. A few weeks later, although she expressed concern that Murray 'will dress me for the part of the Dss of Malfi, even in day clothes', she similarly admitted experiencing pleasure when buying 'new shoes' and the recommended '30/- [blue taffeta] dress' (Woolf 1983: 299, 307). On Woolf's eccentric dress see also R. S. Koppen (2009: 10).
12. I accept Anna Snaith's proposition that the date of the 'Present Day' section can be established by references to Peggy Pargiter's age: '16 or 17 in 1911 and 37 or 38 in this section' (Woolf 2012: lxxii).
13. This is not to suggest that Woolf was uncritically endorsing straightforward narratives about women's progressive emancipation through work. As Evelyn Chan rightly notes, Woolf 'detailed such so-called liberations with unease' (2014: 131).
14. In the original draft, Kitty's self-consciousness is even more pronounced: 'Kitty felt herself even larger than usual', we are told and 'what was stranger, excessively well-dressed'. And 'when Nelly [Kitty's friend] came in' 'all Kitty's fears were confirmed – she was much too well dressed. [*And yet*] It was only the dress she always wore to go out to tea in. But Nelly was wearing [only] a pinafore – which covered her entirely as if she had been doing housework' (Woolf 1977: 131).

15. Years later, Eleanor is finally able to articulate some of these previously undisclosed feelings during another meeting with her cousin: '"You always made some excuse, Nell, for not coming"', her smiling cousin reprimands her. '"Did I? Yes. Perhaps I couldn't afford the clothes"', Eleanor answers while 'smiling back at her. She stooped and picked up one of the white gloves that had fallen on the floor. "That's so silly," said Kitty, looking at the white glove. "Not when you're young," said Eleanor. "When you are young you mind – not looking like other people." She looked at Kitty. She was very well dressed' (Woolf 2012: 835). This scene, set in 1921, was part of the material that Woolf excised shortly before the novel's publication although she seemed to have regretted the omission and thought of reinstating the material when considering Harcourt, Brace's proposition of a Uniform Edition of the text (Woolf 1984: 69). The deleted material has now been made available in the novel's *Cambridge Edition of the Works of Virginia Woolf* (Woolf 2012: 807–55).

16. Throughout the chapter, Woolf repeatedly relates her characters' desire to find and explore shared points of origin in spite of dissimilar socio-economic circumstances. Kitty, for instance, notes that she and Eleanor 'had gone such different ways, they had lived such different lives, since Oxford' (Woolf 1992c: 157). Conversely, Eleanor thinks about shared experiences, the time, for instance, when she and Kitty 'broke the swing together at Oxford' (154).

17. Woolf's interest in exploring the organisation of communities has often been examined. According to Gillian Beer, she aimed 'to find ways of maintaining difference as well as constellation, lest clusters become ordered as hierarchies' (Beer 1987: 87). Mark Hussey (1990: 141–52) and Kirsty Martin (2013: 81–131) have further developed this critical suggestion.

18. Expressions of dictatorial power are identified and listed as 'Hitler's voice', 'the pedagogic, the didactic, the loud speaker strain' in Woolf's essay 'The Leaning Tower' (1940) (Woolf 2011: 261, 272). Against this 'standardizing, regulating discourse', she hoped to develop, as Melba Cuddy-Keane has argued, a notion of a 'literary discourse as an active, not static, mode' (2003: 121).

19. For the critical reception of *The Years* as ostensible 'failure' see also Leonard Woolf (1967: 145–6); Eric Warner (1980: 16–30); Anna Snaith (Woolf 2012: lxxix); James Haule (2009: 241).

20. *The Years*, J. H. Willis suggests, 'became an Authentic American best-seller for 1937, ranking sixth on a list led by such heady company as Margaret Mitchell's *Gone with the Wind* and Kenneth Roberts's *Northwest Passage*' (1992: 290). And B. J. Kirkpatrick confirms that

'18,142 copies' of the first Hogarth edition were printed. Harcourt, Brace initially printed only 10,000 copies. However, there 'were twelve re-impressions totaling 37,900 copies between April and October 1937' (1967: 57–8). Woolf herself also comments in detail on the novel's bestseller status in America in her diary (Woolf 1984: 90–1).

21. The fact that Woolf's photograph had adorned the cover of *Time* magazine shortly before *The Years* was published can only have been conducive to producing such record sales figures – especially in the US. The incident also provides visual evidence that her transformation into cultural icon had been completed. Brenda R. Silver names Woolf's 'location on the borders between high culture and popular culture, art and politics, masculinity and femininity, head and body, intellect and sexuality, heterosexuality and homosexuality, word and picture, beauty and horror', as the reason for her 'elevation to transgressive cultural icon' (1999: 11).

22. Interestingly, in the same diary entry Woolf seems to have made a distinction between two different modes of writing. Here, she thinks in a manner similar to Bowen of novel writing and journalism as incompatible practices. When she announces that she 'shan't become a machine, unless a machine for grinding articles', she accepts the reviewer's work as an activity that is commercially driven. Clearly distinguishable from these journalistic publications is her creative writing that remains untainted by such unworthy concerns as economics. 'As I write', Woolf here claimed, 'there rises somewhere in my head that queer, & very pleasant sense, of something which I want to write: my own point of view' (Woolf 1980a: 107).

23. Duckworth & Co, Gerald's press, had published Woolf's first novels *The Voyage Out* and *Night and Day*. It has often been noted, that his abuse of his half-sisters impacted negatively on their sexual, emotional and professional development. For Virginia, it must have been extremely objectionable, as S. P. Rosenbaum notes, to 'have to submit to Gerald again, and then wait for his approval' when she started her career as a novelist (1995: 13).

24. Acknowledging the 'rapprochement between modernist writers and the marketplace' in general, Ian Willison argues that 'the commercial component of the Hogarth project led inevitably to a rapprochement with the general trade, as not only did Virginia Woolf develop her own canon, but that canon was accepted by the marketplace, with the solid success of her Hogarth *Uniform Edition*' (Willison, Gould and Chernaik 1996: xv).

25. 5,080 copies of *Orlando* were printed on 11 October 1928 in what was the first (not limited) English edition. A week later, Harcourt, Brace

published a first American edition of 6,350 copies. On both sides of the Atlantic, Woolf's novel was re-issued several times before the Hogarth Press released its Uniform Edition in 1933 (Kirkpatrick 1967: 33–5).

26. McKnight Kauffner's contributions to this significant shift in the Woolfs' publicity practices are discussed by Elizabeth Willson Gordon (2010: 179–205).
27. *Flush* followed on 16 November 1932, roughly a year before *Orlando* and *The Waves* were published on 5 October 1933. The Uniform Edition of *The Years* was released on 31 October 1940 and by 1943 the Hogarth Press had also published a Uniform Edition of *Three Guineas*. Information taken from Order Book: Woolf Uniform Editions A–L and Order Book: Uniform Editions M–Z (HPA MS 2750/A/28; HPA MS 2750/A/29).
28. These expressions were used to advertise the 1931 Harcourt, Brace Uniform Edition in America (Anon. 1931: 192).
29. Readers who detect a contradiction in Woolf's thinking about the literary marketplace are well advised to keep in mind John K. Young's perceptive observation that this author, in her role as a publisher, 'was marketing "Virginia Woolf" as a brand name, in an effort to avoid the business mistakes for which she criticises Jane Austen and others in *Room*' (Young 2010: 187). For Woolf, the professional outlook adopted as a publisher and writer was therefore in keeping with the feminist viewpoints she had disseminated in *A Room of One's Own* – the text that contained her most radical and politically challenging observations to date and whose publication coincided with the release of the first titles of the Hogarth Uniform Edition of her work.
30. The expression 'commercial hippogriff' is Leonard Woolf's (quoted in Southworth 2010: 1). Helen Southworth also discusses the various attempts made by the Woolfs (and by other publishers) to negotiate the absorption of the Hogarth Press by other presses. Woolf herself seemed to have been undecided on the question. In 1926 she noted, for instance, that she 'sometimes wish[es]' to 'be quit' of 'the Press' only to change course immediately by stating: 'But then there's the fun – which is considerable' (Woolf 1980b: 70).
31. John B. Thompson defines 'symbolic capital' as 'the accumulated prestige, recognition and respect accorded to certain individuals or institutions' (2012: 8). As editors and publishers, the Woolfs were hoping to do more than just sell books. Clearly, they wanted to be seen as producers of literary culture in the interwar period by carefully cultivating the image of the Hogarth Press as a specialised, prestigious imprint.
32. The 'bestseller's style is uniform and consistent', Leavis argued, characterised by its 'slick technique' that is 'the product of centuries of

journalistic experience'. Elsewhere, she similarly suggested that its 'effect depends entirely on the existence of a set of stock responses provided by newspaper and film' (1939: 218, 234).

33. Although Patrick Collier advises against 'a one-to-one correspondence between' the terms 'patron' and 'reader' that are used by Woolf in this essay (2006: 91), this is precisely how other critics have interpreted Woolf's comments (Dubino 1995: 133).

34. The term 'unknown public' is used in 1858 by Wilkie Collins to describe the sudden increase of literate readers with sometimes rather questionable tastes (1858: 217–22).

35. Lise Jaillant persuasively constructs the image of a more popularist Woolf who was keen to disseminate her political viewpoints as widely as possible in the US. 'Woolf', Jaillant argues, 'tirelessly promoted her pedagogical message and the Modern Library offered her an institutional base to popularise her ideas in America' (2014: 84).

36. Woolf had been asked by Philippa Strachey to give a lecture to the Junior Council of the London and National Society for Women's Service on 21 January 1931. This speech, entitled 'Professions for Women', would be the starting point for the parallel genesis of *The Years* and *Three Guineas* (Woolf 1983: 6, 129).

37. Alice Wood argues that 'in response to the changing literary and political climate, Woolf desired the authority of factual accuracy to carry the weight of her cultural criticism' (2013: 58). Maren Linett has similarly proposed that an impending fascist danger was a pressing reason for Woolf to reconsider her 'modernism of interiority and "vision"' in the 1930s (2002: 349).

Envoi

It is 1956, the height of the Cold War. The year will end in the Suez Crisis and the Hungarian Uprising. Edith Wharton and Virginia Woolf have both been dead for a while, Jean Rhys is all but forgotten and Rosamond Lehmann's career as a novelist is on the wane.[1] Elizabeth Bowen, now in her late fifties, is an acclaimed author and sought-after lecturer, who received a CBE in 1948 and who has just been awarded an honorary doctorate from the University of Oxford. She is deeply immersed in her travelogue, *A Time in Rome* (1960), and also in her 15-year-long love affair with the diplomat Charles Ritchie. In July, she publishes an essay on individuality and subjectivity, 'How to Be Yourself – And Not Eccentric', in *Vogue* to return to a topic that has been occupying her for more than two decades. 'Does fashion help', she had asked in 1937 in a book review when discussing the difficult task of identity formation (Bowen 1950: 113). The *Vogue* piece, published in a politically fraught climate marked by uprisings and suppression of dissident voices, similarly addresses the relationship between conformity and self-assertion and it also discusses fashion's contributions to the complex processes that structure the subject's conflicting desires to conform and dissent.

Indeed, the older Bowen here seems to answer her earlier question by acknowledging her contemporaries' tendency to toe the line: 'on the whole', she observes, 'we dress, behave, run our homes, and conduct our outside existences in the accepted manner – to do otherwise could involve us in needless trouble, or cause us to rile or perplex our neighbours' (2008: 412). But, she interposes, if 'individuality is threatened', if acceptance of norms and social protocols endangers individuation, identity nonetheless seeks an outlet, and it is out of this tension between assimilation and the relational need for self-expression that 'the best of the world we live in' eventually arises (2008: 413). Out of this conflict between the self and the world, that is, emerges something beneficial, something that is constructive for both the individual and the community. And in both cases, in 1937 as much as in 1956, Bowen identifies fashion as an important conveyer of 'shapes, textures, colours', as a producer of 'a concrete vocabulary' with the help of which the subject can create, produce and thereby express individuality and engage with the world (2008: 415). Fashion, in other words, is seen by Bowen as a catalyst for creativity, a cultural incentive that determines individual outlooks, organises relationships between individuals and, by extension, generates cultural capital through the subject's desire for creative expression. And no doubt, Bowen, a politically informed woman, would have been aware that historical processes as complex as the ones she was living through in the 1950s were somehow connected to those microscopic, often localised, energies between individuals she was imaginatively describing by employing the colourful vocabulary provided by the fashion discourse. Dissidence and unorthodoxy, conformity and assimilation – all these are social dynamics that manage 'outer existences', as Bowen called it. It is out of these interpersonal energies that the events of history are made.[2]

This book has shown that fashion was more than a trivial matter for the five selected women writers who tried to find critical acclaim in the interwar period. Without exception they would have agreed with Bowen that fashion was never just the provider of guidelines on what to wear or how to consume the latest sartorial trends. Rather, it was an urgent question for them, offering the opportunity to relate in their writing their thoughts about identity politics and about contemporary gender dynamics. And now that I am coming to the end of this study, I want to propose that it is no coincidence that these particularly focused articulations about fashion's social hermeneutics began to be developed by these writers in the interwar period. According to Alison Light, these were years marked by a 'traumatised relationship to modernity' that 'produced new kinds of conservative as well as radical responses' (1991: 11). It was a historical moment determined by the central conflict 'between old and new, between past and present, between holding on and letting go, between conserving and moving on' (1991: 19). In light of this view that the cultural atmosphere in the years between the wars was characterised by this tension between old and new, the suggestion that fashion can function as a convenient compendium to assess others must have been extremely seductive to the writers included here. Apparent to many contemporaries was its ability to provide structure in a world that seemed randomly organised by the desire to update, transform and modify. Fashion can obviously affirm and restore social structures by sartorially demarcating gender territories, class hierarchies or professional relations. But it also offers endless possibilities for experimenting with new and other versions of the modern self – a psychological entity as concerned with reinvention and innovation as the period that produced it. As a social practice, fashion therefore lends itself to appropriation by both reactionary and progressive outlooks. It has the potential to vary and overhaul but it also gives the impression to confirm and stabilise.

Fashion's dualistic association as consolidator or challenger of established norms was noted and comprehensively discussed by the women novelists included in *Modernism, Fashion and Interwar Women Writers*, writers who can be divided into two different camps depending on whether or not they regarded fashion as a conservative force. Wharton, as we have seen, was thereby unusual in her cultural conservatism that dismissed fashion not as the affirmer of orthodoxies but as a leveller of tastes and appearances that threatens to abolish difference and particularity. For her, the finely shaded world of established customs and traditions was under attack from contemporary consumer culture and its desire to standardise and synchronise aspects of daily life. This was the reason why she regarded fashion as a modernising influence – but one of which she wholeheartedly and determinedly disapproved. In the novels of Lehmann and Rhys fashion conversely functioned as the envoy of patriarchal modes of thinking. Although it signalled a brighter, better future for women who were constantly reminded to purchase and don the colourful, free-flowing garments of the autonomous Flapper, fashion nonetheless functioned, they believed, as the ambassador of a future remarkably similar to the conservatism of a patriarchal past that many hoped was in the process of being dismantled. Rhys, as I have shown, created her struggling protagonists to make readers aware of the discrepancy between those illusionary fantasies of emancipation and progress conjured up by designers' sartorial displays and the unacknowledged conditions determining real experiences of femininity in male-controlled social environments. Her fiction everywhere addresses this conflict between idealising design and socio-economic reality, and it therefore shows very obvious resemblances to Lehmann's *Invitation to the Waltz*, a novel in which patriarchal values are similarly shown to live on in the ubiquitous invitation to women to follow preconceived sartorial and social patterns designed to confirm their socio-economic dependencies on men.

A much more affirmative response to fashion's cultural work came from Bowen. As I have already indicated in these concluding remarks, this writer could see fashion as the facilitator of the subject's desire for creative expression. For her, fashion was intimately connected to the idea of modernity because it had the ability to manifest the subject's immense potential for variation – a prospect that was as exciting as it was occasionally unsettling. Moreover, its ability to visualise in figurative terms the intricately woven social networks and ties that construct modern individuality also fascinated Bowen and encouraged her to relate fashion to connective sociability. Less optimistic about its cultural achievements was Woolf. Her late writing shows fashion's complicity in upholding patriarchal structures and it gives readers glimpses of the consequences that can occur if the desire for structure and organisation, for uniforms and uniformity, creates institutions and socio-political models that assail personal freedoms and individual modes of expression. For all of the writers included in *Modernism, Fashion and Interwar Women Writers*, that is, the engagement with fashion proved such a fertile one because it allowed them to use an expressive cultural manifestation of their time as a means to comment on the social organisation, the political ambitions and cultural misgivings of that very same historical moment.

But fashion, I have argued, also offered these women the possibility to self-reflexively think about their situations as cultural workers in the interwar literary economy. As much as they felt encouraged to use its terminology in their writing to remark on contemporary socio-political circumstances and the organisation of gender hierarchies, they also noted that fashion provided them with conceptual vocabulary with which to deliberate their artistic and professional affiliations with the main cultural impulses of the interwar years. When Bowen writes about conformity and eccentricity in 1956, she is no longer an aspiring young novelist. She is, like her friend Virginia Woolf, part of the English literary canon. During the interwar years, however, all of the women included in this study were trying to establish or consolidate their reputations as professional writers. In response to a burgeoning celebrity culture that turned authors' names into brands, they were attentive to literary fashions and to readers' expectations, and they aimed to define their literary positions and to secure their shares of an expanding, increasingly diversified, literary field. In *Modernism,*

Fashion and Interwar Women Writers, I have shown how such different authors as Wharton or Lehmann self-consciously used fashion terminology to consider these negotiations with the interwar culture industry, and it has been my suggestion throughout that their fiction and criticism often bear marks of these ongoing negotiations on a thematic and sometimes even a formal level. What I have proposed, in other words, was to read the texts they were producing quite literally as carefully crafted textile compositions that reflect their authors' efforts to fashion artistic personas and professional profiles. Bowen, to return to one of her essays for another representative comment, was certainly aware of parallels in the composition of sartorial and textual ensembles: 'To present an appearance, a whole, that shall be not only pleasing but significant ...', she accordingly noted, 'is at least as difficult technically, requires as close a grip by the imagination, as disabused an attitude, as the writing of a book that should be fit to be published' (1950: 112). In both cases – in the successful creation of a social performance and in the writing of a publishable book – the careful management of their public visibility determined these women's attempts at self-styling.

Modernism, Fashion and Interwar Women Writers has taken to heart this suggestion that written compositions can be as elaborately, sparsely or eccentrically adorned as sartorial arrangements by making these women's textual self-stylings central to many of the developed readings. In the cases of Rhys, Lehmann and Bowen, I have argued that a critical attention to stylistic or textual idiosyncrasies is as significant as similarly motivated investigations into strategies for authorial branding through social performances when analysing women writers' engagements with the literary economies of the interwar years. The novels they were writing were the sites on which efforts to affiliate with or depart from contemporary literary traditions become strikingly apparent. As much as fashion determined individual modes of self-styling through clothes, these textual composites expressed rebellion against or accord and compromises with those literary styles perceived to be so dominant as to become fashions in their own right. It is in these individual(ist) modes of textual self-styling that women authors such as Rhys, Lehmann or Bowen knowingly commented on but also defined their positions in the contemporary literary field. And even in those cases (Wharton and Woolf), in which the conceptual engagement with fashion did not seem to leave any clearly observable traces on textual self-stylings, it was nonetheless the reason why these writers thought self-consciously about the role of the women novelist in a market economy that discounted individuality in favour of standardisation – considerations that can be retraced in the manner pursued in the first and final chapter of *Modernism, Fashion and Interwar Women Writers*.

Fashion, I have shown throughout, was principally responsible for shaping the career of these five writers. Whether it was a guideline one was encouraged to follow (Rhys, Lehmann, Woolf), an undesirable cultural affliction (Wharton) or the source of creative energies (Bowen), fashion was part of these women's social and professional realities, and it affected their work on a thematic and sometimes even a formal level. Although the authors themselves might have expressed doubt, if not dislike, of its cultural ascendancy, the novels they were writing show a responsiveness to fashion's imperatives that confirmed its cultural authority. In 1956 Bowen might well be a famous, much-coveted novelist. She consistently travels abroad on behalf of the British Council and reports on events behind the Iron Curtain.[3] But she is still wearing her oversized, fake jewellery and is shying away from the camera. Most importantly, however, she is still writing and thinking about fashion as an index of her culture's desire for conformity and its synchronised longing to express individuality – subjects that obviously continue to be of key interest to both the woman and the writer.

Notes

1. As Emily O. Wittman explains, in '1956, her future literary adviser Francis Wyndham referred to her as "the late Jean Rhys"', believing like most of her contemporaries that Rhys was dead (2014: 185).
2. As Allan Hepburn notes in an essay about Bowen's wartime writing, '[i]ndividual choices, she concludes, have historical consequences' (2009: 134).
3. Some of her essays, such as 'Prague and the Crisis' and 'Hungary', which were written in 1948, but also her observations on youth culture in occupied Germany, 'Without Coffee, Cigarettes, and Feeling' (1955), reveal Bowen's talent for political reportage (2008: 81–99). It is also well known that Bowen was a member of the Royal Commission on Capital Punishment after 1949, a responsibility that required of members significant judiciousness as well as comprehension of the different aspects of this complex public debate.

Bibliography

Angier, Carole (1990), *Jean Rhys: Life and Work*, London: Deutsch.
Anon. (1920), 'Vogue Pattern Service', *Vogue*, 55:4, p. 79.
Anon. (1921), 'Debating Society', *The Girton Review*, 62, p. 3.
Anon. (1923a), '30 Years of the Mode', *Vogue*, 61:3, p. 81.
Anon. (1923b), 'Editorial', *Vogue*, 62:12, p. 18.
Anon. (1924a), 'A Guide to Chic for the Debutante', *Vogue*, 64:1, p. 86.
Anon. (1924b), 'A Guide to Chic for the Business Woman', *Vogue*, 64:6, p. 71.
Anon. (1925), 'Wild Bachelors I Have Met: Some Agonised Entries in the Notebook of a Debutante', *Vogue*, 65:2, p. 70.
Anon. (1926a), 'A Girl with a Past: Anita Loos – Her Story', *Eve: The Lady's Pictorial*, 28 July 1926, pp. 170–1.
Anon. (1926b), *Vogue's Book of Practical Dressmaking*, London: Condé Nast.
Anon. (1927a), 'Edith Sitwell', *Eve: The Lady's Pictorial*, 19 January 1927, p. 127.
Anon. (1927b), 'Mrs Leslie Runciman', *Eve: The Lady's Pictorial*, 20 July 1927, p. 133.
Anon. (1931), 'Uniform Edition: Novels by Virginia Woolf', *Publisher's Weekly*, 10 January 1931, p. 192.
Anon. (1933a), 'The Men who Sold You This', *The Blackshirt*, 24 June to 1 July 1933, p. 4.
Anon. (1933b), 'No Class Distinctions: Fascism Kills that "Feeling"', *The Blackshirt*, 29 July to 4 August 1933, p. 1.
Balla, Giacomo (1914), *Il vestito antineutrale*, Direzione del Movimento Futurista.
Banta, Martha (2003), 'Wharton's Women: In Fashion, In History, Out of Time', in Carol J. Singley (ed.), *A Historical Guide to Edith Wharton*, Oxford: Oxford University Press, pp. 51–88.
Barlow, Jamie (2007), 'No Innocence in this Age: Edith Wharton's Commercialization and Commodification', in Gary Totten (ed.), *Memorial Boxes*

and *Guarded Interiors: Edith Wharton and Material Culture*, Tuscaloosa: The University of Alabama Press, pp. 44–62.
Baudelaire, Charles (1972), *Selected Writings on Art and Literature*, London: Penguin.
Beer, Gillian (1987), 'The Body of the People in Virginia Woolf', in Sue Roe (ed.), *Women Reading Women's Writing*, Sussex: Harvester, pp. 83–114.
Benjamin, Walter (1999), *The Arcades Project*, trans. Howard Eiland and Kevin McLaughlin, Cambridge, MA: Belknap Press.
Bennett, Andrew (2009), 'Bowen and Modernism: The Early Novels', in Eibhear Walshe (ed.), *Elizabeth Bowen*, Dublin: Irish Academic Press, pp. 27–39.
Benstock, Shari (1986), *Women on the Left Bank: Paris, 1900–1940*, Austin: University of Texas Press.
Berman, Jessica (2001a), 'Of Oceans and Opposition: *The Waves*, Oswald Mosley, and the New Party', in Merry M. Pawlowski (ed.), *Virginia Woolf and Fascism: Resisting the Dictators' Seduction*, Basingstoke: Palgrave Macmillan, pp. 105–21.
Berman, Jessica (2001b), *Modernist Fiction, Cosmopolitanism and the Politics of Community*, Cambridge: Cambridge University Press.
Bluemel, Kristin (ed.) (2009), *Intermodernism: Literary Culture in Mid-Twentieth-Century Britain*, Edinburgh: Edinburgh University Press.
Bourdieu, Pierre (1993), *The Field of Cultural Production: Essays on Art and Literature*, Cambridge: Polity Press.
Bourdieu, Pierre (1995), *Sociology in Question*, trans. Richard Nice, London: Sage.
Bourdieu, Pierre (1996), *The Rules of Art: Genesis and Structure of the Literary Field*, Cambridge: Polity Press.
Bowen, Elizabeth (1936), 'The Weather in the Streets. By Rosamond Lehmann', *New Statesman and Nation*, 11 July 1936, p. 54.
Bowen, Elizabeth (1946), *English Novelists*, London: Collins.
Bowen, Elizabeth (1950), *Collected Impressions*, London: Longmans.
Bowen, Elizabeth (1952a), *The Last September*, New York: Knopf.
Bowen, Elizabeth (1952b), *Afterthought: Pieces about Writing*, London: Longmans.
Bowen, Elizabeth (1975), *Pictures and Conversations: Chapters of an Autobiography with a Foreword by Spencer Curtis Brown*, London: Allen Lane.
Bowen, Elizabeth (1998), *The Heat of the Day*, London: Random House.
Bowen, Elizabeth (1999), *The Mulberry Tree: Writings of Elizabeth Bowen*, ed. Hermione Lee, London: Vintage.
Bowen, Elizabeth (2006), *To the North*, New York: Anchor Books.

Bowen, Elizabeth (2008), *People, Places, Things: Essays by Elizabeth Bowen*, ed. Allan Hepburn, Edinburgh: Edinburgh University Press.
Bowen, Elizabeth (2010), *Listening In: Broadcasts, Speeches, and Interviews by Elizabeth Bowen*, ed. Allan Hepburn, Edinburgh: Edinburgh University Press.
Bowen, Elizabeth (2017), *The Weight of a World of Feeling: Reviews and Essays by Elizabeth Bowen*, ed. Allan Hepburn, Evanston, IL: Northwestern University Press.
Bowlby, Rachel (1992), *Still Crazy after all these Years: Women, Writing and Psychoanalysis*, London and New York: Routledge.
Bradshaw, David (1999), 'Hyams Place: *The Years*, the Jews and the British Union of Fascists', in Maroula Joannou (ed.), *Women Writers of the 1930s: Gender, Politics and History*, Edinburgh: Edinburgh University Press, pp. 179–91.
Braudy, Leo (1986), *The Frenzy of Renown: Fame and its History*, New York: Vintage Books.
Britzolakis, Christina (2007), '"This Way to the Exhibition": Geographies of Urban Spectacle in Jean Rhys's Interwar Fiction', *Textual Practice*, 21:3, pp. 457–82.
Brown, Erica and Mary Grover (eds) (2012), *Middlebrow Literary Cultures: The Battle of the Brows, 1920–1960*, Basingstoke: Palgrave Macmillan.
Brown, Judith (2009), *Glamour in Six Dimensions: Modernism and the Radiance of Form*, Ithaca, NY: Cornell University Press.
Buckley, Cheryl and Hilary Fawcett (2001), *Fashioning the Feminine: Representation and Women's Fashion from the Fin de Siècle to the Present*, London: I. B. Tauris.
Burstein, Jessica (2002), 'A Few Words about Dubuque: Modernism, Sentimentality, and the Blasé', *American Literary History*, 14:2, pp. 227–54.
Burstein, Jessica (2012), *Cold Modernism: Literature, Fashion, Art*, University Park: Pennsylvania State University Press.
Cahir, Linda Costanzo (2003), 'Edith Wharton's *Ethan Frome* and Joseph Conrad's *Heart of Darkness*', *The Edith Wharton Review*, 19:1, pp. 20–3.
Campbell, Mary (2004), *Wonder and Science: Imagining Worlds in Early Modern Europe*, Ithaca, NY: Cornell University Press.
Cardon, Lauren S. (2016), *Fashion and Fiction: Self-Transformation in Twentieth-Century American Literature*, Charlottesville and London: University of Virginia Press.
Carr, Helen (1996), *Jean Rhys*, Tavistock: Northcote House Publishers.
Carter, Michael (2003), *Fashion Classics from Carlyle to Barthes*, Oxford and New York: Berg.

Cather, Willa (1988), *Not Under Forty*, Lincoln and London: University of Nebraska Press.

Chan, Evelyn (2014), *Virginia Woolf and the Professions*, Cambridge: Cambridge University Press.

Charles-Roux, Edmonde (1976), *Chanel: Her Life, Her World, and the Woman behind the Legend She Herself Created*, London: Jonathan Cape.

Church Gibson, Pamela (2012), *Fashion and Celebrity*, Oxford and New York: Berg.

Clay, Catherine (2006), *British Women Writers 1914–1945: Professional Work and Friendship*, Aldershot: Ashgate.

Cohen, Lisa (1999), '"Frock Consciousness": Virginia Woolf, the Open Secret, and the Language of Fashion', *Fashion Theory*, 3:2, pp. 149–74.

Collier, Patrick (2002), 'Virginia Woolf in the Pay of Booksellers: Commerce, Privacy, Professionalism, *Orlando*', *Twentieth-Century Literature*, 48:4, pp. 363–92.

Collier, Patrick (2006), *Modernism on Fleet Street*. Aldershot: Ashgate.

Collins, Wilkie (1858), 'The Unknown Public', *Household Words*, 21 August 1858, pp. 217–22

Cooper, John Xiros (2004), *Modernism and the Culture of Market Society*, Cambridge: Cambridge University Press.

Corcoran, Neil (2004), *Elizabeth Bowen: The Enforced Return*, Oxford: Oxford University Press.

Cuddy-Keane, Melba (2003), *Virginia Woolf, the Intellectual, and the Public Sphere*, Cambridge: Cambridge University Press.

Cunningham, Anne (2013), '"Get On or Get Out": Failure and Negative Femininity in Jean Rhys's *Voyage in the Dark*', *Modern Fiction Studies*, 59:2, pp. 373–94.

Cunningham, Patricia A. (2003), *Reforming Women's Fashion, 1850–1920: Politics, Health, and Art*, Kent, OH: Kent State University Press.

de la Haye, Amy and Shelley Tobin (2001), *Chanel: The Couturiere at Work*, London: Victoria and Albert Museum.

Devlin, Kimberly (1985), 'The Romance Heroine Exposed: "Nausicaa" and *The Lamplighter*', *James Joyce Quarterly*, 22:4, pp. 383–96.

DiBattista, Maria and Emily O. Wittman (eds) (2014), *Modernism and Autobiography*, Cambridge: Cambridge University Press.

Dickinson, Emily (1975), *The Complete Poems*, ed. Thomas H. Johnson, London: Faber and Faber.

Doan, Laura (2001), *Fashioning Sapphism: The Origins of a Modern English Lesbian Culture*, New York: Columbia University Press.

Driscoll, Catherine (2010), *Modernist Cultural Studies*, Gainesville: University Press of Florida.

Dubino, Jeanne (1995), 'Creating "The Conditions of Life": Virginia Woolf and the Common Reader', in Eileen Barrett and Patricia Cramer (eds), *Re: Reading, Re: Writing, Re: Teaching Virginia Woolf: Selected Papers from the Fourth Annual Conference on Virginia Woolf*, New York: Pace University Press, pp. 129–37.

Eliot, T. S. (1951), *Selected Essays by T. S. Eliot*, London: Faber and Faber.

Eliot, T. S. (1974), *Collected Poems 1909–1962*, London: Faber and Faber.

Ellmann, Maud (2004), *Elizabeth Bowen: The Shadow across the Page*, Edinburgh: Edinburgh University Press.

Emery, Mary Lou (1990), *Jean Rhys at "World's End": Novels of Colonial and Sexual Exile*, Austin: University of Texas Press.

Evans, Caroline (2003), *Fashion at the Edge: Spectacle, Modernity and Deathliness*, New Haven, CT: Yale University Press.

Evans, Caroline (2013), *The Mechanical Smile: Modernism and the Early Fashion Shows in France and America, 1900–1929*, New Haven, CT: Yale University Press.

Felski, Rita (1995), *The Gender of Modernity*, Cambridge, MA: Harvard University Press.

Flügel, J. C. (1966), *The Psychology of Clothes*, London: The Hogarth Press.

Frisby, David (1986), *Fragments of Modernity: Theories of Modernity in the Work of Simmel, Kracauer and Benjamin*, Cambridge, MA: The MIT Press.

Fryer, Judith (1986), *Felicitous Space: The Imaginative Structures of Edith Wharton and Willa Cather*, Chapel Hill and London: University of North Carolina Press.

Galow, Timothy W. (2010), 'Literary Modernism in the Age of Celebrity', *Modernism/Modernity*, 17:2, pp. 313–29.

Garelick, Rhonda K. (2014), *Mademoiselle: Coco Chanel and the Pulse of History*, New York: Random House.

Garrity, Jane (1999), 'Selling Culture to the "Civilized": Bloomsbury, British *Vogue*, and the Marketing of National Identity', *Modernism/Modernity*, 6:2, pp. 29–58.

Garrity, Jane (2000), 'Virginia Woolf, Intellectual Harlotry, and 1920s British *Vogue*', in Pamela L. Caughie (ed.), *Virginia Woolf in the Age of Mechanical Reproduction*, New York and London: Garland Publishing, pp. 185–218.

Garrity, Jane (2003), *Step-Daughters of England: British Women Modernists and the National Imaginary*, Manchester: Manchester University Press.

Garrity, Jane (2014), 'Sartorial Modernity: Fashion, Gender, and Sexuality in Modernism', in Robert DeMaria, Jr, Heesok Chang and Samantha Zacher (eds), *A Companion to British Literature: Volume IV: Victorian and Twentieth-Century Literature 1837–2000*, Oxford: Blackwell, pp. 260–79.

Geczy, Adam and Vicki Karaminas (eds) (2013), *Queer Style*. London: Bloomsbury.
Gibson, Andrew (2002), *Joyce's Revenge: History, Politics, and Aesthetics in Ulysses*, Oxford: Oxford University Press.
Glass, Loren (2004), *Authors Inc.: Literary Celebrity in the Modern United States, 1880–1980*, New York: New York University Press.
Glendinning, Victoria (1978), *Elizabeth Bowen: A Biography*, New York: Alfred A. Knopf.
Glendinning, Victoria (ed.) (2008), *Love's Civil War: Elizabeth Bowen and Charles Ritchie: Letters and Diaries, 1941–1973*, London: Simon & Schuster.
GoGwilt, Chris (2005), 'The Interior: Benjaminian Arcades, Conradian Passages, and the "Impasse" of Jean Rhys', in Peter Brooker and Andrew Thacker (eds), *Geographies of Modernism: Literatures, Cultures, Spaces*, London: Routledge, pp. 65–75.
Goldman, Jonathan (2011), *Modernism Is the Literature of Celebrity*, Austin: University of Texas Press.
Goldman-Price, Irene (ed.) (2012), *My Dear Governess: The Letters of Edith Wharton to Anna Bahlmann*, New Haven, CT: Yale University Press.
Goldsmith, Meredith (2010), '"Other People's Clothes": Homosociality, Consumer Culture, and Affective Reading in Edith Wharton's *Summer*', *Legacy: A Journal of American Women Writers*, 27:1, pp. 109–27.
Goody, Alex (2000), 'Ladies of Fashion/Modern(ist) Women: Mina Loy and Djuna Barnes', *Women: A Cultural Review*, 10:3, pp. 266–82.
Gordon, Elizabeth Willson (2010), 'On or about December 1928 the Hogarth Press Changed: E. McKnight Kauffner, Art, Markets and the Hogarth Press, 1928–39', in Helen Southworth (ed.), *Leonard and Virginia Woolf: The Hogarth Press and the Networks of Modernism*, Edinburgh: Edinburgh University Press, pp. 179–205.
Gundle, Stephen and Clino T. Caselli (2006), *The Glamour System*, Basingstoke: Palgrave Macmillan.
Hamilton, Cicely (2003), *Diana of Dobson's*, Plymouth: Broadview.
Hammill, Faye (2007), *Women, Celebrity, and Literary Culture between the Wars*, Austin: University of Texas Press.
Hammill, Faye (2010), *Sophistication: A Literary and Cultural History*, Liverpool: Liverpool University Press.
Hanson, Clare (2000), *Hysterical Fictions: The 'Woman's Novel' in the Twentieth Century*, Basingstoke: Palgrave Macmillan.
Hastings, Selina (2003), *Rosamond Lehmann*, London: Vintage.
Haule, James (2009), 'Reading Dante, Misreading Woolf: New Evidence of Virginia Woolf's Revision of *The Years*', in Eleanor McNess and Sara

Veglahn (eds), *Woolf Editing/Editing Woolf: Selected Papers from the Eighteenth Annual Conference on Virginia Woolf*, Clemson, SC: Clemson University Digital Press, pp. 232–44.

Haytock, Jennifer (2008), *Edith Wharton and the Conversations of Literary Modernism*, Basingstoke: Palgrave Macmillan.

Henke, Suzette (1982), 'Gerty MacDowell: Joyce's Sentimental Heroine', in Suzette Henke and Elaine Unkeless (eds), *Women in Joyce*, Urbana: University of Illinois Press, pp. 132–49.

Hepburn, Allan (1998), 'A Passion for Things: Cicerones, Collectors, and Taste in Edith Wharton's Fiction', *Arizona Quarterly*, 54:4, pp. 25–52.

Hepburn, Allan (2009), 'Trials and Errors: *The Heat of the Day* and Postwar Culpability', in Kristin Bluemel (ed.), *Intermodernism: Literary Culture in Mid-Twentieth-Century Britain*, Edinburgh: Edinburgh University Press, pp. 131–49.

Hepburn, Allan (2014), 'A Young Writer Grown Old: Elizabeth Bowen's Autobiographies', in Maria DiBattista and Emily O. Wittman (eds), *Modernism and Autobiography*, Cambridge: Cambridge University Press, pp. 98–112.

Hodgkins, Hope Howell (2016), *Style and the Single Girl: How Modern Women Re-Dressed the Novel, 1922–1977*, Columbus: The Ohio State University Press.

Hollander, Anne (1993), *Seeing through Clothes*, Berkeley and Los Angeles: University of California Press.

Horner Avril and Janet Beer (2011), *Edith Wharton: Sex, Satire and the Older Woman*, Basingstoke: Palgrave Macmillan.

Hughes, Clair (2005), *Dressed in Fiction*, Oxford and New York: Berg.

Humble, Nicola (2001), *The Feminine Middlebrow Novel, 1920s to 1950s: Class, Domesticity, and Bohemianism*, Oxford: Oxford University Press.

Hussey, Mark (1990), '"I" Rejected; "We" Substituted: Self and Society in *Between the Acts*', in Bege K. Bowers and Barbara Brothers (eds), *Reading and Writing Women's Lives: A Study of the Novel of Manners*, Ann Arbor: UMI Research Press, pp. 141–52.

Huyssen, Andreas (1986), *After the Great Divide: Modernism, Mass Culture, Postmodernism*, Bloomington: Indiana University Press.

Inglesby, Elizabeth C. (2007), '"Expressive Objects": Elizabeth Bowen's Narrative Materializes', *Modern Fiction Studies*, 53:2, pp. 306–33.

Jaffe, Aaron (2005), *Modernism and the Culture of Celebrity*, Cambridge: Cambridge University Press.

Jaillant, Lise (2014), *Modernism, Middlebrow and the Literary Canon: The Modern Library Series, 1917–1955*, London: Pickering & Chatto.

Jameson, Fredric (2009), *The Cultural Turn: Selected Writings on the Postmodern, 1983–1998*, London: Verso.

Joannou, Maroula (2012), '"All Right, I'll Do Anything for Good Clothes": Jean Rhys and Fashion', *Women: A Cultural Review*, 23:4, pp. 463–89.

Joannou, Maroula (ed.) (2013), *The History of British Women's Writing, 1920–1945*, Basingstoke: Palgrave Macmillan.

Johnson, Samuel (1977), *Samuel Johnson: Selected Poetry and Prose*, ed. Frank Brady and W. K. Wimsatt, Berkeley: University of California Press.

Joslin, Katherine (2009), *Edith Wharton and the Making of Fashion*, Durham: University of New Hampshire Press.

Kallinay, Peter J. (2013), *Commonwealth of Letters: British Literary Culture and the Emergence of Postcolonial Aesthetics*, New York: Oxford University Press.

Kaplan, Amy (1988), *The Social Construction of American Realism*, Chicago: University of Chicago Press.

Karl, Alissa G. (2009), *Modernism and the Marketplace: Literary Culture and Consumer Capitalism in Rhys, Woolf, Stein, and Nella Larson*, London: Routledge.

Kingsford, R. J. L. (1970), *The Publishers Association, 1896–1946*, Cambridge: Cambridge University Press.

Kirkpatrick, B. J. (1967), *A Bibliography of Virginia Woolf*, London: Hart-Davis.

Knights, Pamela (2008), 'From Lily Bart to Amaryllis: Mrs. Porter's Challenge to Mrs. Wharton', *The Edith Wharton Review*, 24:1, pp. 6–14.

Koppen, R. S. (2009), *Virginia Woolf, Fashion and Literary Modernity*, Edinburgh: Edinburgh University Press.

Kortsch, Christine Bayles (2009), *Dress Culture in Late Victorian Women's Fiction: Literacy, Textiles, and Activism*, Aldershot: Ashgate.

Kracauer, Siegfried (1971), *Die Angestellten*, Frankfurt am Main: Suhrkamp.

Kracauer, Siegfried (1995), *The Mass Ornament: Weimar Essays*, ed. Thomas Y. Levin, Cambridge, MA: Harvard University Press.

Kracauer, Siegfried (1998), *The Salaried Masses: Duty and Distraction in Weimar Germany*, London and New York: Verso.

Kreilkamp, Vera (1998), *The Anglo-Irish Novel and the Big House*, Syracuse, NY: Syracuse University Press.

Latham, Sean (2009), *The Art of Scandal: Modernism, Libel Law and the Roman à Clef*, New York: Oxford University Press.

Leavis, Q. D. (1939), *Fiction and the Reading Public*, London: Chatto and Windus.

Lee, Hermione (2007), *Edith Wharton*, New York: Alfred A. Knopf.

Lehmann, Rosamond (1937), 'Dear Dead Women: English Women's Clothing in the Nineteenth Century. By C. Willet Cunnington', *The Spectator*, 19 November 1937, Literary Supplement, p. 4.

Lehmann, Rosamond (1946), 'The Future of the Novel', *Britain To-Day*, June 1946, pp. 5–11.

Lehmann, Rosamond (1953), 'My First Novel', *The Listener*, 26 March 1953, pp. 513–14.
Lehmann, Rosamond (1981), *Invitation to the Waltz*, London: Virago.
Lehmann, Rosamond (1998), *The Swan in the Evening: Fragments of an Inner Life*, London: Virago.
Lehmann, Ulrich (2001), *Tigersprung: Fashion in Modernity*, Boston: The MIT Press.
Leonard, Garry (1998), *Advertising and Commodity Culture in Joyce*, Gainesville: University Press of Florida.
Lewis, Andrea (2002), 'A Feminine Conspiracy: Contraception, the New Woman, and Empire in Rosamond Lehmann's *The Weather in the Streets*', in Stella Deen (ed.), *Challenging Modernism: New Readings in Literature and Culture, 1914–45*, Aldershot: Ashgate, pp. 81–96.
Lewis, R. W. B. (1975), *Edith Wharton*, New York: Harper and Row.
Lewis, Wyndham (1969), *Wyndham Lewis on Art: Collected Writings 1913–1956*, London: Thames and Hudson.
Light, Alison (1991), *Forever England: Femininity, Literature and Conservatism between the Wars*, London: Routledge.
Linett, Maren (2002), 'The Jew in the Bath: Imperiled Imagination in Woolf's *The Years*', *Modern Fiction Studies*, 48:2, pp. 341–61.
McDayter, Ghislaine (2009), *Byromania and the Birth of Celebrity Culture*, Albany: State University of New York Press.
McKendrick, Neil, John Brewer and J. H. Plumb (1983), *The Birth of a Consumer Society: The Commercialization of Eighteenth-Century England*, London: Hutchinson.
McLoughlin, Kate (ed.) (2013), *The Modernist Party*, Edinburgh: Edinburgh University Press.
Madsen, Axel (1990), *Coco Chanel: A Biography*, London: Bloomsbury.
Mao, Douglas (1998), *Solid Objects: Modernism and the Test of Production*, Princeton: Princeton University Press.
Marsh, Joss (2011), 'The Rise of Celebrity Culture', in Sally Ledger and Holly Furneaux (eds), *Dickens in Context*, Cambridge: Cambridge University Press, pp. 98–108.
Marshik, Celia (2006), *British Modernism and Censorship*, Cambridge: Cambridge University Press.
Marshik, Celia (2017), *At the Mercy of their Clothes: Modernism, the Middlebrow, and British Garment Culture*, New York: Columbia University Press.
Martin, Kirsty (2013), *Modernism and the Rhythms of Sympathy: Vernon Lee, Virginia Woolf, D. H. Lawrence*, Oxford: Oxford University Press.
Marx, Karl (1983), *Capital: Volume 1*, London: Lawrence and Wishart.
Miller, Tyrus (1999), *Late Modernism: Politics, Fiction, and the Arts between the Wars*, Berkeley: University of California Press.

Montagu, Ivor (1934), *Blackshirt Brutality: The Story of Olympia*, London: Workers' Bookshop.

Moran, Joe (2000), *Star Authors: Literary Celebrity in America*, London: Pluto Press.

Mullholland, Terri (2012), 'Between Illusion and Reality, "Who's to Know": Threshold Spaces in the Interwar Novels of Jean Rhys', *Women: A Cultural Review*, 23:4, pp. 445–62.

Nussbaum, Felicity (2005), 'Actresses and the Economies of Celebrity, 1700–1800', in Mary Luckhurst and Jane Moody (eds), *Theatre and Celebrity in Britain, 1660–2000*, Basingstoke: Palgrave Macmillan, pp. 148–68.

Ohler, Paul J. (2006), *Edith Wharton's "Evolutionary Conception": Darwinian Allegory in Her Major Novels*, London: Routledge.

Oliver, Sophie (2016), 'Fashion in Jean Rhys/Jean Rhys in Fashion', *Modernist Cultures*, 11:3, pp. 312–30.

Orgeron, Marsha (2003), 'Making "It" in Hollywood: Clara Bow, Fandom, and Consumer Culture', *Cinema Journal*, 42:4, pp. 76–97.

Osborn, Susan (ed.) (2009), *Elizabeth Bowen: New Critical Perspectives*, Cork: Cork University Press.

Parkins, Ilya (2009), 'Fashion, Femininity and the Ambiguity of the Modern: A Feminist Theoretical Approach to Simmel', in David D. Kim (ed.), *Georg Simmel in Translation: Interdisciplinary Border Crossings in Culture and Modernity*, Newcastle: Cambridge Scholars Publishing, pp. 28–49.

Parkins, Ilya and Elizabeth M. Sheehan (eds) (2011), *Cultures of Femininity in Modern Fashion*, Durham: University of New Hampshire Press.

Paulicelli, Eugenia (2009), 'Fashion and Futurism: Performing Dress', *Annali d'Italianistica*, 27, pp. 187–207.

Pawlowski, Merry M. (2003), 'Exposing Masculine Spectacle: Virginia Woolf's Newspaper Clippings for *Three Guineas* as Contemporary Cultural History', in Karen Schiff (ed.), *Literature and Digital Technologies: W. B. Yeats, Virginia Woolf, Mary Shelley, and William Gass*, Clemson, SC: Clemson University Digital Press, pp. 33–49.

Peel, Robin (2005), *Apart from Modernism: Edith Wharton, Politics, and Fiction before World War I*, Madison, NJ: Fairleigh Dickinson University Press.

Pennell, Melissa (2012), '"Justice" to Edith Wharton? The Early Critical Response', in Laura Rattray (ed.), *Edith Wharton in Context*, Cambridge: Cambridge University Press, pp. 93–102.

Plock, Vike Martina (2010), '"I Guess I'm just Nervous then": Neuropathology and Edith Wharton's Exploration of Interior Geographies', in Laura Salisbury and Andrew Shail (eds), *Neurology and Modernity:*

A Cultural History of Nervous Systems, 1800–1950, Basingstoke: Palgrave Macmillan, pp. 184–203.
Plock, Vike Martina (2017), '"A Journal of the Period": Modernism and Conservative Modernity in *Eve: The Lady's Pictorial* (1919–1929)', in Catherine Clay, Maria DiCenzo, Barbara Green and Fiona Hackney (eds), *Women's Periodicals and Print Culture in Britain, 1919–1939: The Interwar Period*, Edinburgh: Edinburgh University Press.
Pollard, Wendy (2004), *Rosamond Lehmann and Her Critics: The Vagaries of Literary Reception*, Aldershot: Ashgate.
Port, Cynthia (2001), '"Money, for the Night is Coming": Jean Rhys and Gendered Economies of Ageing', *Women: A Cultural Review*, 12:2, pp. 204–17.
Potter, Rachel (2013), *Obscene Modernism: Literary Censorship and Experiment 1900–1940*, Oxford: Oxford University Press.
Price, Alan (1988), *The End of the Age of Innocence: Edith Wharton and the First World War*, London: Robert Hale.
Radin, Grace (1981), *Virginia Woolf's The Years: The Evolution of a Novel*, Knoxville: The University of Tennessee Press.
Rainey, Lawrence (1998), *Institutions of Modernism: Literary Elites and Public Culture*, New Haven, CT: Yale University Press.
Rainey, Lawrence (ed.) (2005), *Modernism: An Anthology*, Oxford: Blackwell.
Rattray, Laura (ed.) (2012), *Edith Wharton in Context*, Cambridge: Cambridge University Press.
Rhys, Jean (1972), *Tigers are Better-Looking with a Selection from The Left Bank*, London: Penguin.
Rhys, Jean (1979), *Smile Please: An Unfinished Autobiography*, London: André Deutsch.
Rhys, Jean (1984), *The Letters of Jean Rhys*, ed. Francis Wyndham and Diana Melly, New York: Viking.
Rhys, Jean (2000a), *After Leaving Mr Mackenzie*, London: Penguin.
Rhys, Jean (2000b), *Good Morning, Midnight*, London: Penguin.
Rhys, Jean (2000c), *Quartet*, London: Penguin.
Rhys, Jean (2000d), *Voyage in the Dark*, London: Penguin.
Rizzuto, Nicole (2001), 'Realism, Form, Politics: Reading Connections in Caribbean Migration Narratives', *Comparative Literature*, 63:4, pp. 383–401.
Roach, Joseph (2007), *It*, Ann Arbor: University of Michigan Press.
Roberts, Mary Louise (2003), 'Samson and Delilah Revisited: The Politics of Fashion in 1920s France', in Whitney Chadwick and Tirza True Latimer (eds), *The Modern Woman Revisited: Paris between the Wars*, New Brunswick, NJ: Rutgers University Press, pp. 65–94.

Rose, Jonathan and Patricia Anderson (eds) (1991), *British Literary Publishing Houses, 1881–1965*, Detroit: Gale.

Rosenbaum, S. P. (1995), *Leonard and Virginia Woolf at the Hogarth Press*, Austin: The Harry Ransom Humanities Research Center.

Rosenquist, Rod (2009), *Modernism, the Market and the Institution of the New*, Cambridge: Cambridge University Press.

Rosenquist, Rod (2013), 'Modernism, Celebrity and the Public Persona', *Literature Compass*, 10:5, pp. 437–48.

Said, Edward (2007), *On Late Style*, London: Bloomsbury.

Saunders, Judith P. (2009), *Reading Edith Wharton through a Darwinian Lens*, Jefferson, NC: McFarland and Company.

Savory, Elaine (1998), *Jean Rhys*, Cambridge: Cambridge University Press.

Shannon, Brent (2006), *The Cut of his Coat: Men, Dress, and Consumer Culture in Britain, 1860–1914*, Athens: Ohio University Press.

Shepherd, Jennifer (2007), 'Fashioning an Aesthetics of Consumption in *The House of Mirth*', in Gary Totten (ed.), *Memorial Boxes and Guarded Interiors: Edith Wharton and Material Culture*, Tuscaloosa: University of Alabama Press, pp. 135–58.

Showalter, Elaine (1977), *A Literature of Their Own*, Princeton: Princeton University Press.

Siegle, Lucy (2011), *To Die for: Is Fashion Wearing out the World?* London: Fourth Estate.

Silver, Brenda R. (1999), *Virginia Woolf Icon*, Chicago: University of Chicago Press.

Simmel, Georg (1971), *On Individuality and Social Forms*, ed. Donald N. Levine, Chicago: University of Chicago Press.

Simons, Judy (1992), *Rosamond Lehmann*, London: Macmillan.

Simons, Judy (1998), 'The Vanishing Hero: Men and Modernity in Rosamond Lehmann's *The Weather in the Streets*', *Critical Survey*, 10:3, pp. 95–104.

Simpson, Kathryn (2008), *Gifts, Markets and Economies of Desire in Virginia Woolf*, Basingstoke: Palgrave Macmillan.

Snaith, Anna (2014), *Modernist Voyages: Colonial Women Writers in London, 1890–1945*, Cambridge: Cambridge University Press.

Sombart, Werner (1902), *Wirtschaft und Mode*, Wiesbaden: J. F. Bergman.

Southworth, Helen (ed.) (2010), *Leonard and Virginia Woolf: The Hogarth Press and the Networks of Modernism*, Edinburgh: Edinburgh University Press.

Spencer, Herbert (1854), 'Manners and Fashion', *The Westminster Review*, LXI, April 1854, pp. 180–208.

Spencer, Herbert (1888), *Ceremonial Institutions*, New York: Appleton and Company.

Staley, Thomas F. (1979), *Jean Rhys: A Critical Study*, Basingstoke: Palgrave Macmillan.
Stead, Lisa (2016), *Off to the Pictures: Cinemagoing, Women's Writing and Movie Culture in Interwar Britain*, Edinburgh: Edinburgh University Press.
Stephenson, Liisa (2010), 'Decorating Fiction: Edith Wharton's Literary Architecture', *University of Toronto Quarterly*, 79:4, pp. 1096-104.
Thacker, Andrew (2003), *Moving through Modernity: Space and Geography in Modernism*, Manchester: Manchester University Press.
Thompson, John B. (2012), *Merchants of Culture: The Publishing Business in the Twenty-First Century*, Cambridge: Polity Press.
Thornton, Edie (2001), 'Selling Edith Wharton: Illustration, Advertising, and *Pictorial Review*, 1924–25', *Arizona Quarterly*, 57:3, pp. 29–59.
Totten, Gary (2012), 'Selling Wharton', in Laura Rattray (ed.), *Edith Wharton in Context*, Cambridge: Cambridge University Press, pp. 127–36.
Truett, Brandon (2014), 'Materializing the Fascist Aesthetic in *Three Guineas*', *Virginia Woolf Miscellany*, 85, pp. 25–8.
Veblen, Thorstein (1994), *The Theory of the Leisure Class*, London: Penguin.
Vinken, Barbara (2005), *Fashion Zeitgeist*, Oxford and New York: Berg.
Vita-Finzi, Penelope (1990), *Edith Wharton and the Art of Fiction*, London: Pinter Publishers.
Warner, Eric (1980), 'Reconsidering *The Years*', *North Dakota Quarterly*, 48:2, pp. 16–30.
Wegener, Frederick (1995), 'Edith Wharton and the Difficult Writing of *The Writing of Fiction*', *Modern Language Studies*, 25:2, pp. 60–79.
Wegener, Frederick (1998), 'Form, "Selection," and Ideology in Edith Wharton's Antimodernist Aesthetic', in Clare Colquitt, Susan Goodman and Candace Waid (eds), *A Forward Glance: New Essays on Edith Wharton*, Newark: University of Delaware Press, pp. 116–38.
Wharton, Edith (1934), *A Backward Glance*, New York and London: D. Appleton.
Wharton, Edith (1988), *The Letters of Edith Wharton*, ed. R. W. B. Lewis and Nancy Lewis, New York: Scribner.
Wharton, Edith (1995a), *The Custom of the Country*, Oxford: Oxford University Press.
Wharton, Edith (1995b), *Madame de Treymes and Three Novellas*, New York: Scribner.
Wharton, Edith (1996), *Edith Wharton: The Uncollected Critical Writings*, ed. Frederick Wegener, Princeton: Princeton University Press.
Wharton, Edith (1997a), *Twilight Sleep*, New York: Scribner.

Wharton, Edith (1997b), *The Writing of Fiction*, New York: Touchstone.
Wharton, Edith (2006a), *The Children*, London: Virago.
Wharton, Edith (2006b), *The Gods Arrive*, London: Virago.
Wharton, Edith (2006c), *Hudson River Bracketed*, London: Virago.
Wharton, Edith (2008), *The House of Mirth*, Oxford: Oxford University Press.
Wharton, Edith (2009), *The Unpublished Writings of Edith Wharton*, ed. Laura Rattray, 2 vols, London: Pickering & Chatto.
Wharton, Edith and Ogden Codman, Jr (1978), *The Decoration of Houses*, New York and London: W. W. Norton & Company.
Whipple, Dorothy (2009), *High Wages*, London: Persephone.
Wilde, Jane Francesca (2010), *Social Studies*, Cambridge: Cambridge University Press.
Willis, J. H. (1992), *Leonard and Virginia Woolf as Publishers: The Hogarth Press, 1917–41*, Charlottesville and London: University Press of Virginia.
Willison, Ian, Warwick Gould and Warren Chernaik (eds) (1996), *Modernist Writers and the Marketplace*, Basingstoke: Palgrave Macmillan.
Wilson, Elizabeth (2005), *Adorned in Dreams: Fashion and Modernity*, London: I. B. Tauris.
Wilson, Richard Guy (1988), 'Edith and Ogden: Writing, Decoration, and Architecture', in Pauline C. Metcalf (ed.), *Ogden Codman and the Decoration of Houses*, Boston: David R. Godine, pp. 133–84.
Winning, Joanne (2013), '"Ezra through the Open Door": The Parties of Natalie Barney, Adrienne Monnier and Sylvia Beach as Lesbian Modernist Cultural Productions', in Kate McLoughlin (ed.), *The Modernist Party*, Edinburgh: Edinburgh University Press, pp. 127–46.
Wittman, Emily O. (2014), '"Death before the Fact": Posthumous Autobiography in Jean Rhys's *Good Morning, Midnight* and *Smile Please*', in Maria DiBattista and Emily O. Wittman (eds), *Modernism and Autobiography*, Cambridge: Cambridge University Press, pp. 185–96.
Wood, Alice (2013), *Virginia Woolf's Late Cultural Criticism: The Genesis of 'The Years', 'Three Guineas', and 'Between the Acts'*, London: Bloomsbury Academic.
Woolf, Leonard (1967), *Downhill All the Way: An Autobiography of the Years 1919 to 1939*, New York: Harcourt, Brace.
Woolf, Leonard and Virginia Woolf (2006), 'Are Too Many Books Written and Published', *PMLA*, 121:1, pp. 253–4.
Woolf, Virginia (1977), *The Pargiters: The Novel-Essay Portion of The Years*, ed. Mitchell A. Leaska, New York: Readex Books.
Woolf, Virginia (1979a), *Mrs. Dalloway's Party*, ed. Stella McNichol, Orlando: Harcourt.

Woolf, Virginia (1979b), *The Letters of Virginia Woolf. Volume 5: 1932–1935*, ed. Nigel Nicolson and Joanne Trautmann, London: The Hogarth Press.
Woolf, Virginia (1980a), *The Diary of Virginia Woolf. Volume 2: 1920–1924*, ed. Anne Olivier Bell, Orlando: Harcourt, Brace.
Woolf, Virginia (1980b), *The Diary of Virginia Woolf. Volume 3: 1925–1930*, ed. Anne Olivier Bell, Orlando: Harcourt, Brace.
Woolf, Virginia (1982), *To the Lighthouse: The Original Holograph Draft*, ed. Susan Dick, Toronto: University of Toronto Press.
Woolf, Virginia (1983), *The Diary of Virginia Woolf. Volume 4: 1931–1935*, ed. Anne Olivier Bell, Orlando: Harcourt, Brace.
Woolf, Virginia (1984), *The Diary of Virginia Woolf. Volume 5: 1936–1941*, ed. Anne Olivier Bell, Orlando: Harcourt, Brace.
Woolf, Virginia (1986), *The Essays of Virginia Woolf. Volume 1: 1904–1912*, ed. Andrew McNeillie, London: The Hogarth Press.
Woolf, Virginia (1988), *The Essays of Virginia Woolf. Volume 3: 1919–1924*, ed. Andrew McNeillie, Orlando: Harcourt, Brace.
Woolf, Virginia (1992a), *To the Lighthouse*, ed. Stella McNichol, London: Penguin.
Woolf, Virginia (1992b), *A Room of One's Own and Three Guineas*, ed. Morag Shiach, Oxford: Oxford University Press.
Woolf, Virginia (1992c), *The Years*, New York: Vintage.
Woolf, Virginia (1994), *The Essays of Virginia Woolf. Volume 4: 1925–1928*, ed. Andrew McNeillie, Orlando: Harcourt, Brace.
Woolf, Virginia (2010), *The Essays of Virginia Woolf. Volume 5: 1929–1932*, ed. Stuart N. Clarke, Boston: Houghton Mifflin Harcourt.
Woolf, Virginia (2011), *The Essays of Virginia Woolf. Volume 6: 1933–1941*, ed. Stuart N. Clarke, London: The Hogarth Press.
Woolf, Virginia (2012), *The Cambridge Edition of the Works of Virginia Woolf: The Years*, ed. Anna Snaith, Cambridge: Cambridge University Press.
Young, John K. (2000), 'Canonicity and Commercialization in Woolf's Uniform Edition', in Ann L. Ardis and Bonnie Kime Scott (eds), *Virginia Woolf: Turning the Centuries: Selected Papers from the Ninth Annual Conference on Virginia Woolf*, New York: Pace University Press, pp. 236–43.
Young, John K. (2010), '"Murdering an Aunt or Two": Textual Practice and Narrative Form in Virginia Woolf's Metropolitan Market', in Jeanne Dubino (ed.), *Virginia Woolf and the Literary Marketplace*, Basingstoke: Palgrave Macmillan, pp. 181–95.
Zakreski, Patricia (2006), *Representing Female Artistic Labour, 1848–1890: Refining Work for the Middle-Class Woman*, Aldershot: Ashgate.

Zemgulys, Andrea (2013), 'Menu, Memento, Souvenir: From Personal Memory to Social Imagination in Jean Rhys's *Good Morning, Midnight*', in Kerry L. Johnson and Mary Wilson (eds), *Rhys Matters*, Basingstoke: Palgrave Macmillan, pp. 21–39.

Zimring, Rishona (2000), 'The Make-Up of Jean Rhys's Fiction', *Novel*, 33:2, pp. 212–34.

Index

Angier, Carole, 106n15
Austen, Jane, 215n29

Bahlmann, Anna (Edith Wharton's governess), 61, 68n4
Balla, Giacomo, *Il vestito antineutrale* (1914), 33n20
Banta, Martha, 42
Barlow, Jamie, 71n22
Barnes, Djuna, 33n22
Barrett Browning, Elizabeth, 128
Barthes, Roland, 43, 69n9
Baudelaire, Charles, 31nn7–8
  'The Painter of Modern Life' (1863), 8, 34n23
Beach, Sylvia, 102
Beer, Gillian, 213n17
Beer, Janet, 71n23
Bell, Clive, 140n4, 140n8
Bell, Vanessa, 140n8, 203
Bellmer, Hans, 105n13
Benjamin, Walter, 8, 9, 34n23
Bennett, Arnold, 162
Benstock, Shari, 102
Berenson, Bernard, 71n24
Berman, Jessica, 36n33, 211n5
Bildungsroman, 101, 108n34, 115
Blackshirt, The (magazine), 210n1
blackshirt uniform, 181–2, 186–7, 209
Bluemel, Kristin, 17
Bourdieu, Pierre, 34n24, 164, 173, 206
  aligns '*haute couture*' with '*haute culture*', 2
  'field of cultural production', 3, 17
  'pseudo-concepts' or 'practical classifying tools', 19
Bow, Clara, 31n6, 70n18, 91–2
Bowen, Elizabeth, 5, 17, 23, 32n17, 142n17, 145–80, 199, 214n22
  argues for the novel's potential for social analysis, 24, 150, 175n9
  becomes established writer in the 1930s, 147, 164, 165, 166, 172

  clothing imagery in, 151–2, 153–62, 175n10, 178n17
  and connective sociability, 20, 22, 27–8, 145–7, 150–1, 153–60, 169, 174n1, 175n9, 176n11, 178n17, 220
  correspondence with publishers and editors of, 28, 146, 168–71
  critical engagement with modernism, 19, 28, 34n28, 67, 138, 145–8, 161–5, 173, 174n2
  critical of book cover designs, 146, 168–9, 172, 180n28
  critical of interwar marketplace, 28, 67, 145, 148, 167, 170–3, 179n26
  and highbrow ambitions, 14, 28, 145, 146, 165–6, 169–73
  identifies fashion as expressive of individuality, 218, 220, 222
  idiosyncratic dress of, 149, 158, 175n7, 222
  'imaginative' versus 'inventive' writer in, 28, 148, 167–8, 169, 180n27
  journalistic work on fashion, 149, 217
  and Nobel Prize in Literature (1963), 180n30
  office politics depicted in, 156–9
  post-war life and reputation of, 217, 222n3
  presents characters externally, 161–3, 174n3
  promotes modernism, 12, 18, 27, 28, 138, 148, 163–5, 173, 178n21
  prose style of, 146, 170–2, 180n29
  and realism, 162–3, 173, 174n2
  relationship between reader and characters in, 160–2
  relationship with Woolf, 145, 147, 162–3
  representation of objects in, 146, 147, 152–3, 163, 175n6
  reviews Rosamond Lehmann's *The Weather in the Streets*, 133, 143n24
  'sartorial connections' in, 27–8, 146, 153, 160, 163, 172

Bowen, Elizabeth (*Cont.*)
  self-conception as a writer, 147–8, 165–8, 169–72, 221
  'ties' in, 20, 146–7, 153–6, 176n12, 177n14
  unperturbed outlook on fashion of, 27, 177n16, 220
  writing for money, 28, 147, 166–7, 171, 172, 179nn23–5
  WORKS
  Ann Lee's and Other Stories (1926), 175n5
  'The Art of Respecting Boundaries', 176n11
  Collected Edition of, 178n19, 180n30
  The Demon Lover (1945), 179n22
  'The Disinherited', 168
  English Novelists (1946), 18
  Eva Trout (1969), 169, 180n28
  Friends and Relations (1931), 150
  'The Happy Autumn Fields', 168
  The Heat of the Day (1948), 133, 155–6, 168, 170, 176n14
  The Hotel (1927), 150
  The House in Paris (1935), 133, 168, 180n28
  'How to Be Yourself – And Not Eccentric', 217
  The Last September (1929), 175n10
  The Little Girls (1964), 174n3, 180n28
  'Pictures and Conversations', 174n2
  'The Poetic Element in Fiction', 150, 153
  'Summer Night', 168
  A Time in Rome (1960), 217
  To the North (1932), 27, 107n24, 146–7, 150–5, 156–63, 165, 169, 174n3, 175n10
  'What We Need in Writing', 179n26
Bowlby, Rachel, 80
Bradshaw, David, 212n7
Braudy, Leo, 31n5, 31n11
British Union of Fascists (BUF), 181–2, 187, 211n5
Brittain, Vera, 211n2
Britzolakis, Christina, 100
Brown, Bill, 175n6
Brown, Erica, 34n25
Brown, Judith, 20–1, 35n31
Browning, Robert, 24
Burstein, Jessica, 21, 35nn30–1
Byron, George Gordon, Lord, 7, 30n4

Cahir, Linda Costanzo, 71n21
Cameron, Alan, 149, 177n16
Campbell, Mary, 36n38
capitalism
  and demand for uniform-looking products, 7, 10, 11, 12, 28–9, 40
  role of fashion and celebrity culture in, 7, 10, 13, 24

Cardon, Lauren S., 36n40
Carlyle, Thomas, 34n23
Carr, Helen, 104n4
Carter, Michael, 69n9
Cather, Willa, 'The Novel Démeublé', 176n13
celebrity culture, 7–13
  and authors, 7, 13, 32n14, 33nn21–2, 36n39, 220
  in the long eighteenth century, 9, 31n12
  and publishers' publicity campaigns, 3
  and women writers, 13, 220
Cézanne, Paul, 72n29
Chan, Evelyn, 212n13
Chanel, Coco, 93
  and celebrity culture, 78
  designing clothes that facilitated movement, 78–9, 105n11
  embodying and promoting female professional success and emancipation, 78–9, 85, 90
  as most important style guide in the interwar period, 77
  treatment of mannequins, 79, 105n11, 105n12
Chatto & Windus, 112, 113, 116, 137, 140n4, 144n26
Christie, Agatha, 6
Church Gibson, Pamela, 8–9
Clay, Catherine, 36n35
Codman, Ogden, Jr., 46, 50, 51, 58, 69n10
Cohen, Lisa, 30n1
Colette, 72n29
Collier, Patrick, 143n21, 143n22, 184, 207, 208, 216n33
Collins (publisher), 124, 137, 144n26, 204
Collins, Wilkie, 'unknown public', 207, 216n34
Conrad, Joseph, 109n35
Constable (publisher), 165, 179n22
Corcoran, Neil, 155, 174n2
Crane, Stephen, 75
crowds, 2, 74
Crowninshield, Frank (editor of *Vanity Fair*), 70n18
Cuddy-Keane, Melba, 213n18
Cunningham, Anne, 108n28
Cunningham, Patricia A., 30n2
Cunnington, C. Willett, *English Women's Clothing in the Nineteenth Century* (1937), 142n17, 149
Curtis Brown, Spencer, 174n3

Darwin, Charles, 49
Devlin, Kimberly, 141n9
Dickens, Charles, 7, 30n4
Dickinson, Emily, 121, 142n16
Doan, Laura, 33n22
Dreiser, Theodore, 36n40

Driscoll, Catherine, 79, 91
Duckworth, Gerald, 200, 202, 203, 214n23
Duncan, Isadora, 72n29

Eliot, George, *Middlemarch* (1871–2), 129
Eliot, T. S., 17, 21, 33n20
    'Tradition and the Individual Talent', 58, 70n19
    The Waste Land (1922), 59, 94
Ellmann, Maud, 152, 162, 174n2
Emery, Mary Lou, 103n2
Evans, Caroline, 31n9, 84, 86, 104n10, 108n31
Eve: The Lady's Pictorial (magazine), 143n23

fascism
    detrimental to individuation, 28, 186–7
    and reliance on sartorial signifiers, 28, 181–2, 187, 198, 210n1
fashion
    and adaptation versus differentiation, 2, 13, 20, 35n29, 48, 53, 76, 110, 112, 122, 125, 130, 136, 149, 196–7, 209, 217–19
    and affiliations, 1, 20, 21–2, 35n32, 36nn33–4
    and broader questions of taste, style and appearance, 2, 10, 30
    and 'dress', 43–4
    in evolutionary theory, 47–9
    and fascism *see* fascism and reliance on sartorial signifiers
    and female professional competence, 33n19, 93–7, 107n24, 120, 157–9
    Fordist aesthetics in, 86–7
    and gender politics, 4, 14–16, 22, 27, 29, 188–91
    and identity formation, 1, 6, 13, 22, 219
    and impersonality, 21
    as male-dominated discourse, 16, 34n23
    and the (modernist) novel, 23–5, 36n38
    mounting influence of, 9–10, 30, 47, 64, 222
    and novelty, 7–8, 9–10, 11–12, 23, 31n9, 36n36, 39, 40, 41, 50, 68n5, 111, 146
    offering fantasies of transformation and improvement, 74, 77–9, 81–6, 96
    politically motivated appropriations of, 2, 29, 185
    relationship with celebrity culture, 7–9
    and social hierarchies, 48–9, 83, 106n16, 190
    typecasting in, 86–7, 124
    and uniformity, 1, 10, 11, 30, 39, 49, 53, 73, 86–7, 106n20, 106n21, 112, 157–8, 182–3, 188, 193–4, 195–6, 210n1, 220

Faulkner, Willian, 36n40
Fitzgerald, F. Scott, 31n10
Flapper couture, 26, 79, 90, 219
Flaubert, Gustave, 109n35
Flügel, J. C., 16, 34n23, 117, 141n14, 156–7
    'great masculine renunciation', 14–15, 33n20, 212n10
    The Psychology of Clothes (1930), 14, 89, 106n16, 190
Ford, Ford Madox, 26, 73, 75, 109n35
Forster, E. M., 18, 34n28
Fry, Roger, 140n4, 140n8
Fryer, Judith, 51, 70n15
Futurism, 33n20, 60

Galsworthy, John, 162
Garelick, Rhonda K., 78
Garrick, David, 9
Garrity, Jane, 23, 36n34, 85, 106n17, 106n20, 140n8, 141n13
Gaskell, Elizabeth, 128
Gibbons, Stella, 32n16
Gibson, Andrew, 141n13
Gibson Girl, 79, 82
Girton Review (college newsletter), 139n2
Glass, Loren, 33n21
Glendinning, Victoria, 140n6, 149
Glyn, Elinor, 70n18
GoGwilt, Chris, 97
Goldman, Jonathan, 11
Goldsmith, Meredith, 43
Goody, Alex, 33n22
Gordon, Elizabeth Willson, 215n26
Grant, Duncan, 140n8
Greene, Graham, 167
Grover, Mary, 34n25

Hall, Radclyffe, 33n22, 205
Hamilton, Cicely, *Diana of Dobson's* (1908), 83, 106n17
Hammill, Faye, 32n16, 33n18, 35n31, 36n39
Hanson, Clare, 143n18
Harcourt, Brace (publisher), 198, 213n15, 214n20, 214n25, 215n28
Harper's Bazaar (magazine), 179n25
Hastings, Selina, 113, 140n6
Haule, James, 213n19
Haytock, Jennifer, 62
Hemingway, Ernest, 33n21, 36n40, 205
Henke, Suzette, 141n9
Hepburn, Allan, 45, 52, 166, 171, 175n9, 179n23, 179n25, 222n2
Hitler, Adolf, 186, 211n2, 213n18
Hodgkins, Hope Howell, 32n16
Hogarth Press, 14, 23, 29, 139n1, 190, 198
    begins to print Uniform Edition of Woolf, 178n19, 199, 201–6, 207, 215n25, 215n27

Hogarth Press (*Cont.*)
  relationship with commercial publishing, 199, 201–2, 204–6, 214n24, 215n26, 215n30, 215n31
Hollander, Anne, 43
Hollywood star culture, 3, 7, 31n6
Horner, Avril, 71n23
Hughes, Clair, 43
Humble, Nicola, 34n25, 140n5
Hussey, Mark, 213n17
Hutchinson, Mary, 185
Huxley, Aldous, 140n4
Huxley, Thomas Henry, 49

Imagisme, 21
Inglesby, Elizabeth C., 152
intermodernism, 17, 18
interwar period
  and 'conservative modernity', 218
  and gender politics, 1, 4, 29, 90–3, 96, 124, 127
  literary field of, 3, 5, 6, 10–11, 16–19, 34nn26–7, 221
  and mass culture, 10–11
  social and cultural change during, 1, 116, 127, 131
It (movie) (1927), 70n18, 91–2

Jaffe, Aaron, 11, 57, 77, 148
  'imprimatur', 5–6, 39, 41, 146
Jaillant, Lise, 208, 216n35
James, Charles (designer), 185, 211n3
Jameson, Fredric, 5, 11
Jameson, Storm, 211n2
Joannou, Maroula, 34n26, 85
Jonathan Cape (individual and publisher), 170, 172, 178n19, 179n22, 180n28, 180n30, 204–6
Joslin, Katherine, 42–3, 68n4
Joyce, James, 15, 17, 34n28, 78, 148, 164
  Ulysses (1922), 21, 33n20, 59, 60, 141n9

Kallinay, Peter J., 77, 104n8
Kaplan, Amy, 14, 68n6
Karl, Alissa G., 89, 100, 107n22
Kauffer, E. McKnight, 202, 215n26
Kirkpatrick, B. J., 213n20
Knights, Pamela, 67n2
Knopf, Alfred A., 176n12
Knopf, Blanche W., 177n16, 180n30
Koppen, R. S., 32n15, 212n11
Kortsch, Christine Bayles, 129
Kracauer, Siegfried, 10–11, 32n14, 34n23, 40, 86, 107n26, 157–8
  'salaried-bohemians', 94–5, 107n27, 177n15
Kreilkamp, Vera, 174n2

Larsen, Nella, 36n40
Latham, Sean, 75
Lawrence, D. H., *Women in Love* (1920), 35n30, 36n34
Leavis, Q. D., 207, 215n32
Lehmann, John, 138n1
Lehmann, Rosamond, 5, 10–11, 17, 19, 23, 103, 104n6, 110–44, 145, 148, 217, 221, 222
  abortion motif in, 135
  associates fashion with patriarchal values, 16, 27, 111–12, 113, 115, 123–4, 142n17, 219–20
  being trivialised as a writer, 116, 140n5, 141n10
  biography of, 110, 138n1, 140n6
  clothes and fashion imagery in, 117, 119, 122, 123, 131, 141n14
  collaborations with other women writers, 112, 132–6
  comments on Woolf's writing style, 126–7
  commercial success of, 113, 115, 132, 137, 143n23
  as design-conscious writer, 116, 119–20, 124, 127, 129–30
  emphasis on communality and women's experiences in, 110, 111, 112, 131, 132, 135, 136, 144n25
  Girton letters of, 113–14, 121, 122–3, 141n13
  identifies fashion as producer of feminine types, 111–12, 120, 122
  interest in stylistic experimentation, 116, 137, 140n5
  intertextual dialogue with Rhys, 134–6, 137
  intertextual dialogue with Woolf, 27, 112, 125, 127–30, 137, 143n18
  knitting imagery in, 128–30
  literary aspirations of, 110–11, 112, 125, 137–8, 140n3
  on literary trends, 10–11
  and 'modish modernism', 27, 112–13, 132, 137–8
  'patterns' in, 110, 111, 120, 122–3, 132, 141n15
  preoccupation with clothes, 110, 113–15, 139n2
  promoting modernism, 12, 18, 27, 28, 126, 138
  relationship with Elizabeth Bowen, 133, 143n24
  relationship with literary marketplace, 110, 111, 130, 137–8
  self-conception as an author, 111, 125, 131, 136
  tries to befriend Jean Rhys, 134
  uses sartorial tropes to represent writing and authorship, 121–2, 124

WORKS
 The Ballad and the Source (1944), 139n1
 Dusty Answer (1927), 132, 139n1, 140n5, 143n18, 143n23
 The Echoing Grove (1953), 144n25
 The Gypsy's Baby and Other Stories (1946), 139n1
 Invitation to the Waltz (1932), 27, 111–12, 115–25, 127–31, 135, 136, 137–8, 139n1, 140n5, 142n15, 219
 No More Music (1939), 139n1
 A Note in Music (1930), 115, 139n1
 The Weather in the Streets (1936), 112, 115, 123, 124, 133, 134–6, 137, 139n1, 142n15
Lehmann, Ulrich, 68n5
Lelong, Lucien, 105n10
Lewis, Andrea, 135
Lewis, R. W. B., 62, 70n18
Lewis, Wyndham, 15, 33n20, 140n4
 'The Caliph's Design', 32n15
Light, Alison, 218
Linett, Maren, 212n7, 216n37
Listener (magazine), 140n3, 179n25
London, Jack, 33n21
Loos, Anita, 32n16
 Gentlemen Prefer Blondes (1925), 3, 70n18
Loy, Mina, 33n22

Macaulay, Rose, 34n28
McLoughlin, Kate, 36n33
Mademoiselle (magazine), 166
Mailer, Norman, 33n21
Mansfield, Katherine, 35n28
Mao, Douglas, 174n4
Marinetti, F. T., 15
Marshik, Celia, 22, 30n1, 75, 83, 96, 106n19, 108n29, 108n33, 141n12, 174n1
Martin, Kirsty, 213n17
Marx, Karl, 159–60
 'commodity fetishism', 153, 160
Maupassant, Guy de, 109n35
middlebrow literary culture, 16–19, 34n25, 65, 113, 140n5, 167
Miller, Tyrus, 34n27, 178n18
Mitchell, Margaret, 213n20
modernism (male)
 and celebrity culture, 11, 12, 25, 33n21
 challenging cultural hegemonies through the use of fashion, 15, 33n20
 and commercial literature, 5–6, 12, 17–19, 40
 dissemination and promotion of, 5–6, 11–12, 18–19, 77, 102, 164–5
 and early twentieth-century dress designs, 20–1, 35n31
 and exclusivity, 5, 11–12, 13, 28, 102

 and novelty, 11, 40, 41, 65, 173
 preoccupation with interiority, 19, 28, 138, 146, 148, 161–2, 173
 as prestige commodity, 11, 18, 32n15, 34n24, 173
Mosley, Sir Oswald, 181, 182, 187, 211n5, 211n6
Mulholland, Terri, 108n30
Murray, Ronald (Woolf's dressmaker), 185, 212n11

National Socialism (NSDAP), 186, 187
New Statesman (magazine), 179n25
Nicolson, Harold, 211n5

Ohler, Paul J., 50, 69n14
Oliver, Sophie, 104n9
Orgeron, Marsha, 92
Osborn, Susan, 180n29

Parker, Dorothy, 32n16
Parkins, Ilya, 35n29, 36n32
Patou, Jean, 78, 86
Paulicelli, Eugenia, 33n20
Pawlowski, Merry M., 189
Peel, Robin, 59, 71n21
Pennell, Melissa M., 71n23
Philipps, Wogan, 125, 139n1, 143n19
Pictorial Review (magazine), 62, 71n22
Pollard, Wendy, 140n4, 141n11
Port, Cynthia, 89
Pound, Ezra, 12, 17, 21, 148
 'Make it new', 11
Proust, Marcel, 144n26
Public Order Act (1936), 181–2
Punch (magazine), 138n1

Radin, Grace, 212n9
Rhys, Jean, 17, 23, 73–109, 110, 111, 137, 217, 221, 222
 abortion motif in, 135
 ageing in, 87–9
 alcoholism of, 134
 artistic and intellectual development of, 76, 98–102
 associating fashion with patriarchal values, 16, 26, 219
 clothes and fashion imagery in, 81–3, 84, 86–9
 commercial and popular success of, 76, 102, 108n33
 disparity between fantasy and reality in, 74, 85, 87, 90, 91, 219
 as 'dissident' or 'marginal modernist', 25–6, 77, 102, 109n36
 emancipation, 26, 74, 82–6, 87, 90, 91, 93–4, 96, 97
 and fashion's optimistic narrative about women's socio-political progress

Rhys, Jean (*Cont.*)
 and idealising fantasies of selfhood, 83–6, 88–9, 90, 104n7, 106n18, 107n22, 219
 love of clothes and fashion, 67, 73, 103n1, 106n14
 narrative perspective in, 99
 and naturalism, 75
 nonconformity in, 76–7, 102–3
 polyvocality in, 100–1
 as postcolonial writer, 77, 102, 103n2, 104n9
 relationship with modernism, 76–7, 102, 109nn35–6
 relationship with Rosamond Lehmann, 134
 spatial imagery in, 79, 80–1, 91, 95–7, 108n31
 standardised images of femininity in, 86–7, 107n27
 stylistic eccentricity of, 26, 67, 76–7, 100–2, 109n36
 women's exploitation depicted in, 74–5, 80–1, 104n4, 105n13, 106n15, 108n29, 108n34
 'work' depicted in, 90–1, 93–4, 95–7
 works as a mannequin, 26, 73, 82, 106n15
 WORKS
 After Leaving Mr Mackenzie (1930), 74, 75, 76, 82, 83, 87–8, 93–4, 95, 98, 99
 'Chorus Girls' (unfinished), 107n21
 'Down Along' (autobiographical fragment), 104n3
 'Fears' (autobiographical fragment), 104n6
 Good Morning, Midnight (1939), 74, 76, 80, 82, 84, 88–9, 95, 96–7, 98, 99, 100, 101, 105n13, 106n18, 108n29
 Green Exercise Book (unpublished), 108n32
 'Illusion', 82–3, 85–6, 87, 106n19
 The Left Bank (1927), 73, 79, 109n35
 'Mannequin', 79, 81, 84, 86–7, 95–6, 105n12
 Quartet (1928), 73, 74, 75, 76, 80, 82, 95, 98, 99, 105n13, 107n27
 Smile Please (1979), 106n14, 106n21
 Triple Sec (unfinished), 106n18
 Voyage in the Dark (1934), 83, 103n2, 104n5, 108n33, 135–6
 Wide Sargasso Sea (1966), 26, 77
Richardson, Samuel, 36n37
Rilke, Rainer Maria, 72n29
Ritchie, Charles, 175n7, 177n16, 217
Rizzuto, Nicole, 104n5
Roach, Joseph, 31n6
Roberts, Kenneth, 213n20
romance novel, 14, 27, 113, 115, 137, 141n9
Rosenquist, Rod, 13, 17–18

Sackville-West, Vita, 140n8, 185, 211n5
Said, Edward, 99
Savory, Elaine, 104n4
Schiaparelli, Elsa, 78
Sheehan, Elizabeth, 36n32
Shepherd, Jennifer, 43, 72n27
Showalter, Elaine, 135
Siddons, Sarah, 9
Silver, Brenda R., 214n21
Simmel, Georg, 20, 34n23, 35n29, 122, 125
Simons, Judy, 116, 139n1, 140n5
Simpson, Kathryn, 200
Sinclair, May, 132
Sitwell, Edith, 15, 33n22
Snaith, Anna, 81, 212n9, 212n12, 213n19
Sombart, Werner, 9–10, 11, 34n23, 39, 40, 68n5, 152–3, 176n11
Southworth, Helen, 202, 215n30
Spencer, Herbert, 34n23, 39, 50, 52, 106n16
 aligns 'taste' with the educated and cultural elite, 49
 associates differentiation with progress, 48
 associates fashion with copyism, imitation and conformity, 48, 49, 51
 on ceremonial dress, 48, 190
 Ceremonial Institutions (1879), 48–9
 'Fashion and Manners', 47–8, 49
Staley, Thomas F., 103n1
Stead, Lisa, 107n23
Stephenson, Liisa, 69n11
Stevens, Wallace, 21
Strachey, Alix, 186–7
Strachey, Lytton, 144n26
Strachey, Philippa, 216n36
Stratton-Porter, Gene, 60, 65, 67n2
 Laddie: A True Blue Story (1913), 37–9, 40, 62
Stravinski, Igor, 72n29

Tatler (magazine), 53
Tennyson, Alfred, Lord, 129
Thacker, Andrew, 80
Thompson, John B., 206, 215n31
Tiller Girls, 86
Time and Tide (magazine), 36n35
Todd, Dorothy, 140n8, 203
Totten, Gary, 71n22
Truett, Brandon, 190

uniforms, 28–9, 181–2, 185–7, 189, 190, 196, 209, 212n8, 220

Vanity Fair (magazine), 70n18
Veblen, Thorstein
 conspicuous consumption, 7
 conspicuous leisure, 69n12
 The Theory of the Leisure Class (1899), 47
Victor Gollancz Ltd. (publisher), 147, 165, 178n22

Vinken, Barbara, 30n3, 69n13
Vionnet, Madeleine, 78
Vita-Finzi, Penelope, 69n7, 72n26
Vogue (magazine), 53, 111, 114–15, 122, 142n15, 154, 166, 176n11, 179n24, 179n25, 203, 217
   advice for business women in, 159
   advice for debutantes in, 140n7
   advocating change and variation, 116
   'clothes sense' promoted by, 117
   'Pattern Service', 117, 118
   as producer of idealised womanhood, 116
   relationship with Bloomsbury modernism, 140n8
Vogue's Book of Practical Dressmaking (1926), 119, 122

Wallace, Alfred Russel, 49
Warner, Eric, 213n19
Warner, Sylvia Townsend, 140n4
Waugh, Evelyn, 72n29
Wegener, Frederick, 56, 61
Wells, H. G., 162, 205
Wharton, Edith, 5, 14, 17, 19, 23, 26, 32n15, 36n40, 37–72, 73, 111, 120, 172, 183, 184, 199, 209, 217, 221, 222
   and architecture and interior design, 41, 45–6, 50, 58
   and art of collecting, 45, 51–2
   associates fashion with imitation and vulgarity, 50–2
   commercial success of, 40–1, 61–2, 67n2, 71n22, 137
   critical of modernism, 6, 12, 25, 39, 40, 41, 57–61, 65–6, 70n20, 72n29
   criticises fashion's tendency to standardise tastes and forms, 25, 39–40, 53–5, 182, 219
   criticises 'novelty', 50, 52, 58, 60, 65
   dislikes surface impressions, 45, 46–7, 52
   distinction between 'fashion' and 'dress' by/in, 42–5, 47, 55
   fears decline of artistic standards, 39, 41, 57–8, 65, 67n1
   importance of tradition emphasised by, 56, 57–9, 65, 219
   and 'individualist' style in art, 41, 57, 58–9, 62, 63–4, 66, 69n7, 72n29
   influenced by evolutionary theory, 47, 49–51, 52, 58, 69n14
   on interwar literary marketplace, 25, 39, 56–61, 65, 66, 68n6, 70n17
   late work of, 62–3, 71n23
   and literary realism, 25, 44, 46, 63–4, 71n21, 71n25, 72n26
   and love of designer dresses, 39, 44, 45, 47. 68n4
   management of sewing workrooms during the First World War, 42, 69n8
   objects to publicity campaigns for Woolf's *Orlando*, 3–4, 65, 201
   receives honorary degree from Yale University, 64
   rejects celebrity authorship, 37, 40, 65
   synchronises reflections on sartorial and literary fashions, 43, 55–6, 64
   on 'taste', 50, 51–2
   uses clothes to represent characters' socio-economic circumstances, 42, 43, 44
   WORKS
   The Age of Innocence (1920), 61, 62, 71n24
   The Children (1928), 53–4, 62, 71n23
   The Custom of the Country (1913), 50–3, 61, 63, 64, 70n14, 70n15
   The Decoration of Houses (1897), 45–6, 50, 51, 58, 69n10
   Disintegration (unfinished novel), 55
   Ethan Frome (1911), 70n21
   The Glimpses of the Moon (1922), 62
   The Gods Arrive (1932), 59–60
   'The Great American Novel', 39, 50, 67n1, 69n12
   The House of Mirth (1905), 42, 43, 44, 72n28
   Hudson River Bracketed (1929), 56–7, 59, 62, 63
   The Mother's Recompense (1925), 55, 62, 71n22
   Summer (1917), 43
   'Tendencies in Modern Fiction', 57, 70n20
   'The Touchstone', 55
   Twilight Sleep (1927), 62, 70n16
   The Writing of Fiction (1925), 42, 46, 56, 57, 58–9, 62, 63–4, 69n7, 71n25
Whipple, Dorothy, *High Wages* (1930), 92, 93, 101, 107n25
Wilde, Jane, Lady (Speranza), 44
Wilde, Oscar, 33n20, 107n21
Willis, J. H., 202, 213n20
Willison, Ian, 214n24
Wilson, Edmund, 71n23
Wilson, Elizabeth, 7
Winning, Joanne, 34n24
Wittman, Emily O., 222n1
women novelists
   affiliations among, 23, 36n35, 65–7
   and association with mass culture, 13–14, 33n18
   and domesticity, 13–14
   'dual literacy' of, 128–9, 130
   as fashion critics, 16, 22, 29, 218–20
   and highbrow ambitions, 15–16
   and (male) modernists, 12, 13, 23
   self-images of, 3, 6, 220–2
   social performances of, 3, 15, 222
   writing practices of, 3, 13–14, 29–30, 32nn16–17, 65, 221–2

Wood, Alice, 216n37
Woolf, Leonard, 206, 213n19, 215n30
  comments on Mosley's BUF, 187
  correspondence with Jonathan Cape, 204–5
Woolf, Virginia, 3, 7, 17, 19, 23, 32n15, 35n28, 78, 113, 121, 125–31, 132, 135, 137, 138, 140n8, 145, 163, 164, 165, 181–216, 217, 221, 222
  artistic work depicted in, 127–8, 131
  associates sartorial insignia with social hierarchies, 48, 183, 190–1, 193, 195–6, 197–8, 220
  'clothes complex/fear' of, 185, 200
  comments on Dorothy Todd, 203
  commercial success of, 198–9, 200, 202, 213n20, 214n21
  on conspicuous dress, 29, 183, 189, 191, 193, 194–6, 197, 210, 212n11, 212n14
  on contemporary celebrity culture, 7, 199–200
  critical of sartorial politics in totalitarian regimes, 28, 182–3, 187, 190, 198, 209, 220
  criticises patriarchal culture, 131, 183, 185, 189, 190, 197, 208
  distinction between 'Georgian' and 'Edwardian' writers by, 66
  dressmaking vocabulary in, 128, 129, 143n20
  as editor and publisher, 23, 29, 184, 201–2, 206
  encounters fascism in Germany, 186–7, 211n4
  examines how clothes coordinate individuals in social configurations, 28–9, 182–3, 188–91, 193–6, 209–10, 213n15
  and Femina-Vie Heureuse Prize, 199
  'frock consciousness' in, 191, 193–6
  importance of individual in, 28, 182–3, 185, 196, 198, 209, 220
  interested in her readers, 131, 207–8, 210
  intertextuality in, 129
  knitting imagery in, 128–9
  on Lehmann's writing, 126
  Monks House scrapbooks, 188–9, 195, 212n8
  relationship with literary marketplace, 29, 65, 131, 143n22, 173, 184–5, 200–1, 203–4, 204–6, 207–8, 214n24, 215n29, 216n35
  reviews Wharton's *The House of Mirth*, 72n28
  and uniform cultural productions, 28–9, 182, 183–4, 185, 199, 201, 207, 208–10
  on uniforms, 29, 190, 196, 209
  uses clothes to indicate historical particularity and everyday experiences in *The Years*, 192
  worries about being 'out of fashion', 11
  WORKS
  'Angel in the House', 13–14
  'Anon', 207
  'Are Too Many Books Written and Published', 206–7
  'Character in Fiction', 162
  The Common Reader (1925), 202
  Flush (1933), 199, 215n27
  Jacob's Room (1922), 202
  'The Leaning Tower', 213n18
  Mrs Dalloway (1925), 30n1, 202
  'The New Dress', 1, 30n1, 193, 209
  Night and Day (1919), 202, 214n23
  Orlando (1928), 4, 18, 65, 143n22, 199, 200, 201, 202, 214n25, 215n27
  'The Patron and the Crocus', 207, 216n33
  A Room of One's Own (1929), 32n17, 142n16, 143n18, 200, 202, 208, 215n29
  'Society of Outsiders' in, 197, 198
  Three Guineas (1938), 29, 48, 182, 183, 186, 188, 190, 193, 194, 195, 197, 198, 207, 208, 209, 210, 212n9, 212n10, 215n27, 216n36
  To the Lighthouse (1927), 27, 112, 125, 126–31, 143n19, 143n21, 199, 202
  Uniform Edition of, 29, 178n19, 184, 185, 199, 201, 202–7, 208, 210, 213n15, 214n24, 215n25, 215n27, 215n28, 215n29
  The Voyage Out (1915), 202, 214n23
  The Waves (1931), 215n27
  The Years (1937), 29, 143n20, 182, 183, 187–8, 189, 191–9, 200, 208, 209, 210, 211n6, 212n9, 212n12, 212n14, 213n15, 213n16, 213n19, 213n20, 214n21, 215n27, 216n36

Yeats, W. B., 72n29
Yezierska, Anzia, 36n40
Young, John K., 202, 215n29

Zakreski, Patricia, 128
Zemgulys, Andrea, 109n36
Zimring, Rishona, 104n7, 105n13, 108n34
Zola, Émile, 75
  Nana (1880), 104n5

EU representative:
Easy Access System Europe
Mustamäe tee 50, 10621 Tallinn, Estonia
Gpsr.requests@easproject.com

www.ingramcontent.com/pod-product-compliance
Lightning Source LLC
Chambersburg PA
CBHW061710300426
44115CB00014B/2632